The Making of the 20th Century

This series of specially commissioned titles focuses attention on significant and often controversial events and themes of world history in the present century. Each book provides sufficient narrative and explanation for the newcomer to the subject while offering, for more advanced study, detailed source-references and bibliographies, together with interpretation and reassessment in the light of recent scholarship.

In the choice of subjects there is a balance between breadth in some spheres and detail in others; between the essentially political and matters economic or social. The series cannot be a comprehensive account of everything that has happened in the twentieth century, but it provides a guide to recent research and explains something of the times of extraordinary change and complexity in which we live. It is directed in the main to students of contemporary history and international relations, but includes titles which are of direct relevance to courses in economics, sociology, politics and geography.

The Making of the 20th Century
Series Editor: CHRISTOPHER THORNE

Titles in the Series include

China and the World since 1949

The Impact of Independence, Modernity and Revolution

Wang Gungwu

ST. MARTIN'S PRESS NEW YORK

Contents

50145

Abbreviations

(used in text, notes and guide to further reading)

C.C.P.	Chinese Communist Party
C.P.S.U.	Communist Party of the Soviet Union
G.P.C.R.	Great Proletarian Cultural Revolution
K.M.T.	Kuomintang
P.L.A.	People's Liberation Army
P.R.C.	People's Republic of China
P.R.G.	Provisional Revolutionary Government
SEATO	South-East Asia Treaty Organisation
U.N.	United Nations
U.S.A.	United States of America
U.S.S.R.	Union of Soviet Socialist Republics

Preface

THE origins of this book are very humble. It began as a historian's notes on the roots of China's foreign policy. Each time I was called upon to lecture in this subject, I added to the notes and modified them. In the meantime, I was lecturing on China in a course on the history of revolutions and also attending numerous seminars and discussion meetings organised by the Contemporary China Centre of the Australian National University. More and more I was drawn to attempt some kind of contemporary history which might be a little more than an extended essay in interpretation. Finally, I was persuaded that it might serve as a useful introduction to the study of China. By that time, I was away from teaching and administrative duties, spending my study leave at Oxford. Thus through the beautiful summer of 1975, between sitting in my study at All Souls and walking in the Parks, I gathered my thoughts together to write. I could not have been intellectually further from revolutionary China than I was that summer, but there was the time and the quiet to write. For that, I am grateful to the College. And because my wife and two daughters patiently waited for me to finish while the summer 'wasted away', they really spurred me to get my draft written in time.

Although the book was written mainly in Oxford, I could not have written it without the opportunities to read, listen, discuss and teach that the Australian National University has provided for me. Having lived for most of my life in south-east Asia, where facilities for the study of contemporary China are spectacularly lacking, I have benefited enormously from my colleagues in Canberra who have long worked on current Chinese affairs, and from students who enjoy the freedom to satisfy their curiosity about China and its fast-changing society and history. I mention a few names here, not to have them share the responsibility for what I have written, but merely to let them know how much their work here over the years has stimulated and inspired me: Bruce Kent for asking me to share his revolutions course; Fred Teiwes for his dedication to political studies; Stephen FitzGerald for his many insights; Pierre Ryckmans for his deep love of Chinese culture; Enid Bishop and Y. S. Chan for making our China library such an excellent one; Gordon White, Audrey Donnithorne, Ian Wilson and Colin Mackerras, who helped me more than they know. Finally, my wife Margaret read the manuscript several times and saved me from many errors of fact, grammar and style. It seems such a paltry thing merely to dedicate the book to her, but she will know how much of the book is really hers.

Canberra   WANG GUNGWU

To Margaret

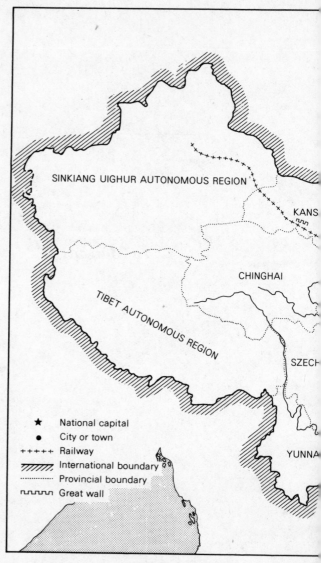

SINKIANG UIGHUR AUTONOMOUS REGION

KANS

CHINGHAI

TIBET AUTONOMOUS REGION

SZECH

YUNNA

★ National capital
● City or town
+ + + + + Railway
▨▨▨ International boundary
········· Provincial boundary
� Great wall

Modern China: provinces and major cities.

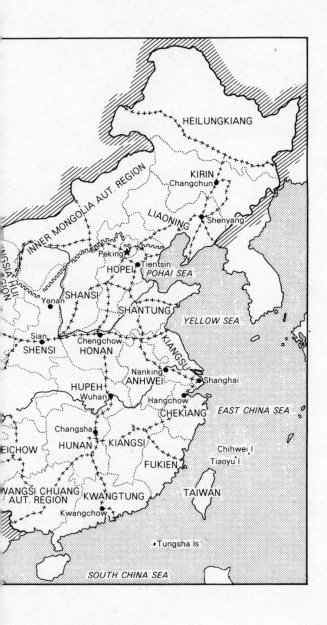

1 Introduction

THE transformation of China is one of the remarkable stories of the twentieth century. In 1900, it was well on the way to its fall as a great empire; by the mid-1920s, it was a drastic failure as a republic; then, after a brief effort at recovery between 1928 and 1937, its war with Japan brought it to the verge of becoming a puppet state of Japan or even being swallowed up altogether. In 1945, after Japan was defeated, China was proclaimed one of the world's five Great Powers, with a permanent seat in the Security Council with the U.S.A., the U.S.S.R., Great Britain and France. The propulsion to the forefront of world politics was premature as the country drifted into civil war and the economy was paralysed by galloping inflation. Then, again with astonishing suddenness, the Nationalist Government was thrown out and the People's Republic of China was established. This new regime, led by the Chinese Communist Party, quickly forced a new consensus and set the course for a distinctive revolution. Within a few years, it had begun to live up to the Great Power status thrust upon China in 1945. The transformation has been one of many twists and turns and the outcome was never as certain as it appears today, but that it was remarkable has never been in doubt.

This volume is an attempt to present some of the main changes in China since 1949. It outlines the efforts to change and tries to identify the internal and external policies and events which have produced important changes as well as those which have served as significant obstacles to change. In doing this, special attention has been paid to three themes: the desire to assert independence, the problems of modernity and the determination to make revolution. Change in itself is not remarkable in a century when change is demanded and is taking place almost everywhere. What is remarkable is the magnitude of China's problems and the challenge China offers to accepted models of change. The transformation has been dramatic, and this order of historical change, involving such an old and continuous civilisation, such a large area and some 800 million people, simply cries out for explanation. The events are of course too recent for anyone to tell the full story. The basic data are still fragmentary and have not been systematically gathered together, the thoughts of the main protagonists can only be broadly outlined and guessed at, even the narrative of events must still have many important gaps. But there is enough for a brief history of the striking developments and for preliminary efforts at explanation. And what is striking is the complex conditions that determine the nature and quality of change in China, the interplay of foreign and domestic policies underlying specific changes, the conflicts between ideas and actions that have propelled the country to rapid change and the traditional as well as the externally determined factors that have inhibited the speed and range of change.

The writing of contemporary history involves a high degree of selection. The themes selected – independence, modernity, and revolution – represent broad goals open to a wide variety of definitions. In this introduction the significance of each of these goals to the Chinese will be outlined briefly.

Independence is a deceptively simple goal. In practice, a full measure of it is exceedingly difficult to achieve. It has at least three major components which the Chinese today consider essential: it presupposes sovereignty; sovereignty requires freedom from interference; and, for a large and proud country, that freedom can only be guaranteed by its equality in strength with the strongest. This extended meaning of independence is not necessary for most countries. Smaller nations have to be content with independence as defined in international law and as guaranteed by bigger nations or by alliances. The Chinese would recognise that this is perhaps all that small nations can hope for, but would not accept such a limited form of independence for China. The reasons for this are rooted in China's history. They stem from traditional perceptions of China's place in the world, that is, the parts of the world directly relevant to China.

So much has been written about this traditional view which was so vital to Chinese relations with all non-Chinese that only a brief survey is necessary.[1] The view has been variously described in terms of China's position in a 'world order' of its own making, or in terms of China's centricity and the long-assumed superiority of its values and institutions, or in terms of the paradox that China had the capacity to make a form of universalism disguise its isolation. There is some truth in all these descriptions, although none of them would be true for the whole length of pre-modern Chinese history. In particular, it is quite anachronistic to describe China as isolated before the tenth century A.D.[2] The Chinese Empire was far from isolated before the T'ang dynasty (618–906). It had received a large number of foreign traders and visitors and welcomed many foreign faiths, ideas and material goods. Buddhism from India took root during this period. Zoroastrians, Nestorians, Manichaeans, Jews and increasingly large numbers of Muslims (Persians, Arabs, Turks) traded and settled there. China was expansive and tolerant and, if it seemed proud of its centricity and made universalist claims for its civilisation, there was no contradiction with reality.

The situation changed after the tenth century. China had become weak and defensive. By the thirteenth century, Chinese claims to superiority had been much diminished by the lack of political and military power. Neo-Confucianism, the philosophy which emerged when the Chinese Empire was in decline, still carried a universalist frame, but tied as it was to a dwindling empire, it was little more than a framework for philosophical speculation.[3] Yet after the Mongol conquest of the whole of China in 1276, the first time that all of China came under foreign rule, the surviving universalism took on a new significance. The succeeding Chinese Ming dynasty (1368–1644) endorsed neo-Confucianism as the new orthodoxy and also sought to legitimise itself by returning to the rhetoric and the institutions of the Han (206 B.C.–A.D. 220) and T'ang dynasties, thus ensuring that neo-Confucianism would carry all the claims of the great empires of the past. Unfortunately, most of the Ming emperors were inclined to a defensive isolation. For the first time, foreign trade was actively discouraged and private foreign travel for Chinese actually prohibited.[4] This was at a time when other peoples, especially in Western Europe, were advancing rapidly in technology and the sciences. By the sixteenth century, when a new set of adventurous foreigners arrived off the coast of China, there had developed a growing unreality in Chinese perceptions of all foreign nations.[5] The limiting nature of the neo-Confucian language of politics and history had induced the Chinese leaders to foster views about China's centricity which must necessarily be the source of myth. What was beginning to take root was the idea of an invulnerable China, strong because of its cultural superiority, rich because of its large population and self-sufficient because of its extensive cultivated lands.

This myth reached its climax during the Manchu Ch'ing dynasty (1644–1911). The Manchus were non-Chinese, leading a partially Chinese military confederation. They were a small minority ruling over the Han Chinese majority: the justification for this was found in the political universalism of neo-Confucianism, the practical result was the successful integration of Manchu military and political acumen with Chinese administrative genius. This success reinforced the Chinese assurance of the Empire's greatness and invulnerability.[6] It confirmed the assumption that all changes in the world outside were relative and temporary compared with the centricity of China, which history had shown to be absolute and permanent. Thus there was never any need to consider a concept like independence when China held a central position based upon strength and wealth. And as long as the Empire was thriving, China was more than independent. It was not only sovereign and free from interference; it was also more equal than others. This was the Chinese heritage in the nineteenth century. It was a view that had to be modified greatly by the beginning of the twentieth century, but it was never rejected by the Chinese. How much was modified and why the Chinese still expect a high level of independence will be considered in the following chapter.

The second theme concerns the idea of modernity. This idea is far from simple. For one thing, it is always relative and sometimes totally subjective. The Chinese today realise that it is not helpful to make arbitrary comparisons about the modernity of one era and that of another; for example, it would be pointless to say that Ch'ang-an in the seventh century A.D. was more *modern* than London in the fourteenth century. What is needed is a scientific basis for relating modernity with progress, and this they feel they have found in historical materialism. Thus modernity moves through the stages of historical development, the capitalist stage being more modern than the feudal and the socialist stage more modern than the capitalist. Again this is not necessarily true for all countries. 'Developed' countries have little doubt about what is modern, and 'undeveloped' countries equate 'development', that is, being like the 'developed', with modernity. In Asia, this modernity meant imitating the West, or Westernisation, and many leaders of smaller, economically dependent countries have this in mind when they want to modernise.* Thus the Chinese remain in an ambiguous

* The Chinese have long rejected the idea of 'Westernisation', and even of 'modernisation' and 'development', especially when the Western capitalist or mixed-economy model is intended. The difference, however, between the earlier rejection couched in terms of the return to Chinese ideals and values and the later rejection in terms of Marxist dialectical materialism, became apparent only in the late 1920s; see Chapter 2 below.

position. They do not deny the modernity of Western technology and may concede the higher economic growth and standard of living produced by superior technology, but seek to avoid subordinating themselves by mere imitation. Part of their fervent quest for independence spills over into the search for the scientific progress which would not require them to acknowledge the superiority of other peoples but only the objective criteria for attaining a higher stage of history. This ambiguity towards the West also derives from China's history, from its perception of its cultural superiority for twenty centuries.

The origins of this sense of superiority have already been outlined. The isolationism of the Ming dynasty survived into the following Ch'ing dynasty and into the early nineteenth century. It strengthened the myths of superiority, but restricted the conditions under which large-scale and continuous technological innovation and economic diversification to sustain China's vast population would be encouraged.[7] On the contrary, with increasing administrative and educational centralisation and control during the Ch'ing dynasty, the sense of China's invincibility was transmitted to more and more Chinese. It became more pervasive and immanent, and, through its appearance of timelessness, began to appear more real and contemporary. Thus the Chinese did not have the idea of modernity and did not need it so long as they felt that their civilisation was superior. In this way, when the idea came to be accepted, it became associated with the idea of superiority. This was an uncomfortable association. If what was modern was superior, then those who were modern were superior to those who were not. It then followed that it was necessary to catch up with those who were more modern in order not to be regarded as inferior. Thus among the 'superior' élite classes in China at the beginning of the twentieth century, the pressure to modernise became more and more difficult to resist. Their efforts to agree on what modernity meant were at the base of some of the major conflicts in China before 1949. A survey of these appears in Chapter 2.

The third theme is that of revolution. The Chinese seem to have been quite clear what this meant in 1949. It meant the violent struggle led by the C.C.P. which established the People's Republic of China. This revolution was successful. But ever since then, the idea has grown that this revolution was only a beginning and that there are more revolutions to come. This begins to blur the picture of the revolution as a means to an end and of the revolution as a long and continuous process towards an ideal communist society which becomes neither a definable nor a foreseeable end. It then is unclear whether revolution, in fact, becomes an end in itself and is equated with a permanently revolutionary society. Thus the idea becomes fluid and elusive, moving from the questions of how and when it determines that a society had moved from one stage to another and how and when anyone could be sure that the revolution has been completed.

There are no real Chinese roots for the idea of revolution. The Chinese today acknowledge that the idea was derived from the ideas of Marx and Engels and that its first great success was the October Revolution which Lenin brought to Russia. Here the Chinese would agree with most other revolutionaries that the October Revolution was the culmination of a historical process which began with the bourgeois revolutions in England, the U.S.A. and France. Thus the linear descent of the Chinese Revolution from the October Revolution placed the Chinese in a global context and brought China into the forefront of world history. But, significantly, the Chinese remained troubled by the idea that the revolutionary process could not be traced through Chinese history and several keen efforts have been made to re-examine this.[8] Firstly, they traced its Chinese inspiration to the Taiping Rebellion (1850−66), and opened up the fascinating question of whether this rebellion was the crucial conjunction between traditional peasant uprising and modern revolution. In their enthusiasm, they went further back to analyse the class nature of all previous peasant uprisings, reaching back to the first of its kind, the uprising of Ch'en Sheng and Wu Kuang at the end of the third century B.C. It was at this point that Marxist historiography was worked in to show that the First Empire of Ch'in (256−207 B.C.) was not merely a brilliant political achievement but also marked the climax of a transition from one stage of history to another.[9] The first emperor, Ch'in Shih-huang, represented the newly emerging feudal class in finally overthrowing the survivors of the slave-owning aristocracy. He thus played a clearly revolutionary role. In this indirect way, and only after decades of intensive debate, it has been decided that the Ch'in dynasty provided China's first clearly identifiable revolution. This is not simply an issue of 'sinicising' Marxist historiography nor one of merely legitimising the Marxist 'world-view' for China. It brings the very idea of revolution close to home and makes revolution concrete, familiar, understandable, and alive, and attempts to alter fundamentally the perspectives of most Chinese peoples towards the revolutionary process.[10] The difficulties experienced in finding roots in Chinese history for an essentially alien idea deserve close attention.

How the idea of revolution was first introduced into China at the turn of the twentieth century and the tortuous course it took among the Chinese élites before 1949 will be explored in the next chapter.

The three themes outlined here do not account for all the changes that have occurred in China since 1949. They do, however, help to identify the main areas where the Chinese were clearly committed to policies of change, and thus provide a useful basis for considering what changes have occurred and what have not, and even how these changes measure up to the goals the Chinese had determined for themselves. A warning note should be sounded here. For the purpose of the account that follows, the three themes have been given roughly equal weight. This does not reflect the rhetoric and publicised purposes of the People's Republic of China. If repeatedly declared goals were the main criteria, the Chinese certainly assigned the highest value to revolution. This is especially true if the widely read texts of Mao Tse-tung (1893−1976) were to serve as a guide to what is of ultimate importance. This fact cannot be ignored. Mao Tse-tung was the key figure in providing a coherent and essentially consistent vision for the Chinese Revolution.[11] But he was not simply a revolutionary fanatic. On the contrary, his was a most complex personality and his thoughts ranged from the sublime to the most banal. He was profoundly Chinese and understood the great traditions of China, yet he was ruthless about the Chinese past and quite ready to undermine the values the Chinese have long been proud of. He has been described as a romantic visionary, yet he was something of an embodiment of the rationality and earthiness of the Chinese people. He has been called a nationalist at heart, yet there is no doubt he was a convinced Marxist−Leninist who seemed willing to accept the dynamics of historical change as perceived in the West as necessary for China's future. That he could be all this without apparent self-conflict is a source of wonder and bewilderment to both admirers and critics. But his manifold influences on events and policies remind us not to oversimplify the range and quality of change in China since 1949. Independence and modernity may seem only to be the means to revolution, but it would inhibit our understanding of change to subsume the first two under an all embracing concept of revolution.

It is also tempting to relate the three themes to the visibility of the leading personalities concerned.[12] For example, independence could easily be linked to Chou En-lai (1898−1976), the person most openly active in establishing China's place in the world; modernity to Liu Shao-ch'i (b. 1898) before 1966, the man who seemed to have cared most for careful and steady progress; and revolution to Mao Tse-tung as the chastiser of all who might forget what the whole thing was all about. Such linkages are plausible, but it will not greatly help this study to assign individual responsibilities for specific changes. Attention will be focused here on the phenomena, not on the heroes. Finally, in a brief study of China, it is the Chinese point of view that will be looked at most closely. There will be no attempt to provide all sides of any specific question. Such a perspective influences the periodisation adopted here. For the developments since 1949, the dividing dates between chapters are 1953, 1958, 1966 and 1971. These dates reflect domestic changes somewhat more than external events and have been chosen to bring out the contrasts between phases of marked change. But they are not meant to suggest that, in this study, only Chinese initiatives would be emphasised. Quite clearly there are important differences in the three themes where initiatives are concerned. However much the Chinese may wish to take the initiative in all three areas, it is inevitable that, where issues of independence are concerned, initiatives could just as easily come from outside; similarly, with some aspects of modernity. Perhaps only in the theme of revolution can it be argued that the pace of change, whether realisable or not, is determined largely within China. But before the Chinese 'stood up' in 1949 and began to take initiatives, they were tossed in storms not of their own making. The next chapter will briefly sketch this turbulent historical background to the C.C.P. victory.

2 New Pressures for Change: Historical Background up to 1949

THE idea that Chinese civilisation could claim to be timeless and universal and that the Chinese Empire could preserve its own time-scale of dynastic and cyclical change following periods of stability was hard to change. Throughout most of the nineteenth century the world outside appeared to the Chinese to be restless and uncertain. In the minds of the Sino-Manchu mandarinate there was still the assurance that, however strikingly the world might be changing and however these changes may appear to threaten China, the Empire had the resources within itself to handle such threats and could even afford to ignore such changes. To this mandarinate, it seemed futile to try to relate to foreign values that were dynamic but misguided, and quite unnecessary to respect and learn from traders, soldiers and missionaries who might only be temporary irritants on the China coast. If these intruders saw themselves as progressive and inventive, it was on some other time-scale and did not contradict the fundamental centricity of China's place in the world. What the Sino-Manchu élites failed to grasp for a long time was that the economic and technological advances in the West had made nonsense of China's sense of invulnerability. There had been a fundamental change in power relations, and it became increasingly urgent to recognise the world for what it was. But it took several wars from the first Anglo-Chinese ('Opium') War of 1840–2 to the Sino-Japanese War of 1894–5 to persuade the mandarins that the Ch'ing Empire was no longer an equal among the great empires.[1] By the end of the century, a few men began to realise that the Empire's independence was nominal, that it was justly considered backward and that something radical had to be done. Ultimately, it was not merely that Chinese pride was hurt; it was a sense that a long-unchallenged understanding of China's place in the world had been largely undermined.

It was really quite a fall from the assurance of centricity to the anxieties about national independence. Questions of sovereignty, equality and freedom from interference had to be considered afresh in terms of the idea of 'the family of nations' which China was forced to accept by the 1860s. But, to begin with, most of the 'nations' China had had to deal with were, in fact, empires, most notably the British, the French and the Russian, but also the Dutch, the Spanish (till 1898), the Portuguese, the Austro-Hungarian and eventually the German, the American, the Belgian and, not least, the Japanese.[2] Thus when the 'self-strengtheners' and reformists from Tseng Kuo-fan (1811−72) and Tso Tsung-t'ang (1812−85) to K'ang Yu-wei (1858−1927) and Liang Ch'i-ch'ao (1873−1929) sought to change China,[3] they were mainly concerned with equality in wealth and military strength and certain aspects of modernity, like more efficient political institutions and scientific education. Even when Sun Yat-sen (1866−1925) and his youthful followers first pronounced on the need for 'nationalism', they still identified China with other empires.[4] And the only part of their platform which attracted wide appeal was their determination to replace Manchu aristocrats with more modern Chinese élites. It was really not until the fall of the Ch'ing dynasty and the establishment of the Republic of China in 1912 that serious doubts about China's independence began to come to the fore. To begin with, the Republic was immediately threatened with the loss of Outer Mongolia and it was apparent that Manchuria, Tibet and even Turkestan (Sinkiang) were equally vulnerable. Fears had first been aroused by Russo-Japanese activities in Manchuria and by the Japanese takeover of Korea in 1910, but, during the First World War, the Japanese presence in Shantung and other Japanese demands (notably the Twenty-One Demands of 1915) made it quite clear that there was not merely the question of being unequal but the much more serious matter of the erosion of Chinese sovereignty within Han China itself. The danger became even more real when the Chinese saw, at the end of the war, the break-up of the Ottoman and Austro-Hungarian Empires and the partial dismemberment of the Tsarist Empire in Europe. It became all the more ominous to note that Tibet was beyond direct Chinese control and Japanese ambitions in Manchuria were increasingly blatant.[5]

The first question of independence, therefore, concerned China's sovereignty and its boundaries. On this, the Chinese found they had quickly to reject the nationalism that would have led to the redrawing of the map of China. They had to espouse a nationalism that would justify the retention of the boundaries of Ch'ing China. This meant that they would have to identify with the successes and failures of the Ch'ing dynasty and to assert the continuity with the whole length of Chinese history. It would also require that they reaffirm the universalism that legitimised their claims to preserve the Ch'ing polity unimpaired, however unreal and erroneous that might have been. It would imply that the Neo-Confucian justification of Manchu minority rule over the Han Chinese majority could be simply reversed to justify once again the Han Chinese majority rule over non-Han minorities, which must now, in international usage, all be redefined as Chinese.[6]

In practice, of course, relations with the large minorities who occupied distinct territories on the borders of China remained difficult. All Chinese leaders were uncomfortable with the *fait accompli* that eventually produced the independent nation of Mongolia. If that were accepted, what of the Mongol lands in Western Manchuria and Inner Mongolia? What of the Turkic tribes of Sinkiang and, even more vexing, what of the Tibetans in the provinces of Hsi-tsang (Tibet), Hsi-k'ang (now absorbed into Tibet and Szechuan) and Ch'ing-hai (Chinghai)? And there were several other more or less 'sinicised' tribes in south-west China and in Manchuria for whom claims of nationhood might yet be made. In one respect, Sun Yat-sen and later nationalists had no problems. The Han Chinese needed no convincing that narrow definitions of the nation-state did not apply to China. They identified totally with the heritage of the Ch'ing dynasty. Thus the errors of the Ch'ing were their errors; these they had to rectify. Similarly, the humiliations of the Ch'ing were also their humiliations, and the stronger the emotional response to these humiliations, the greater would appear the affirmation of the continuity with Ch'ing China. The Chinese were supported in this, somewhat ironically, by the practices of international law. The Great Powers insisted that the new Republican government honour all the treaty commitments of the Ch'ing and this strengthened the Chinese claim to all the territories of the Ch'ing. What was more significant, however, was that the Chinese attitudes towards the boundaries of their sovereignty were both wider and more limiting than normally understood elsewhere. They were wider in that more kinds of peoples and cultures were included in the 'nation' and distinct steps had to be taken to try and prevent 'Great Han chauvinism' from destroying the wider appeals of the new nationalism to the millions of non-Han Chinese. At the same time, they were more limiting in that the sense of continuity with traditional China burdened the country with many of the past pretensions and disadvantages of a polity with universalist, even imperialist, claims. An example of the former was the persistence of descriptions of the minority peoples which implied that they were 'barbarians' and therefore not the equals of Han Chinese. An example of the latter was the long insistence that countries like Korea, Vietnam, Burma and several others in south and south-east Asia had been 'lost' to the aggressive Great Powers and the way this was indicated in maps and textbooks until recent years.[7]

There was another aspect of sovereignty which related to the questions of both equality and freedom from interference. This concerned the Unequal Treaties signed with Britain, France, Russia, U.S.A., Japan and other powers, which were forced upon the Ch'ing from 1840. On this matter most Chinese leaders would agree, and the task of trying to have them revised had begun even before the fall of the Ch'ing dynasty. During the first Republican period of 1912–27, the Ministry of Foreign Affairs spent more time on this problem than on any other single issue. Small gains were made with regard to the Western Powers and high expectations were raised by the high-sounding declarations of the U.S.S.R. soon after Lenin and the Bolshevik Party seized power.[8] But there could have been no significant improvement in China's position as long as any one of the Powers continued to make gains at China's expense. Thus the pressures exerted by Japan in Manchuria (now Liaoning, Kirin and Heilungkiang), Shantung, Inner Mongolia and Fukien nullified any satisfaction that might have been obtained through long-drawn-out negotiations with other Powers. And as long as Japan was still advancing into China, the most-favoured nation clause in the Unequal Treaties encouraged all others to drag their feet.

In any case, a more crucial weakness lay in China's disunity. This had become acute after the death of Yuan Shih-k'ai, the first effective President of the Republic, in 1916. The era of the warlords from 1916 to 1927 was not a time to expect the Powers to make concessions. On the contrary, the competition for power between different groups of warlords actually invited intervention in the form of loans and military assistance. In fact, the Republic was in a far worse position than the Ch'ing Empire. By 1917 the legitimacy of the government in Peking was being questioned and China's status as an independent nation was in many ways a fiction. It became imperative that China be reunified if the heritage of the Ch'ing was to have meaning and if there was to be any progress towards sovereignty within China itself. This was well understood, especially by the time China's position had reached its nadir in 1925–6, when anarchy would certainly have followed if some unification had not been in sight.[9] This was the chief reason for the widespread enthusiasm when the Kuomintang forces in the Northern Expedition brought a limited unity to China in 1927. It was also the reason why this new government, after its formal establishment in Nanking in 1928, had such an uphill battle for China's independence for the next ten years.[10] It was only the beginning of the upturn after ninety years of steady decline in China's prestige and power.

The K.M.T. victory led by Chiang Kai-shek (1887–1975) was seen as a victory for nationalism. This was to produce the first condition for independence – national unity. But the unification was far from complete: only the eight provinces of central and south China could be said to have been safely in Nationalist hands and even here Chiang Kai-shek was challenged by his former allies, the Chinese Communist Party (C.C.P.), in at least five provinces. The remaining provinces were still in the hands of various warlords. Although most of them did acknowledge allegiance to the Nanking government, this was more formal than real. Nevertheless, the new regime acted vigorously to assert the independence of China through diplomacy and through further pacification campaigns against the C.C.P. and some of the recalcitrant warlords. By 1936, only two main forces stood in the way: the C.C.P. in the north-west (after having being defeated in south China and being forced on the Long March to Yenan) and the Japanese in Manchuria and key parts of north China. Now came the truly testing period. Should Chiang Kai-shek continue with his policy to crush the C.C.P. first and then lead a united China against Japan or should he go ahead with a truce with the C.C.P. and lead a United Front against the Japanese straight away? Chiang Kai-shek preferred the first course, but when some of his allied generals turned against him at Sian in December 1936 he was forced to adopt the second. It was a fateful decision which led to a full-scale war with Japan. The only positive gain in this decision was the initial success in uniting almost all Chinese behind the central government for the first time in twenty years.[11] If Chiang Kai-shek could have led the country to victory, his leadership of a unified China would probably have been assured. This was his second chance to unify China, the first having been in 1926–8. It was, of course, something of a gamble; being allied with the C.C.P. was recognised by the K.M.T. as an enormous risk. It was also one that did not come off. China under Chiang Kai-shek was successively defeated and the Japanese split the country into two and created a puppet Nanking government for the Japanese half in 1940.[12] It took another five years for the Japanese to be defeated after they had taken on the U.S.A., the British and other empires in Asia. When the Second World War came to an end in 1945, Chiang Kai-shek looked as if he had been given his third chance to bring the whole of China under a single government. This might be considered the best chance he had ever had, for the Japanese war had made a major contribution to China's unification. It had cleared the field of all other competitors except one. Only the C.C.P. now stood in the way.

Other conditions for China's independence had also been fulfilled. China was at least in theory recognised as an equal of the Great Powers by being given a permanent place in the Security Council of the United Nations. The Unequal Treaties had all gone during the war and the opportunities for future interventions in China's internal affairs now seemed negligible. And, no less important, China's sovereignty over Manchuria and Taiwan, and indeed implicitly over all of Ch'ing China with the exception of Outer Mongolia, was widely acknowledged.[13] Whether the victory went to the K.M.T. or to the C.C.P., the independence of China looked assured.

The long struggle to attain this independence underlined several things for the Chinese. Firstly, a nominal independence in international law was meaningless. Secondly, unification was essential and this could only be obtained through military successes followed by full political and administrative control. Thirdly, nothing less than the Ch'ing territorial heritage was really satisfactory. Fourthly, only equality in power with the strongest countries in the world could guarantee China's sovereignty and its freedom from outside interference. These were lessons which were learnt by both the K.M.T. and the C.C.P. and after the C.C.P. victory in 1949 they were to sustain the People's Republic of China (P.R.C.) in its continued straining for the fullest possible independence for China.

For most of the Chinese élites during the first half of the twentieth century independence was not enough. What was to replace the cultural superiority that had been so much a part of the traditional heritage? Although they conceded by the end of the nineteenth century that the idea of over-all superiority was probably false, they still retained a keen sense that China had once been more advanced than others and therefore there was no reason why its backwardness in certain fields should not be temporary and rectifiable. The idea that there was nothing fundamentally wrong with Chinese civilisation was kept alive well into the twentieth century. All the Chinese needed to do was to locate the areas that had fallen behind and work hard in these areas to catch up with China's rivals and enemies. The 'self-strengtheners' in the middle of the nineteenth century had not succeeded in actually catching up, so the reformists of the 1890s and 1900s wanted to go further. But it was still largely a question of identifying larger areas of backwardness and making more sacrifices in order to remedy what was lacking. So strong was this faith in the basic strengths within Chinese civilisation that even Sun Yat-sen, the most radical leader of his time, was forced to fall back on traditional virtues to support his ideas for a political revolution. With this background in mind, it is understandable why, up to 1912 and perhaps not until the May Fourth Movement in 1919 when there were nation-wide demonstrations against the betrayal of China by its Western allies at Versailles, what was modern was perceived only as specific examples of Western progress. The concept of modernity was untranslatable, and 'modern' was for several decades rendered in Chinese as the sound 'mo-teng'.[14]

The insistence on concrete examples reflected the pragmatic and practical side of Chinese civilisation. The first and most urgent need in the 1850s had been better guns and ships. When these did not seem to have been good enough to overcome the enemy, the mandarins re-emphasised the moral qualities of leaders and their men. They turned to other concrete Western examples: more thorough military training, a better grasp of international diplomatic practice and the enemy's psychology, and a more scientific education for officers and engineers. When these in turn seemed inadequate, the mandarins observed the keen business and administrative methods of foreign merchants and bankers and noted the efforts of coastal Chinese to master them in their own businesses. The efficiency and profitability of these modern organisations seemed to provide the basis for Western wealth and strength. Thus the mandarins went through a period of experimentation with various kinds of 'officially-supervised merchant-managed' industries and trading companies, and even gave some encouragement to Chinese private enterprise. But catching up in this piecemeal fashion did not seem to work; certainly it did not produce the quick results which the Chinese wanted, and the defeat by Japan in 1894–5 underlined this all too clearly. The time had come for more fundamental reform. A radical but abortive attempt by K'ang Yu-wei in 1898 was followed by a violent reaction symbolised by the Boxer Rising in 1900. Both reflected a growing impatience with the efforts at concrete solutions to specific problems which did little to restore the sense of superiority that the Chinese so regretted losing. But the pragmatism of the mandarins prevailed. Although they agreed that change was urgent and introduced very much more radical measures after 1901, they again concentrated on concrete examples of Western progress: modern schools and new universities and colleges, with the emphasis on new subjects, replacing the traditional learning which culminated in the imperial examinations; more foreign training for the most brilliant young men was introduced; steps towards constitutional and parliamentary government encouraged; more banks, more mines, better communications were established.[15] As the list of modernising items grew, together with greater expectations, there grew also a deeper dissatisfaction with the underlying cultural heritage as a whole. During the 1900s, the cumulative effect of five decades of deliberate change in technology and institutions had left a strong impression and the idea of progress had become meaningful. A new readiness to acknowledge the superiority of the West began to emerge. But even then, the most radical proposals of Sun Yat-sen were centred on specific remedies: replacing the Manchu monarchy with a Chinese republic, speeding up the establishment of democratic institutions and building railways and new industries on a large scale.[16]

Sun Yat-sen did achieve his first objective. The Ch'ing dynasty fell and the Republic was proclaimed in 1912. But he did not achieve political power. The old mandarins, both civil and military, survived. They accepted the necessity of continued reform and recruited younger 'modernisers' into their government, but they reacted against any radical change in the political structure. Once again, Chinese pragmatism seemed to have produced a stop – go quality in their attitudes towards modernity and change; that is, so far and no further, until the next crisis pushed the leaders to take the next leap forward. But this was now to change. The old mandarins survived, but not the old order, or their capacity to control the course of affairs. The authority of the government soon disintegrated and the conditions of near-anarchy between 1916 and 1927 brought about a new and unexpected freedom.

It was not the kind of freedom that made it possible to pursue systematic modernisation. It was more a breakdown of central control, so that different regions and enclaves were free to experiment and even innovate according to their respective interests.[17] For example, the Treaty Ports of Shanghai, Canton (Kwangchow), Tientsin, and Hankow (Wuhan) became not only centres of considerable industrial and commercial progress but also centres of political and intellectual freedom. Also, regions under warlord control, like Manchuria, Shansi and several provinces in south and central China (notably Kwangtung, Hunan, Fukien, Chekiang and Kiangsu), had the autonomy to encourage economic development to support their local interests. In quite unexpected ways, many forces were released to press for modernisation in many different directions. More than at any other period in modern Chinese history, foreign 'modernisers' were allowed to come and help: engineers, scientists, businessmen, doctors, school teachers, and significantly, university teachers in the fields of humanities and social sciences.[18] It became a decade when, willy-nilly, attitudes towards modernity were transformed.

But, as has been pointed out in Chapter 1, modernity has always been a difficult and elusive concept. It is relative and can be pointlessly subjective. K'ang Yu-wei was radical in one direction, Sun Yat-sen in another. Yen Fu (1854—1921) was cautiously modern while Liang Ch'i-ch'ao, Liu Shih-p'ei (1884—1919) and Chang Ping-lin (1868—1936) ranged far and wide without being certain what kinds of modernity they should settle for.[19] And there were hundreds of others who were converted and reconverted, who tasted at every spring — some became fanatics, others became sceptical and even cynical, and yet others settled back with relief into the Chinese tradition. As more and more of the Chinese élites claimed to be modern, irreconcilable differences about what modernisation meant began to appear. Whether in the manifold new policies being introduced by central and provincial governments or in the critical and political writings of numerous intellectuals and students, a large variety of proposals were made and concepts introduced. Almost every well-known Western writer, thinker, scientist or politician with a new idea or a new technique was looked at and borrowed from, some more thoroughly than others, some quite uncomprehendingly. Also, at the same time, almost every period of Chinese history was scrutinised for analogies which might help the leaders decide between one course of action and another. And not least, Chinese traditional concepts that were thought to be revivable were used, either directly to help the process of change, or indirectly to ease the acceptance of some alien idea.

In short, once modernisation became respectable, even fashionable, it was no longer true to say that the Chinese élites did not try hard enough to bring modernity to China. In some ways, they tried too hard, either to find the one set of Western ideas that opened all doors, answered all questions and promised to modernise painlessly, or to bring together into some Chinese mixture a variety of traditional and foreign ideas and procedures that could be tried experimentally in quick succession. The fertility of the earnest modernising minds in the 1910s and the 1920s was amazing. Both in print and in action, they provided a measure of, on the one hand, the determination of the administrative élite, and, on the other, the utter helplessness and irrelevance of unstructured intelligence. After at least a decade of a confusing 'enlightenment', it became necessary to wonder where this was leading China to.[20] The kind of freedom associated with the condition of disorder (*luan*) was not one most Chinese cared for. It was abnormal for China not to have a purposeful centre which guided the general course of events. The Chinese were not so modern as to forget the key lesson of their history, that ultimately it was political power and authority that mattered and that this could only be achieved through victory on the battlefield.

It was therefore not surprising that modernity came once again to be linked directly with modern arms and training and the revenues to pay for them. The one new factor that came to be appreciated was a need to find a new ideology on which to build a new kind of political organisation. At this stage, the ideology may broadly be called nationalism, although it ranged from varieties of warlord patriotism to varieties of revolutionary nationalism.[21] Whatever form it took, nationalism was more or less modern. The least modern was that of the warlords, which was often based mainly on the refurbishing of neo-Confucian ideology strengthened by a rhetoric not far from that of Napoleon, Bismarck and the modern patriotic 'samurai'. Against them were ranged the radical nationalists, until 1925 led by the ever-undaunted Sun Yat-sen. Their radicalism had been intensified by years of frustration and desperation, but also encouraged by new insights about the nature of China's backwardness. The K.M.T. was the party they gathered around, and each time it was reorganised it appeared that the modern was that which was the most radical. By 1922 the K.M.T. had accepted help from the U.S.S.R. and had taken under its wing the newly formed Chinese Communist Party. Between them they aroused enough support to oust the warlords from power in 1927. Afterwards, the K.M.T. turned on the C.C.P. and threw out all Soviet advisers.[22] The competition from then on until 1949 was mainly between the K.M.T. of increasingly right-wing radical nationalism and the C.C.P. of revolutionary nationalism.

A clear-cut struggle for power now took the place of the free-for-all quest for modernity. Modernity was no longer the open-ended vista of new possibilities that it had promised to be. Both the main protagonists claimed to be modern and modernisation was thereafter largely a question of changes and improvements made within two given frameworks. Indeed both now claimed to lead the Chinese Revolution. As parties of revolution, their struggle will be taken up later in the chapter. As for the modernity they both claimed, a brief summary of the developments from 1928 to 1949 follows.

Much has been made of the political conservatism of the Nanking government after 1923. In Chinese terms, there seem to have been a resurgence of neo-Confucian values and an attempt to build a new mandarinate. Yet there was clearly also a growing middle class who were on the whole progressive in outlook and who contributed steadily to the country's economic and technological development. Modern education became more widely accessible and modern skills were encouraged where possible not only in indigenous small-scale factories covering a wide range of light industry but also in agriculture and rural workshops. Furthermore, the new political and administrative élites consisted increasingly of men who had been trained in the most modern available techniques of government. They included men who managed mines, railways, large-scale industry, and also men who had learnt how to handle the growing urban working classes. In contrast, the outlawed C.C.P. was driven deep into the remoter countryside and forced to survive with the help of the most deprived peasant communities. There it had to learn to start afresh, to use the most unpromising conditions to struggle for what it believed were the most modern and scientific objectives. The party had become fragmented and had regrouped in pockets of resistance against the modern armies of Chiang Kai-shek. It was sustained by some international support (mainly Soviet-backed) and by the fierce conviction that its goal of the communist society was the ultimate modernity in the light of history, but otherwise it was isolated from the centres in and out of China which were setting the contemporary standards of modernity.[23]

Thus both the K.M.T. and the C.C.P. lived with their contradictions. For the K.M.T., the industrialising cities were modernising far faster than the countryside and had opened up an unbridgeable gap between the new Westernised élite and the majority of the Chinese people. And in the rural areas which it controlled the regime failed to implement the land reforms it had promised and left the social structure much as it had found it, that is, in the hands of traditionalist local leaders and skilful exploiters of the peasantry. As for the C.C.P., it found the peasantry it depended on was largely unmoved both by the high-sounding and sophisticated debates among the modernising literati in the urban centres and by its own alien theories of a proletarian revolution. It had to devise new ways to mobilise some very tradition-bound people and prepare them for a modern world. It had to start with basic ingredients like literacy and land reform and introduce the peasants gradually to modern ideas of social discipline and political action. And in time its leaders began to recognise that modernity was not an end in itself. It was but a means to obtain the ultimately modern end of a communist society. From this experience, the C.C.P. built its armies and discovered its own ways to win the war against the K.M.T., not by modern arms alone but chiefly by a modern spirit.

Both the K.M.T. and the C.C.P., of course, claimed to have led the Chinese Revolution. Both would acknowledge that revolution was an alien idea, despite the ancient ancestry of the term *ko-ming* used to translate it. But because *ko-ming* raised analogies with the past, it produced some ambiguity. This was especially true of Sun Yat-sen's 1911 Revolution. It encouraged many of his early supporters to believe that the revolution was mainly the violent overthrow of the Ch'ing dynasty, something like a dynastic change. This was not, of course, what Sun Yat-sen meant. He too had analogies in mind. But his model was a combination of the English, the American, and the French revolutions, with a distinct preference for the American because it was wholly successful. But there were two elements of the traditional term which were easily understood, the element of violence and that of a righteous struggle. Under Chinese conditions, non-violent changes of dynasty were rare. Even the several palace coups were usually bloody, and they were not dignified by the term *ko-ming*. *Ko-ming* was first used by historians to describe the successful overthrow of the tyrant Chieh of the Hsia dynasty by the founder of the Shang dynasty, T'ang (about the fifteenth century B.C.). Later, it was used to describe the more heroic and successful victories against tyrants by founders of dynasties like those of the Han, the T'ang and the Ming. By extension, it also from time to time became loosely used to describe most founders of dynasties. But violence leading to victory was taken for granted and there was also the implication of righteousness and legitimacy.[24] Sun Yat-sen never had any doubts that the revolution he proposed was righteous and would be violent. He was ready from the start to buy arms for all the discontented who had come to join his party. The fact that he was amateurish in war was not as striking as the complete confidence he had in his cause. It was his cause which made his idea of revolution different from the traditional Chinese *ko-ming*.

Sun Yat-sen's *Three Principles of the People* (1924) was developed rather slowly from the ideas he first formally propounded in 1905. The three are translated usually as Nationalism, Democracy, and People's Livelihood. They were not original, nor were they entirely alien to the Chinese. In their basic forms, Nationalism could be taken to stem from the pride of being Chinese and People's Livelihood had first been crudely equated with the old slogan, 'the tiller should own his land'. Only the idea of people's rights in Democracy could be said to have been new. But the repeated emphasis on *min*, meaning people, was revolutionary in conception and in effect. Whatever Sun Yat-sen might have meant by people, it became a vital, almost a liturgical, part of his revolutionary movement and also one of the links it had with the *jen-min* (also people) in the People's Republic of China.

The continuity between Sun Yat-sen's K.M.T. and the C.C.P. founded by Ch'en Tu-hsiu (1879—1942) and Li Ta-chao (1889—1927) went further than this.[25] The C.C.P. was founded in 1921, sixteen years after the T'ung-meng League (the precursor of the K.M.T. in 1905). Although intellectually apart, it was asked by Lenin and the Comintern to come together with the K.M.T. in action. From 1923 to 1927 the two parties were in alliance. Both the parties had become increasingly uneasy with the alliance after Sun Yat-sen's death in 1925, but they stayed together long enough to ensure the success of the Northern Expedition, which ended the era of the warlords. For a few months in 1927, when two rival centres had been established in Nanking and Wuhan, the C.C.P. had hoped to control the centre at Wuhan with the left wing of the K.M.T. But this was not to be. Not only did the right-wing K.M.T. under Chiang Kai-shek order the destruction of the C.C.P. and its trade-union allies in Shanghai and elsewhere, but even the left-wing K.M.T. turned against them. In desperation, the Party tried to order its own military insurrection at Nan-ch'ang (capital of Kiangsi) in August 1927 and, when this failed, attempted a bold but futile gamble with the 'Canton commune' of December that year.[26] A series of further disasters followed during the next ten years. But 1927 was the major parting of the ways. The K.M.T. victors began to impose their new order: their revolution was now the only genuine one, victory having conferred upon it legitimacy. The C.C.P. were the rebels to be pacified or destroyed. On the run, the Party lost its original leaders and changed its leadership several times. Ch'en Tu-hsiu had been ousted, Li Ta-chao executed by the warlords in Peking, and a succession of young and passionate men all proved inadequate to the task of preserving the Party's authority. Only Mao Tse-tung and Chu Teh (1886–1976) in their Kiangsi Soviet and Chang Kuo-t'ao (b.1897) in his O-Yü-Wan Soviet (mainly in north-eastern Hupeh) provided a safe enough base to plan the Party's recovery. Even there, the soviets faced a grim struggle for survival and finally the Party had to abandon these bases and escape to the north west, to a new consolidated base at Yenan in Shensi province. Altogether the bitter years of defeat, encirclement and retreat lasted from 1927 until 1936.[27]

They were critical years for revolution in China. Firstly they transformed what had been something close to a consensus about a nationalist anti-imperialist revolution backed by all progressive forces (which Sun Yat-sen had painfully constructed) into a bitter and bloody polarisation of all those who still called themselves revolutionaries. There had been one revolution against all conservatives and reactionaries. Now there were only revolutionaries left; one set of them was in control and the other was on the run. Secondly, while all were revolutionaries, some were obviously more revolutionary than others. But how much more revolutionary was exceedingly difficult to define. If the C.C.P. had insisted that Marxist–Leninist–Stalinist principles and practices were more revolutionary, it would have encountered incomprehension, scepticism, even hostility among the people. The party worked among the peasantry, and such principles and practices would have been too alien. Its methods of winning confidence and support had to be gradual. It concentrated on land reform and measures to improve health, welfare and education. It criticised the Nanking government, but it did not separate itself from Sun Yat-sen's *Three Principles*, especially the third principle of People's Livelihood, which it claimed was similar to that of socialism and was a principle the C.C.P. was carrying out. In fact, the major criticism of the K.M.T. which it encouraged was that the K.M.T. leaders had betrayed Sun Yat-sen's revolutionary principles. The K.M.T., in turn, claimed to have been more revolutionary by being more true to the vision of Sun Yat-sen. Sun Yat-sen, after all, had been enshrined, his image was everywhere, his works distributed widely and at all levels; summaries and commentaries were being studied. Sun Yat-sen wanted China to be unified, prosperous and strong, and the K.M.T. was publicly committed to this very desirable end. Sun Yat-sen wanted China to be modern, and the K.M.T. was building factories, railways, ships, schools and universities, modern housing, efficient office blocks in all the main cities of China and was clearly far more modern than the 'rural bandits' that the C.C.P. had become. And, above all, Sun Yat-sen was Chinese and wanted China to develop its essential Chineseness. How could the C.C.P. claim to be loyal, the K.M.T. was to ask, when all its ideas came from two bearded Germans and the leaders of a country that held on to its influence in Mongolia and its imperialist interests in Manchuria?[28]

The Chinese who understood revolution as *ko-ming* would have seen that the K.M.T. had won a violent but righteous struggle and were legitimately trying to crush C.C.P. 'rebellion'. They would have found it more difficult to comprehend the idea which both the K.M.T. and the C.C.P. emphasised, that the revolution was not yet complete, the C.C.P. sometimes going further to add that the revolution had only just begun. The two parties emphasised the same idea for obviously different reasons and used the word revolution in different senses: the K.M.T. meaning that its victory in 1927 was only the first step and the C.C.P. that it was the Chinese people led by the C.C.P. that would eventually win the struggle. The ambiguity was deliberate and, like many other ambiguities of this period, stemmed from Sun Yat-sen himself. It originated from Sun Yat-sen's will and testament which ended with the words, 'The Revolution has not yet been completed. Our comrades must still continue to strive their utmost.' They were the two most quoted lines of Sun Yat-sen, appearing beside most of his photographs, which hung in every public building in the country, and read at every formal K.M.T. meeting and most national functions. The lines were simple enough and fully comprehensible in 1925. Indeed the key battles had yet to be fought. Much was still to be done. But the lines were quoted for decades after victory. They then expressed the warning that the victory in 1927 was only partial. A large part of China was still under warlord control, the imperialist powers were still threatening China's integrity and the dangerous Soviet-aided communists were still at large. That the lines were quoted so often also reflected the fact that the Nanking government was dominated by one party and by only one faction in the party, that this faction favoured tight military control, and that it believed that a long period of political tutelage was needed before democratic rule could be introduced. But, among the more radical members of the K.M.T. and the communist critics of the government, the lines were quoted to remind the country that no democracy was in sight and no steps had yet been taken to carry out Sun

Yat-sen's third principle of People's Livelihood. Until this was done and some measures were taken to bring social justice to the people, the revolution was indeed far from complete.[29]

The Sino-Japanese War (1937–45) united parties that had been bitter enemies, who now appeared to have postponed their respective efforts at revolution. In fact, the unity did not go far.[30] Deep suspicions remained to undermine all efforts at collaboration: the K.M.T. was afraid that the C.C.P. would not really fight the Japanese but would simply use the opportunity to strengthen itself for the ultimate struggle to seize national power from the K.M.T.; the C.C.P. feared that the K.M.T. leaders did not really want to fight the anti-communist Japanese and would seize any chance to make a deal with them. Perhaps fortunately for both parties, the Japanese were caught in their own rhetoric and had gone too far in their drive for empire to exploit the underlying conflicts to the full. They wanted China to be weak and liked the Chungking government's brand of nationalism not much more than the C.C.P.'s communism. Also, they did win over some factions of the K.M.T. and were able to fly the K.M.T. flag over their puppet government, led by Wang Ching-wei (1883–1944) at Nanking.[31] In so far as this did confirm the C.C.P.'s suspicions about the K.M.T. leadership, it helped immediately to distract the Chinese from a truly united anti-Japanese effort. In the long run, however, it justified the C.C.P. decision to become self-sufficient and fend for itself as much as it could and prepare against K.M.T. treachery as well as Japanese attacks. Thus the War became not only a patriotic but also a revolutionary war, and the C.C.P. used every opportunity to highlight the class contradictions which could lead the landlord, industrialist and financial supporters of the K.M.T. to national betrayal.

The War, therefore, did not distract the C.C.P. from its ultimate goals. On the contrary, it was seen as a useful if not necessary stage of preparation for greater struggles ahead. By fighting on the side of patriotism, the C.C.P. legitimised its recruitment, its arms and its extension into new areas of military and political control. But there was nothing cynical about this. China's independence and freedom from imperialism, and not merely Japan's at that, was a major goal. So also was the excellent chance to bring technology, industry, education and more modern cultural values to the rural areas of north and north-west China. And, not least, the war justified the training of disciplined armies and made it easier for the C.C.P. to convince the new troops that ultimately the war was against China's class enemies outside and within

China itself.[32]

It is here that Mao Tse-tung's adaptations of Marxist – Leninist theory to Chinese circumstances and the military and political strategy he evolved to serve that theory became crucial.[33] The C.C.P. did not suffer from the K.M.T.'s indecision as to whether Japan as China's enemy was more dangerous than the K.M.T.'s own enemy, the C.C.P. The United Front strategy that the C.C.P. employed made the priorities clear: of the two enemies, Japanese militarists had to be destroyed first, but Chinese militarists and their supporters were no less dangerous and at no time should their enmity be lost sight of. Therefore, throughout the war, the C.C.P. fought one war while preparing for the next. More decisively, it recognised that winning the first war, against Japan, was not within its powers but must await the combined allied forces outside China, while winning the second war, against the K.M.T., had to be achieved largely by its own efforts. The course was exceedingly clear. It was the second war that determined the re-volutionary future of China and it was for that they must steel themselves.

And, no less decisively, the C.C.P. leaders realised that the second war had to be won not only on the battlefields. They would have to offer not only a good patriotic record and honest soldiery but also a social and economic programme and an honest and efficient administration that fundamentally challenged the corrupt and demoralised regime in Chungking. Victory in battle had to be accompanied by an organised force for reconstruction. And this the C.C.P. leaders set out vigorously to produce, at Yenan and in the various Border Regions under their control, and to prove conclusively to the country as a whole that they had done so.[34]

When the war ended, several factors appeared to make the C.C.P. a credible alternative government. Its armies were large and mobile and its appeal to the peasantry in northern China was widespread. The U.S.S.R. had seized the north east (Manchuria) from the Japanese and opened it for the C.C.P. armies to use as a safe base. The U.S.A., which had begun as intermediary, was more open to accusations that it was replacing the Japanese as the imperialists who wanted to prop up the reactionary K.M.T. government as its puppet in Nanking. The K.M.T. struggled to re-establish its authority in the occupied zones, but was singularly unsuccessful in north-east and north China and was disastrous in its failure to stem the rapid rise in post-war inflation. Thus the resumption of the civil war in 1946 came at a time when the C.C.P.

was no longer on the defensive but was well poised to counter-attack – not merely militarily, but also politically and in terms of saving China from total economic collapse.[35] While it surprised many how quickly the C.C.P. would win, it did not surprise many that it would eventually do so.

During this final stage, both the K.M.T., backed openly by the U.S.A., and the C.C.P.,backed less openly by the U.S.S.R.,called for more sacrifices in order to 'complete' the revolution. But the only meaning to the word 'complete' that mattered was which side would win. The two lines of Sun Yat-sen's will remained ambiguous, but two points may be made, arising from the ambiguity, which are specially relevant to the chapters which follow. The first is that the Chinese have lived with the idea of revolution since the beginning of the century and, for most of them even today, it is apparent that revolution is a long and tortuous process that has to progress slowly and by stages. It is a struggle that has always to contend with enemies both inside and outside China. And the struggle always has to be an extended one because, as outlined briefly above, there are great contradictions in modern China. The second point is a question for the C.C.P. revolutionaries who won in 1949. There has never been a completed revolution in China. How is the revolution to proceed after victory? Obviously it has always been premature to say that the revolution has been completed. If this has been so, how and when will it be possible to say that the revolution is complete? Will the revolution ever be complete?

3 Building a New Model, 1949 – 53

CHINA emerged from the Second World War as – nominally – one of the Great Powers. This was flattering to the Chinese, but it was undeserved at the time. China did not have the cohesion, the wealth or the authority to play a Great Power role. The Chinese people were not prepared for the new place in world politics which President Roosevelt and others had seen for them. Only one role seemed credible in 1945: China as the grateful partner of the U.S.A., growing strong under American tutelage and with American support, one day taking its rightful place at the side of the Western democracies.[1] Such a role would have fitted in well with other trends in Asia. Japan would be kept weak and disarmed, Thailand would be forgiven its wartime relations with Japan, and the other territories in Asia were to be successively decolonised by Britain, France, the Netherlands and the U.S.A. Just as the Western nations had withdrawn from China, so they would eventually withdraw from Asia as imperial powers. New kinds of nation would be created, all indebted to the West for making them more or less independent and all friendly trading partners in a new Asia. Precisely what role China would play in the Asian neighbourhood was uncertain, but it was generally expected that it would lead the way in seeking rapid economic development in the world capitalist system. The successful democratic and capitalist China would be a major bulwark against the hostile rival economic system represented by the U.S.S.R.

It is not clear how much this picture of China's role impinged on the Chinese during the civil war which followed the Japanese surrender. The Nationalist government emphasised China's Great Power status and this gave added prestige to its leader, Chiang Kai-shek. The friendship of the U.S.A., the most powerful nation in the post-war world, was thought to provide political capital. Certainly the prospect of aid and trade to speed up the reconstruction of China's broken-down economy looked promising to the Chinese business and professional élite, who would be the first to profit. For the Nationalists, China's new status seemed a fitting climax to more than twenty years of effort to regain international respect. That this should have come with a vision of progress and future greatness defined largely in American terms was not inappropriate since the U.S.A.'s was the most striking success story among nations in modern times. China's leaders at the time were confident that they could carry the Chinese people with them if they could unite the country under their political control.

This turned out to be more difficult than most people expected. By 1947 the Nanking government showed that it was failing to adjust to the demands of post-war reconstruction. Its credibility as the government of unity suffered from an image of corruption and ineptitude in the cities and repression in the countryside. The factionalism within the K.M.T., the increasing disenchantment of liberal democratic groups outside the party, the fierce opposition of the ruthless and purposeful C.C.P. helped to erode further its claims to legitimacy.[2] Finally disastrous failures to control inflation left most Chinese ready, although uneasily so, for a change.[3] The decisive question, as the Chinese would themselves have seen it, was settled on the battlefields. And here the better disciplined and more determined armies of the C.C.P. supported by a sympathetic peasantry turned out to have a distinct advantage. In 1948 the Nationalist armies were being soundly defeated in Manchuria and North China.[4] By the middle of 1949, the civil war was all over apart from mopping-up operations in the south and west and the many offshore islands. On 1 October 1949, the People's Republic of China was proclaimed.

This bare outline hides the drama of four incredible years, the four most dramatic in modern Chinese history and comparable to the first four years of the French Revolution and to the events of 1917 in Russia. There is as yet no study which does justice to the period that produced one of the major transformations in the international politics of Asia and there are still many unexplained events and speculative 'ifs and buts' about the K.M.T. defeat and the C.C.P. victory.[5] Was it merely a bitter civil war, or was it a peasant victory over urban power, a Leninist defeat of feudal-bourgeois forces, an indomitable Maoist 'Yenan spirit' overwhelming a crude élitist nationalism, superior men outmanœuvring technologically advanced arms? Or was it a Stalinist conspiracy which undermined the ideals of New Deal diplomacy? Or good Chinese patriots destroyed by Japanese greed and ambition? Or dissolute and selfish Chinese leaders committing political suicide? Or, on the broadest canvas, was it part of the unstoppable international communist brotherhood burying a desperate capitalism? Obviously, of the above, there was more of some and less of others and obviously, until enough is known,definitive judgements are not yet possible. However, for the understanding of how the lessons of victory were applied to the years of reconstruction, it is valid to emphasise those factors the victors have stressed. The C.C.P. interpretation of its own victory was certainly relevant to the way its new government was going to rule China, to the new model of the independent, modern and revolutionary state it was going to give the world.

The first authoritative statement on the C.C.P. victory was made by Mao Tse-tung on 30 June 1949, some three months before the P.R.C. was founded, in his *On the People's Democratic Dictatorship.*[6] Among various things, he quoted Sun Yat-sen to explain the victory: 'we must arouse the masses of the people and unite in a common struggle with those nations of the world which treat us as equals'. The turning-point was, of course, 1921 when 'the vanguard of the Chinese proletariat learned Marxism – Leninism after the October Revolution and founded the Communist Party', but he summed up the fundamental lessons of C.C.P. victory, which would determine future policies of the P.R.C., as 'uniting the working class, the peasantry, the urban petty bourgeoisie and the national bourgeoisie and forming a domestic united front under the leadership of the working class', and 'allying ourselves with the Soviet Union, with the People's Democracies and with the proletariat and the broad masses of the people in all other countries'.

Another succinct statement is found in Chou En-lai's Report to the People's Political Consultative Conference on the First Anniversary of the P.R.C.:[7]

What lessons can we learn from this? The most important lesson is: such a big victory can never be an accidental phenomenon of history, but is the inevitable outcome of the numerous revolutionary struggles of the Chinese people during the past century. Such an enormous, swift and thorough victory cannot be conceived apart from the selfless support of millions of people.

This victory of the Chinese people is entirely different from all the 'unifications' in China's history. Formerly, there were this and that sort of 'unifications', but the unifiers were either the oppressors of the people from the start or else became so afterwards. Therefore, they could not but collapse after a little while. Today the unity among the Chinese people has emerged for the first time. The people themselves have become masters of China's soil, and the rule of the reactionaries in China has been irrevocably overthrown.

Thus the new leaders were able to say that a genuine revolutionary movement had overcome one which had long betrayed its own revolutionary goals. They rejected all that the K.M.T. government had stood for and promised to create eventually nothing less than a new Chinese society. But the first steps they took were to proclaim that they would govern by the principles of New Democracy which were generally inclusive and conciliatory, and most of the early speeches and slogans gave weight to the theme of harmony and unity. This can be clearly seen in the composition of the People's Political Consultative Conference (1949–54), the predecessor of the National People's Congress, which included the representatives of most existing political parties, including the 'Revolutionary Committee' of the K.M.T., as well as those of the surviving 'patriotic' capitalists and 'progressive' intellectuals of the major urban centres.* This Conference met on 21–30 September 1949. It adopted the Organic Law of the Central People's Government, a Common Programme for the reconstruction of China, elected a Central Government Council and enabled the P.R.C. to be formally proclaimed on 1 October 1949.

Similarly, non-C.C.P. and non-party individuals were appointed to other executive branches of government at national, provincial and local levels. Also, large sections of the administrative and technical élites were retained, mostly in their respective departments, and the more independent intellectual élites with Western liberal affiliations were invited to make their skills available for the revolutionary cause. So also were the managers and engineers in trade and industry and the educational and cultural staffs in schools, colleges, universities, libraries and museums. The initial indication was that the adjustments required would be relatively gradual and painless. While these suggest that there was a divergence between revolutionary theory and reformist practice, this is more apparent than real. It was politically sound to be conciliatory in 1949 and the early 1950s when the task of unification was not complete and the liberation of Taiwan was still imminent; and it was desirable that, if at all possible, no available skill should be lost where there were urgent tasks of national reconstruction ahead. What was important was that the C.C.P. leaders underlined from the beginning that the New Democracy was to remain 'under the

---

* This was extended to organs of executive power. For example, of the 63 members of the Central People's Government Council (1949–54), 29 were not members of the C.C.P.; and of the 26 heads of ministries and commissions in 1949–50, 11 were not members of the C.C.P.

leadership of the working class', the vanguard of which was the C.C.P., and that the revolution would eventually be deep and thorough.[8] The early years were a period of transition. For China's transformation, for the building of socialism, tougher measures would be necessary and would soon follow. There was no compromise where the dictatorship of the proletariat was concerned.

The new government recognised that there was much to be done, that it had only taken 'the first step in a long march of ten thousand *li*'.[9] And the long march now included travelling with a number of friendly and hostile nations engaged in a bitter Cold War which must necessarily involve China. There were questions of what cultural and technical baggage to carry, how quickly the country could recover from the damage caused by inflation and civil war and how to ensure that China could get on to the next step of 'building socialism'. For all this, the new leaders needed 'a peaceful environment', and they outlined their foreign-policy objectives accordingly. They wanted to protect China's independence; they wanted cordial relations with foreign governments whose attitudes were friendly; and consistent with the policy of all Chinese governments since the end of the nineteenth century, they wished to protect the rights and interests of the overseas Chinese. More unusually, they declared that China would work for lasting international peace and friendly co-operation between all countries – an objective which all governments piously subscribe to.[10]

None of the above objectives could be described as revolutionary, nor did they depart from traditional Chinese foreign policies. Only in one objective did the Chinese strike a new note: this was their declared intention to unite with the U.S.S.R. and other communist states and governments in the struggle against the imperialists and in particular the U.S.A. This was a truly remarkable addition to China's foreign policy. It marked off the new government from all previous Chinese governments. The underlying assumption seemed to have been that China needed revolution in the same way that the whole world needed revolution, that the U.S.S.R. led the world in revolution and China's revolution was in total accord with that of the U.S.S.R. Such an assumption could not have been more different from the China that was and could not have moved further away from all the values and institutions of Chinese history.

What was unmistakable was that China had recognised that its internal development had initially to depend on its alignment with an external power, something that all weak and developing nations were forced to accept. Like all countries, China expected the dependence to be necessary but temporary, and of course it had a better chance than most of achieving the reliable independence it wanted so much. All the same, it was significant that a foreign-policy decision was to play a major role in development during the first years of the P.R.C. It emphasises the truism in modern history that war and diplomacy determined the future of weak and undeveloped countries more decisively than that of strong and prosperous ones. For most of Asia since the beginning of the nineteenth century, major Western powers, later including Russia and the U.S.A., provided the foreign-policy decisions which divided much of the continent between themselves and thus contributed conclusively to the direction of growth of each of the countries which came under their respective influence or domination, in many cases, even long after these countries gained their 'independence'.

China, however, had been different. No one power was able or willing to determine the course of its development even though China was no less weak, divided and technically backward than India, Indonesia and other Asian countries. But, unlike the others, China had been the target of such divisive and confusing international rivalries that no single foreign war or foreign-policy decision could determine the course of development and no single power could have been depended on to lead the way. Some degree of polarisation between the road to capitalism favoured by the K.M.T. and that towards socialism chosen by the C.C.P. had begun after 1928, but it really was not until the U.S.S.R. declared war on Germany and the U.S.A. declared war on Japan in 1941 that the choice for China between these two powers became increasingly clear. By the end of the war, these were the two to emerge as stronger than ever before: it must have been with some relief that the Chinese in 1945 found that they would, if they wished, only have to choose between the U.S.A. and the U.S.S.R. Not surprisingly, after a century of playing one power against another with a marked lack of success, the new leaders saw little merit in adopting a policy of calculated neutralism. They probably considered themselves fortunate that the choice had become such a simple one.

It is still being asked whether the C.C.P. might not have chosen to attract U.S. friendship rather than to depend on Soviet assistance if the U.S.A. had not appeared to side with the K.M.T. during the civil war of 1946–9.[11] Had the U.S.A. been more aloof from the K.M.T., the P.R.C.'s relations with the U.S.A. might have been marginally better. If the U.S.A. had been more friendly to the P.R.C. the Chinese leaders might have done marginally better in their bargaining with Stalin and gained more Soviet help. But what seems not to be in doubt is that the U.S.A. would never have given the P.R.C. any material assistance if it had associated itself with Soviet international objectives. Also Soviet response could hardly be cool since the C.C.P. success was true to the revolutionary goals which the U.S.S.R. declared it wanted. Given the sharing of these goals, China would have been grateful to have had a powerful ally like the U.S.S.R. to lean towards.

Hence the policy of 'leaning to one side'. By this, the impression was certainly given that China acknowledged that revolution was where the U.S.S.R. was. Yet there were hints already that the equation was not that simple. In stressing that Marxist–Leninist theory had to be married to concrete Chinese experience, Mao Tse-tung and Ch'en Po-ta (b. 1904) had opened the way to possible Chinese innovations in future revolutionary practice.[12] Also, in the first flush of victory, it was to be expected that the contributions of Mao Tse-tung Thought to the securing of that victory were emphasised. It must have seemed that what was most important were the lessons of Chinese victory: how to capture power by one's own efforts – that was the key step to revolution. Here was the lesson for colonial Asia, the continent where China's experience might be specially relevant. But it was also clear at the same time that capturing power was one thing, retaining that power and building socialism to ensure that the revolution would be fully carried out was quite another. For the latter, the C.C.P. recognised that the fraternal assistance of the U.S.S.R. was essential. What better way than to take the achievements of the greatest revolution in modern times and turn them into the models for China? The Soviet revolution was after all the revolution to point the way for all revolutions. China was most fortunate in having not only a ready-made body of theoretical literature to adapt and use but also a powerful state machine (recently steeled in a great European war!) complete with successful blueprints and ex-perienced technicians and administrators to stand by its side. What more could a modern revolution ask for?

The Chinese did not hesitate. Immediately after China's clear declaration of policy, on 2 October 1949, the U.S.S.R. was the first country to recognise it, followed the next day by Bulgaria and Romania, and the day after by Poland, Hungary and Czechoslovakia, and then by all other communist countries – East Germany, North Korea, Outer Mongolia, Yugoslavia and Albania in November. By the end of October China's first ambassador was appointed to the U.S.S.R.

He was Wang Chia-hsiang (1907 – 74), a senior party man, one of the young men trained in Moscow and sent to lead the Chinese party in 1931, and his appointment underlined the debt to the U.S.S.R. Although non-Communist countries also began to recognise the P.R.C. by the middle of December: first Burma and later that month India, and in January 1950 another ten more including Britain, the Scandinavian countries, Pakistan, Ceylon and Afghanistan, the Chinese left no doubt that they would continue to lean heavily to one side, and that other 'friendly' countries could not sway them from their purpose. Mao Tse-tung had gone to Moscow in December 1949, a finely calculated display of commitment, accompanied by the determination to get the best for China with negotiations at the highest possible level. In February 1950, a treaty of friendship, alliance and mutual assistance was signed, and an agreement that the U.S.S.R. would provide long-term credits to China, and that China would leave certain Manchurian railways and port arrangements in Soviet hands for a few years.[13]

The negotiations were far from easy. Siding with the U.S.S.R. had its difficulties. Several Chinese leaders, notably Mao Tse-tung himself, were not fully trusted by Stalin, nor could the Chinese be sure that they would not have to pay too high a price for Stalin's help. In order to win Stalin's trust, China would have to assure him that it would be whole-hearted in modelling itself on the U.S.S.R. and the Chinese people would have to be persuaded to show a degree of friendship to their Soviet comrades that they had never shown to any foreigners before. This was all the more challenging a task because the Russians had not had a good press in China.[14] Tsarist Russia was certainly unloved; Russian literature portrayed a decadent and backward society and Soviet literature had little appeal except to communists and left-wing intellectuals. The Russian language was relatively unknown; and what was available to read on Soviet society and economy was far from impressive. Then there was the Soviet policy towards Outer Mongolia and the Soviet raiding of Manchurian factories during the last days of the war, which had been widely publicised right up to 1949. It was obvious that a great deal of pressure would have to be exerted to reorientate the Chinese to become friends of the U.S.S.R., and this the Sino-Soviet Friendship Association, established five days after the P.R.C. was proclaimed, and headed personally until 1954 by the second most important leader in China, Liu Shao-Ch'i himself, was expected to do.[15] The speed with which this association extended itself across the country and the force of the campaigns the association sponsored marked the recognition that the task was both a difficult and a vital one.

A great deal has recently been made of Mao Tse-tung's difficulties with Stalin and the mainly technical nature of his decision to lean to the side of the U.S.S.R. There is even the implication that the U.S.A.'s insistence on supporting the Nationalist government in Taiwan and withholding recognition from the P.R.C., its intransigence and its series of provocative acts and statements embittered Mao Tse-tung and made him all the more determined to woo a distrustful Stalin. An equally convincing argument could, in fact, be made for the view that Stalin's suspicions of the C.C.P. leaders drove them to harden their attitude towards the U.S.A. more openly, to act and speak more provocatively than they really had to, to mobilise anti-U.S. opinion among the Chinese in order to arouse them to show more friendly feelings towards the unknown Russians. Much depends on whether we accept the massive evidence pointing to China's determination to eschew compromise, to reject 'the third road' between the side of imperialism and the side of socialism, even before P.R.C. was established and long before U.S. intransigence could have made any difference.[16] The Chinese leaders had understood that the politics of the Cold War would automatically extend to China, where Soviet and U.S. interests were directly involved. Whether Mao Tse-tung had been altogether happy to go cap in hand to Moscow, he had, as early as his days in Yenan, accepted the orthodoxy of Stalinism as a necessary stage in world revolution and nothing that had happened during the immediate post-war years, not even Stalin's willingness to deal with Chiang Kai-shek and failure to anticipate the C.C.P. victory, could have changed his perception of the U.S.S.R's historic role. It was in this context that he had long prepared for the uphill task of converting the Chinese people to a sense of trust and friendship with the Soviet peoples. This task was eased by the start of the Korean War in June 1950, only nine months after the P.R.C. was founded. Within a few days, the U.S.A. brought the war close to China by openly reinforcing the Nationalist forces in Taiwan and thus confirmed that it was an enemy of the P.R.C. Anti-U.S. campaigns thereafter became easier to organise, and their slogans became more realistic and concrete.[17]

The decision to side with the U.S.S.R. was a fateful one. It had serious repercussions for the P.R.C. in the United Nations, in the U.S. intervention in Korea and the Taiwan Straits, and in the Cold War which spread rapidly over most of east and south-east Asia. But it also had a positive impact on China's internal development. This is not to suggest that Soviet assistance and support determined the successes of this period; more important factors were the C.C.P.'s old organisational skills and mobilisation experiences. What was crucial, however, was the confidence that the Soviet backing gave to China's sense of security and sovereignty and the way this enabled the Chinese to concentrate on the immense task of national reconstruction.

This task of reconstruction had to begin with the country's reunification. The People's Liberation Army (P.L.A.) continued to overcome K.M.T. forces in southern and western China. By April 1950, only two sizeable territories, Taiwan and Tibet, were still outside their control. The former the Chinese were preparing to liberate when the Korean War began. But U.S. commitment to its defence made liberation by force impossible. The latter came under Chinese control when the P.L.A. marched into Tibet in October 1950. Although in Chinese terms unification was yet to be completed, China was effectively unified by the end of 1950.

In 1949, the Soviet road to socialism was the most modern road to follow. It was one based on a highly centralised state and a planned economy which emphasised the development of heavy industry and the rapid collectivisation of agriculture. Translated into Chinese terms during the first four years, this meant extending party as well as P.L.A. control over all regions and provinces and reorganising a unified bureaucracy, starting afresh to build up heavy industry and carrying out basic land reforms throughout the country.

The first task was obviously to bring order to the newly conquered territories and out of the financial and economic chaos of the civil war period. At the centre was the Government Administration Council and this the party dominated from the start. Outside were the six Regional Political and Military Committees, mainly created by P.L.A. officers and political commissars who governed the regions on behalf of the centre.[18] Their immediate tasks were clear. The K.M.T. forces which surrendered were quickly absorbed into the P.L.A. or disbanded, and the officers and men retrained and indoctrinated to make them useful soldiers, workers or peasants. A new security structure was created to liquidate all 'enemies of the state'. Everywhere, people's courts were established to dispose of landlords, profiteers and corrupt representatives of traditional authority in the most public and dramatic ways. Specially trained political cadres sifted out the common criminals and potential dissidents for re-education and reclassification. In contrast with the conciliatory measures at the highest levels, swift justice and severe punishment were the norms where resistance from below was concerned. Gentler methods of rehabilitation and corrective labour became more usual later on. Within a few months of conquest, each region or province was pacified. The speed with which the new organs of authority brought order to the near anarchy produced by decades of weak and corrupt provincial governments was astonishing. These organs encouraged the release of pent-up feelings for freedom and revenge among the ordinary people, especially among the peasantry, and excesses and dubious justice occurred everywhere and were later admitted, but there was also no doubt as to the nation-wide relief at the quick return to order.

Financial and economic order were more difficult to attain. The most important instruments used to create the new centrally planned economy were the People's Bank of China, the investment and insurance companies of the Ministry of Finance and the key economic agencies and trading corporations, but they would take several years to bring the whole economy under direct supervision.[19] The most immediate job was to restore confidence in the modern industrial sector and this had largely to be left in the hands of the 'national bourgeoisie', that is, the capitalists and their managerial and technical staff. They were allowed to retain their say in production, in both local and foreign trade, and in most areas of internal transportation. Although no reliable figures are available, estimates that the private sector accounted for well over half of gross production in 1949–50 seem quite acceptable.[20] The state was content during the first two years to try to obtain a monopoly of banking and finance facilities and ultimately of all foreign trade. It would then, through the overhauling of the tax structure, the registering of all properties, the revision of all the laws concerning industry, commerce and communications, and a thorough review of the wage structure in relation to the labour resources of the country, gradually take over control of the private sector. The second area in which the state moved quickly to full control was the area of heavy industry, the key to the Soviet model, and it was relatively easy to do this in areas like the north east where the Japanese had made a good start some twenty years earlier. By 1952, it was estimated that the state controlled 80 per cent of heavy industry and 90 per cent of the country's foreign trade.[21]Another notable area which the state began to control was prices, not only wholesale prices but by the end of the first four years most retail prices as well. This brought an end to the run-away inflation of 1947–9. By 1951, it was claimed that the peasant purchasing power had risen by at least 40–50 per cent throughout the country.[22]

Once there was order, it was but a short step towards increased productivity. Here the Chinese recognised that new planning skills and technology were needed, especially in the realm of heavy industry. A start had been made in north-east China, where Kao Kang (c. 1902–c. 1954) had, with the help of the first batches of Soviet advisers, introduced measures similar to those of state capitalism employed in the New Economic Policy stage of Soviet development. With the newly reorganised industrial units, from mining and steel to machine-manufacturing, there was a dramatic rise in productivity. It was not long before other industrial centres adopted the practices tried out in the north east: first in the coastal cities of Shanghai and Tientsin, then in Wuhan in central China, then in the south at Canton and, equally important, in the industries moved into the undeveloped interior provinces, especially of Shensi, Honan, Szechuan and Hunan. Where heavy industry and high levels of planning were concerned, the Soviet model clearly paid off. After various delays and adjustments, a formal Soviet-type state planning board under the chairmanship of Kao Kang was set up in October 1952 and the first Five-Year Plan for industrial and agricultural development was announced soon afterwards.[23]

The delays in adjustments were partly due to the three-year gap between the liberation of the north east and that of the south and west, but also partly due to the unevenness of development between the coastal regions and the interior and to some of the unexpected emergency needs arising from the Korean War. What was to become an even more fundamental difficulty in the kind of Soviet planning methods employed was consideration of the special investment needs for Chinese consumer industries and agriculture. Here the size of China's rural population, the subsistence level of most of its farm plots, the almost total lack of mechanisation and the exceptional vulnerability to natural disasters like drought, floods and locusts created problems which even the thirty years of Soviet experience with planning could not solve. The Chinese had, of course, foreseen that agriculture and the peasantry would be the country's great source of strength if they were not allowed, through unsuitable methods of planning, to become its great source of weakness. If their development failed to dovetail with the plans for large-scale capital investment in heavy industry, they could become major obstacles to national productivity as a whole.

Thus one of the first major measures of the new government, long promised before it came to power, was an agrarian reform law.[24] This was something which the C.C.P. had had plenty of experience of in north China and it was largely a matter of standardising practice and extending the reforms into new regions as they came under the new government's control, thus enabling all new lands to be redistributed in preparation for the next stage of co-operative farming. The law was adopted in June 1950 and much of the redistributed land was organised into units cultivated by 'mutual-aid teams'. The immediate successes in land reform were encouraging. By the middle of 1952, the reforms had progressed so well that new plans for collectivisation could be drawn up and hundreds of thousands of small agricultural co-operatives were expected to be established during the next three years. Agriculture became a greater focus of attention as more production surpluses were needed for the state to finance and pay for the increasing numbers of factories and for heavy industry. Partly because of these pressures for capital accumulation, but partly also because of inadequacies in distribution and transportation and the alarming rate of urbanisation during the last years of the Nationalist regime, the peasantry was strongly urged to stay on the land and plans were devised to return most of the new urban migrants to their rural homes. Again, although there were dislocations and failures due to haste and errors in planning, especially in the south and west, the purposefulness of the reforms and the earnestness of the dedicated cadres of the C.C.P. seemed to have overcome much of the resistance to the changes.[25]

The initial restructuring of both town and countryside and the rise in the productive capacity of industrial workers and the newly established rural co-operatives were impressive. Within four years of the P.R.C.'s foundation, it looked as if the Chinese had already achieved a transformation of traditional society. One new set of laws followed another: freeing peasants from landlords; guaranteeing workers against arbitrary sackings and penalties and offering opportunities for retraining and reassignment; gradually introducing free health, low rents, stable prices and more equitable wage-structures; permitting some worker participation in industrial management; and pressurising criminals, gamblers, secret-society members, prostitutes, opium addicts, other social outcasts and even 'counter-revolutionaries' to turn themselves into useful citizens. Not least, the government implemented a Marriage Law not only in urban areas but also in the country-side.[26] For the first time, polygamy, child marriage and concubinage were effectively banned and real progress was made to give equal rights to women at home and at work. In the face of the rapid changes in social and economic conditions, it is understandable why Kuo Mo-jo (b.1892), the president of the Chinese Academy of Sciences, celebrated the first anniversary of the P.R.C. with a poem that included the line, 'several thousand years of feudalism dug out by the roots'. Although somewhat premature, it reflected an enthusiasm for radical change which was already widely shared.

But rapid change on such a large scale with an inadequate and poorly trained administrative infrastructure must lead to much waste, if not great unevenness, in development. The new government was soon made aware of the continued gap between theory, law and good intentions on the one hand and the persistence of inefficient and corrupt practices on the other. Once the main fighting in the Korean War had ended in July 1951, the government in the north east (that is, in the provinces that took the brunt of the war) opened the first campaign to improve administrative performance.[27] This was the 'Three-Anti' campaign against waste, corruption and bureaucratism among government officials at all levels. This was so effective that it became a national campaign and also a model for the later campaigns against businessmen and entrepreneurs, and then against artists, intellectuals and teachers. Early in 1952, there followed the 'Five-Anti' movement against bribery, tax evasion and three other ways of cheating the state of property and materials. Less publicly but no less fiercely, fresh campaigns had started against bourgeois values in the arts, literature, science and humanistic scholarship. Although less tangible and more controversial than re-educating criminals and opium addicts, the methods employed to break down attitudes and undermine intellectual independence were initially almost as effective.[28] The problem of correct intellectual commitments became increasingly urgent as the new government stepped up its efforts in the cultural and educational fields. Hundreds of thousands of primary and secondary schools had to be reorganised to use new syllabuses and textbooks and thousands more new ones needed new teachers. Extension courses, and adult literacy and basic education were also much encouraged and greatly in demand. Then there was the urgent need for the political reorientation of the élites which had recently submitted to the regime. And, at the apex, there were the hundreds of institutions of higher education and technical training attempting quickly to produce the skilled personnel the country needed, and to train enough people to staff the hundreds of institutions that were being started. On top of this, as revolutionary theory and practice demanded, all these teachers and trainees had to become familiar with Marxist – Leninist philosophy and the Thought of Mao Tse-tung.[29] Special efforts had to be made to ensure that older educated élites did not transmit their scepticism concerning the regime but were won over to the side of the revolution.

Indeed, at the higher levels during this period of thought-remoulding much of the exhortation to change consisted of a judicious mixture of revolutionary rhetoric and traditional idioms. The greater part of the emphasis was on persuasion and rational debate and, although the need to control thought was regarded as urgent from the start, the pressure on the non-communist intellectuals was moderate. Even a radical party theoretician like Ch'en Po-ta quoted Confucius and Mencius and resorted to pithy old sayings to urge his audience to work harder and more honestly for China. And a Westernised scientist like Li Ssu-kuang (1889–1971), the geologist, academician and Minister of Geology (from 1952), could in one place decry the absurdities of 'bourgeois science' and in another quote one of the oldest Chinese justifications for scientific knowledge, the highly 'idealist' Confucian references to 'the investigation of things, the acquisition of knowledge, the sincerity of thought and rectification of mind, the cultivation of one's self, the regulation of one's family and the ordering of one's state that leads to the peace and tranquillity of all under heaven'. Such appeals to tradition were understandable and appeared to satisfy the majority of the élites who had stayed behind to support the regime. Most of them adapted themselves readily and many threw themselves with enthusiasm into teaching and writing for the Revolution. But even while much was being made of the 'brainwashing' campaigns of this period, astonishingly large support was forthcoming from the older élites, enough to suggest a small renaissance of scholarship and creative experimentation for a few years. By 1953, the impression had been created that the New Democracy of the P.R.C. was broadly based and tolerant of a wide range of opinions provided they were not anti-government and provided they were more or less couched in Marxist language.[30] Indeed the Chinese leaders showed themselves to be realistic, flexible and concerned to demonstrate that, while their revolution would transform Chinese society, they also valued continuity and would harness various parts of China's past to achieve their ends.

The pressing task for the C.C.P. was still to get on with the business of building socialism on the Soviet model and, given the grimness and unfamiliarity of this model, it was probably technically wise not to overstress the eventual discontinuities of the revolution. The speed and extent of Sovietisation was never alarming, but it was soon obvious how much China would have to depend on Soviet expertise and supply of equipment and materials to get the first Five-Year Plan (1953–7) off the ground. By 1952 it was noted that 72 per cent of all foreign trade was with the U.S.S.R. and most of the remainder with other communist countries.[31] Admittedly, the dependence was accentuated by the trade embargoes imposed on China by the U.S.A. and its allies as a result of the Korean War and, though China's foreign trade with non-communist countries did improve in the following years, the figures indicate the key feature in China's isolation. It was an isolation which China struggled for the first four years to break out of. But while the isolation lasted, China could only have been grateful for the Soviet assistance which made it possible for it to get started. The question of whether China trusted Soviet friendship in the early 1950s is less important than that of whether China wanted any alternative. Despite the recent bitterness in Sino-Soviet relations, all the evidence still suggests that China was genuinely committed to adopting the Soviet way to 'socialist transformation' even after Stalin's death in March 1953, and for several more years there were no doubts about the Soviet model for China's main industrialisation plans. The difficulties lay in the socialisation of small-scale labour-intensive industrial and agricultural units and this was something which the Chinese did not expect the Soviet model to solve. There was, in any case, no serious discrepancy between the different rates of industrialisation and agricultural collectivisation until after 1954, and there was certainly no question that, during the first four years, China would have achieved less were it not for the steady Soviet support received.

Where there was doubt about the Soviet model, this did not arise so much from the model itself as from the Chinese self-image of its rehabilitation from a century of humiliation, its historical distrust of non-Chinese formulas for modernisation and its confidence in its capacity to direct its own revolution. Two features of this self-image are striking. Firstly, China could not see itself even in 1949 following the U.S.S.R. in the way that Poland, Hungary, Bulgaria and Romania (or even the more developed Czechoslovakia and East Germany) had done a few years earlier. The analogies with these countries of Eastern Europe would have been most inappropriate and the U.S.S.R. was never a model in that sense. This was obvious not only because Eastern Europe shared something of a common heritage with Russia and was more economically comparable whereas China was more correctly described as 'poor and blank', but also because China's Communist Party did not feel that it had depended on Soviet help for its success. It is significant that right from the start the Chinese insisted on comparing their problems in the 1950s to those of Bolsheviks during the first two decades after 1917 and repudiated the examples of Eastern Europe whenever and wherever they could.[32]

The second feature of the doubt was less obvious but perhaps no less apparent to the culturally and politically sensitive Chinese leaders. This stemmed from the fact that the U.S.S.R., for all its proclaimed respect for the nationalities within it, was obviously Russian in the most important things. That a revolution with universalist appeal should acquire unique Russian features tied to its location, its size and its history seemed quite natural to the Chinese,who had so strongly stressed the concreteness of their own revolutionary successes. It should be no surprise if the Chinese would seek very early on to separate the non-transferable parts of the Soviet experience. That they were alert to some of the problems that might arise can be seen in the contrast between the speed with which they imported and digested industrial plants and technological skills and their very complex and ambiguous response to the reading of Soviet ideological polemics from Lenin to Stalin, of Soviet development debates and of Soviet literature and history.[33] Also, on the surface, the C.C.P. in 1949 appeared to be a Stalinist party, not only in its rules, its structure, its type of personnel, its discipline, but also in most of its rhetoric, its work-style and its control over party history. But Stalin's vast power, his individuality, his Russianness was something else again; Stalin could not be simply substituted at the head of the C.C.P. by Mao Tse-tung or Liu Shao-ch'i, nor would either of these men have thought it necessary to act like latter-day Stalins. The C.C.P. would have understood that the Stalinist features of the party would also have to be modified, and even ironed out, although it was premature to attempt to do that before the party's power within China had been consolidated.

Thus the Chinese recognised that their victories in China had to be safeguarded externally by a powerful ally. It was fortunate that this ally shared the same sorts of revolutionary goals and it was possible to put aside for the moment China's own role in world revolution and let the U.S.S.R. carry that responsibility at that stage. What was more urgent and vital was China's sovereignty and security, and the first four years after 1949 were devoted to laying sound foundations for both. China's sovereignty depended on the unification of all of China and international recognition that the People's Republic of China was the sole government of China. That sovereignty it saw as complete only when its representatives sat in the United Nations in place of those of the Nationalist government it had ousted. But the Korean War brought the most unfortunate consequences. At one blow, the tide of recognitions was halted and the question of its seat in the U.N. was blocked by the U.S.A. and its allies. For the next four years, the closest China got was in November 1950 when its delegate Wu Hsiu-ch'uan (b. *c.* 1908) spoke at the Security Council meeting against the armed aggression of the U.S.A. against Taiwan, a territory of China. The bitterest moment was when he had to speak while 'the so-called representatives of the Chinese K.M.T. reactionary remnant clique' were allowed 'to sit unashamed here in our midst, professing to be representing the Chinese people'.[34] Indeed he was right to protest that 'without the participation of the lawful delegates of the People's Republic of China, representing 475 million people, the United Nations cannot in practice be worthy of its name'. But his passionate plea went largely unheeded. There were echoes here of China's long humiliating experiences with the Western-dominated international system. Once again, China's enemies were manipulating the system to deny China's rightful place in it. From Unequal Treaties forced on China by superior arms to an unjust exclusion from the formal international stage, also it would appear through superior arms in the Taiwan Straits, China was being thwarted and its sovereignty was being laid open to doubt. Although China could not have foreseen in those early years that its failure was to extend for more than twenty years, nothing could have been more frustrating than to be subjected to a system which allowed its enemies to act as if there were two Chinas.

As for China's security, it is doubtful if the U.S.A. would have invaded China or encouraged the Nationalists in Taiwan to do so with their full support. But the Chinese could not discount that possibility after their experiences fighting the American forces under the U.N. command in Korea. Most of all they were convinced that the possibility of nuclear blackmail was even more real and that they could only rely on Soviet protection for a limited period without China in fact becoming the client-state of the U.S.S.R. that it was already accused of being. At no time did the policy of 'leaning to one side' imply any intention to remain subordinate to the U.S.S.R., and both Mao Tse-tung in 1950 (after two months in Moscow) and Liu Shao-ch'i in 1953 (after three months in Moscow) took special care to avoid any impression of inequality even when they were most directly seeking treaty guarantees and financial assistance.[35] It must have become obvious during those troubled and dangerous first years of the P.R.C. that, even without the reminders of history, China could not really 'stand up' in the way it expected to, as long as it did not have its own capacity to ensure its own security. A start was made in 1949–53, internally with national reconstruction and rapid industrialisation along Soviet lines, and externally with the Soviet alliance and fresh efforts to take the diplomatic initiative outside the framework of the U.N. But already there was an awareness that, given its past and given the aggressive enemies it had, the only safety for China lay in becoming a nuclear power.

Thus in terms of independence, modernisation and revolution, China's achievements by 1953 were modest. Its independence was limited by the U.S. Seventh Fleet and the existence of the Republic of China, as well as by the need for Soviet assistance in so many fields, the recognition of the Mongolian People's Republic and the acceptance of Soviet garrisons at Port Arthur. Its modernisation hinged on modelling itself on the U.S.S.R., on the heavy industry it would help China to build, on the administration it would train the Chinese to man and use, and on the skilled manpower it would provide to help inexperienced Chinese counterparts learn what a modern industrial economy should be like. As for revolution, there was a moment of glory when China could itself appear as the model for all anti-imperialist wars in colonial Asia, as the answer to how to achieve power under Asian conditions, but the moment was brief. The U.S.S.R. quickly reasserted its claim to be the fountain-head of revolution, the ultimate model for all who wanted revolution.[36] The Chinese were forced to recognise that until they were themselves fully independent and could modernise in their own distinctive way, they could not provide a revolution for others to emulate.

4 Towards Independence, 1953 – 8

THE many heads of state and prime ministers who have made their way to Peking and then been given an audience with Mao Tse-tung have often been compared with tribute missions visiting the imperial Chinese court. This is the sort of historical analogy that is not always helpful in understanding China today. For then one would have to say that Mao's visit to Moscow in 1949 would put China in a similar tributary position vis-à-vis the U.S.S.R. This is obviously not so even to the Chinese at the time. Nevertheless, it was significant that Mao Tse-tung, who had never been abroad before, went to Moscow in December 1949 to pay his respects to Stalin, and personally dedicated an article on 'The Greatest Friendship' to Stalin on his death in March 1953.[1] No less significant then was the fact that Mao Tse-tung made one more trip abroad, also to Moscow, in November 1957, and never left China again. Without making too much of Mao Tse-tung's admiration for Stalin, it should be emphasised that the desire to 'learn from the Soviet Union' in the 1950s was deep and genuine and that China was ready to admit its dependence on the leading nation of the socialist world. The dependence could only be temporary, however, and mainly a means to an end. Both countries recognised that China's size and history would ensure that it would ultimately be independent, even assertive in world affairs. In the meantime, a treaty of friendship and alliance, a special relationship and a debt of gratitude might enable the two countries to remain on the same side against the same enemies.

Until 1953, however, the Chinese leadership were not confident as to how much longer it would be before their independence was universally recognised, and when there would be only one China in the United Nations. With Malenkov and a younger leadership in the U.S.S.R. and with the formal signing of the Korean War armistice, China was much better placed to make a fresh start to counter the American and Taiwan propaganda that it was just another 'satellite-state'. Attention was first focused on the United Nations partly to return to the lost momentum of recognitions (twenty-six nations between October 1949 and June 1950) and partly to gain a place in the conference to settle the problems of Korea.[2] For the former there was no success at all. In addition, for the next two years the United Nations agreed by a large majority to postpone discussion of the issue of China's admission: in 1953, by 44 votes to 10 with 2 abstentions; in 1954, by 45 votes to 7 with 5 abstentions. But while *de jure* recognition was hard to achieve, *de facto* negotiations on trade and war proceeded more smoothly.[3] Japan was eager to normalise relations with China; although it was rebuffed, it did open up a regular and increasingly successful trade. France was still smarting from having French properties in China requisitioned, but it did welcome the chance to trade without political commitments. Thus China was assured that *de facto* relations were forthcoming and these could provide political leverage later on. More significantly, China was invited to participate in the Geneva Conference on far-eastern problems in April 1954.[4] Although this was outside the U.N. framework, it was gratifying to the Chinese that all the key U.N. countries were present and it was the only China at the table.

The Geneva Conference marked a major turning-point in China's international affairs, especially in the image Chou En-lai projected of a basically patient and reasonable nation on the side of the oppressed and poorer nations of Asia against the Western powers. The new image has been described as the result of fresh Chinese thinking about the U.N., of a more sophisticated view of how to win friends there and the recognition that American hostility could not be stormed but could be overcome by long-term strategy. But what was perhaps more important was the realisation that China's independence should not only be measured by getting Taiwan out of the U.N. but also by China's ability to manœuvre successfully where major international issues were concerned. Chou En-lai's performance at Geneva was an eye-opener for those who had only seen China as the 'aggressor' in Korea, backed by the U.S.S.R., and who expected China to be equally 'aggressive' in other parts of Asia, especially in south-east Asia. The independence from Soviet manipulations was now obvious: Stalin's death and the uncertainties of the new Soviet leadership made it easier to perceive this. The confidence that there was only one China that mattered, especially for the countries of Indo-China and their neighbours, also came through clearly. It was an excellent beginning to China's campaign to show that its exclusion from the United Nations was due only to the irrational hatred of the U.S.A. and merely demeaned that organisation and made it far less effective as a guardian of world peace.

So successful was Chou En-lai that the U.S.A. had to make counter-moves to check his progress and plan in turn for a protracted struggle to 'defend' Taiwan[5] and protect Western interests and pro-Western élites in south and south-east Asia. This had become so obvious that, by August 1954, the Chinese were saying,

[Aggressive circles in the United States] are now in the midst of schemes for signing a 'bilateral treaty of mutual security' with the traitorous Chiang Kai-shek group. They are trying to whip together a so-called 'Northeast Asian Defence Alliance' embracing the reactionary forces in Japan, the Syngman Rhee clique and the Chiang Kai-shek group. They are making every effort to bring round Britain and France, trying to coerce certain countries in the Western Pacific and Southeast Asia into organizing a 'Southeast Asian Defence Community'. Without a doubt the P.R.C. is the chief target at which this series of sinister moves by the United States' aggressive circles is aimed.[6]

The results of the American initiatives were slightly different and did not involve Japan and South Korea. The Manila Treaty was signed in September establishing the South-East Asia Treaty Organisation (SEATO), but in December, the U.S.A. did finalise the Mutual Defence Treaty with the K.M.T. government in Taiwan. Apart from being aimed at China and patently provocative, the two moves signalled that many countries in the region and ex-colonial powers like the U.S.A., Britain and France would always regard the P.R.C. as the enemy. Although China was not really impressed by SEATO, it was furious at the Taiwan Treaty.[7] The former was something it could hope to neutralise through diplomacy just as it had successfully headed off any possibility that key Asian countries like India, Indonesia and Burma might join it. The latter, however, was a direct challenge to China's legitimacy, and it saw the treaty as a most blatant example of interference in China's internal affairs. But there was no simple way out of the Taiwan problem. The more determined the Chinese were to 'liberate' Taiwan, the more committed the U.S.A. became to using the Seventh Fleet to defend the island. Unification would have to be achieved by force and the force to match that of the U.S.A. was something the Chinese did not have. In fact, if the U.S.A. really threatened China, or allowed Taiwan to use American missiles against the mainland, China would have had to admit that it depended on the U.S.S.R. to provide a nuclear umbrella. By this time, this was a kind of dependence that China was less willing to count on. Thus the Taiwan Treaty was a sharp reminder, even as China's international status improved, that it could never feel safe as long as there was another China for people to look to and as long as it had to depend on another country for its own security.

There were, of course, reassurances which gave the P.R.C. leadership confidence. Within the country, a series of elections at local, provincial and national levels had produced the 1141 deputies who met at the First National People's Congress in Peking in September 1954.[8] A new constitution was adopted, Mao Tse-tung was formally confirmed as Chairman of the P.R.C. and various reports by Liu Shao-ch'i and Chou En-lai were officially made the bases for foreign and domestic policies. The Constitution was formal and elaborate, but it was drawn up on the premise that it served a period of transition and reflected 'the general desire of the people as a whole to build a socialist society'. The central point was, however, unequivocal. The 1949 victory was led by the C.C.P. and the system of new democracy was one of 'people's democratic dictatorship'. And firmly singled out for mention in the preamble was the 'indestructible friendship with the great Union of Soviet Socialist Republics and the People's Democracies'. And if this was not reassuring enough, a few days after the Constitution was adopted and the new Chairman, the Standing Committee of the Congress and the State Council appointed, a large delegation from the U.S.S.R. led by Khrushchev and Bulganin arrived to attend the fifth-anniversary celebrations on 1 October.[9] They confirmed full Soviet support for China's position in the United Nations and its claims to Taiwan as an integral part of China and reaffirmed Soviet willingness to protect China from attack. In a series of communiqués, more credits were agreed to, and more assistance for the building of new industrial plants, railways and naval craft. Also it was agreed that Port Arthur would be returned to China and the Sino-Soviet joint-stock companies which Stalin had insisted on would be transformed into Chinese enterprises so that China could feel that it was a little less dependent on the U.S.S.R.

But these were not the only issues to matter. Implicit in the U.S. treaty with Taiwan and the SEATO countries were two conflicting pictures of China. The first picture focused on China as an aggressive communist power seeking to bring all other Asian countries under totalitarian rule on behalf of the global conspiracy orchestrated by the U.S.S.R. The second emphasised a post-imperial China which hankered after restoring its traditional tribute system. According to the latter, most of its neighbours had acknowledged China's suzerainty and were to be found on the maps which the Republic of China had produced after 1912 to strengthen its claim that China had 'lost' territory to the Western imperial powers during the nineteenth century. The two pictures formed an effective two-pronged attack. Either way, China appeared the dangerous neighbour, and anti-Chinese propaganda concentrated on blurring the two pictures so that they seemed to reinforce each other. China thus became the aggressive post-imperial power which was also communist and serving the will of the U.S.S.R. Chinese 'aggression' in Korea was invoked to support this, so also was Chinese backing for North Vietnamese 'aggression' on South Vietnam, Laos and Cambodia and even the threatened Chinese 'invasion' of Taiwan: all a prelude to China's plan to dominate all of east, south and south-east Asia. And to add to the picture of threat, a subtler and more credible campaign was launched on two areas where China's position was indeed ambiguous:[10] the question of Tibet's autonomy and the problem of the millions of overseas Chinese in south-east Asia. On these two matters, China's words and actions were more open to doubt. The first posed a problem for the Indians, who had inherited British interests in Tibet, and the second for the nationalist élites of the newly independent south-east Asian states. On both counts traditional interpretations of China's sovereign rights and responsibilities sat uncomfortably with progressive anti-imperialist ideas about self-determination. Particularly embarrassing to China was the rebellion in Malaya which was not merely communist and modelled on Maoist guerrilla tactics but also supported largely by people who were ethnically Chinese.

It was in this context that Chou En-lai attended the conference on Asian and African States in Bandung in April 1955.[11] Despite anti-Chinese propaganda and a prevailing sense of doubt among most of the pro-Western countries which attended the conference, Chou En-lai performed brilliantly. He was able to do so because he had prepared the ground carefully for a year beforehand. In particular, he had for a long time ceased to criticise India and had arranged for an amicable agreement about Chinese rights in Tibet; he had paid Nehru and U Nu a visit in June 1954; he had opened up successful trade negotiations with the three key countries of India, Burma and Indonesia; he had entertained both Nehru and U Nu in China; and he had started preliminary discussions about the nationality of overseas Chinese with Indonesia so that, at Bandung, he was able to announce with the Indonesian Prime Minister that a treaty on this potentially explosive subject had been signed. And, to cap it all, also at Bandung, he was able to arrange meetings with the representatives of North Vietnam, Laos and Cambodia to publicise the assurance given to Laos and Cambodia that neither North Vietnam nor China would interfere with their internal affairs. It was altogether a spectacular achievement for China to offer a new start with all its southern neighbours, based not upon traditional tributary terminology nor upon communist jargon but upon the Five Principles of Peaceful Coexistence defined according to the standards of international law.

Nevertheless, neither the issue of Tibet nor that of the overseas Chinese was fully resolved. Suspicions remained, partly because it was already well known that numerous Tibetans were dissatisfied with the actual practice of autonomy, and also because even more overseas Chinese remained ambivalent about their loyalties and many were openly enthusiastic about the new-found Chinese power and some of China's revolutionary ideals.[12] So both these issues which impinged on traditional concepts of China's sovereignty over the territories and peoples of the Ch'ing empire and over the Chinese status of all who could claim to be ethnic Chinese remained to plague China's international relations for many more years to come. In this way, the problems were comparable to that of Taiwan. And on such matters, the Chinese, whether ethnically Han or not and whether inside or outside the P.R.C., have been burdened by their complex history and traditions and remained vulnerable to determined efforts to embarrass them and question their sincerity. This was something of a tragedy for the prospects of peace in south and south-east Asia in the 1960s. Whether the Chinese could have done more in the 1950s to dispel doubts about their ultimate intentions is difficult to determine. Certainly their own propaganda at the time against the U.S.A. and its 'lackeys' in Asia, their resentment against the lies and distortions in the propaganda against China, their aggressive-sounding revolutionary rhetoric, their determination that China should never again bow its head to the bullying cries of stronger nations all contributed to the continuing tensions in the region. It is possible that, however sincere the Chinese might have been in the post-Bandung years about peaceful coexistence in Asia, there was no way to escape from the necessary, even though sometimes indirect, struggles that China would have to endure in the next decade with the U.S.A. and its allies. From the success that Chou En-lai enjoyed at Bandung, it certainly was not obvious that it would take another twenty years before China could establish new relationships with its southern neighbours.*

As it turned out, the three years after Bandung were some of the most peaceful and constructive for China. Although its independence was still imperfect, these were years when it could look forward to improvements in its international position. The U.N. vote on postponing the debate on China's admission improved only slightly: in 1956, 47 votes in favour to 24 against (with 9 abstentions); in 1958, 44 votes in favour to 28 against (with 9 abstentions). But these were years of decolonisation, especially in Africa, and China could look forward in time to a new batch of U.N. members to support them. Recognition by new states also came slowly. To the original twenty-five nations which recognised China before June 1950, only Nepal was added in 1955 and only three Arab states in 1956: Egypt, Syria and Yemen. It was not until 1958 that three more Muslim nations joined in (Iraq, Morocco and Algeria), but the recognition of and by Algeria was a dramatic initiative, since Algeria was not yet independent, and the provisional government was still 'in exile'. Also particularly satisfying was the recognition that year by Cambodia. Cambodia was in the neighbourhood and sought a closer relationship, and Prince Sihanouk seemed to have learnt to speak the same political language. Furthermore, the old colonial powers of Britain and France had come into conflict with the U.S.A. over the Suez crisis, and the U.S.S.R. was grateful for China's support when it ran into difficulties in Hungary. All this was most satisfactory. But even more significant was that the decline of the old imperialist powers was accompanied by the rapid rise of the U.S.S.R. as a nuclear power. This surely would be the turning-point for the socialist camp, as Mao Tse-tung put it, 'the East Wind prevailing over the West Wind'.[13] Of all the skills that the U.S.S.R. had to offer, this was the most important. With Soviet help, China could produce its own bomb more quickly. In 1956, the U.S.S.R. promised to establish a Joint Institute for Nuclear Research, and an agreement was signed to co-operate with all the socialist countries. All at once it seemed that China's freedom from dependence was in sight. Nuclear power involved marvellous science and technology, and was the highest symbol of modernisation and progress. It served the revolution,

---

* Relations were established with Cambodia between 1958 and 1971, and with Laos in 1962, but these were expected ever since the end of the Geneva Conference of 1954 and certainly since Bandung in 1955. The really significant *new* relationships had to await the recognition by Malaysia (May 1974), the Philippines (June 1975) and Thailand (July 1975).

speeding it along to hasten the end of decadent capitalist forces. But it could not but appear to others, not only to the U.S.A. and its allies but also to the U.S.S.R., that a China with the bomb might bring into play in international politics an enigmatic and incalculable factor that neither of the two Super Powers could control. The very impatience for China to be wholly independent when there was obviously a deep and unrelieved grievance over Taiwan and where there was likely to be a reawakened pride in China's capacity to lead the downtrodden coloured peoples of the Afro-Asian world was understandable, but it was enough to make China's enemies shudder and even its friends wonder.

It is far from certain whether China pressed the Soviet leaders to give it the bomb or whether the Soviet leaders urged the Chinese to leave the bomb to them. What is certain is that by August 1958, the Soviet leaders had been tested and found wanting.[14] The doubts about Khrushchev's nuclear policy had begun the year before and had been reinforced by his obvious interest in the end of nuclear testing which he made public early in 1958. At the same time, American military support for the K.M.T. government in Taiwan had been increasing and Sino-American talks at Geneva had become bogged down. It seemed to the Chinese leaders a good time to find out how much they could rely on Soviet help if and when they should really need it. Khrushchev, now the Soviet leader in every respect, went to Peking on 31 July and talked anxiously to Mao Tse-tung. Sino-Soviet relations had not been going well, though the first Chinese nuclear reactor had been operating with Soviet help; the Soviet model was being challenged by the Great Leap Forward campaigns and the new plans to push ahead with 'People's Communes'. The meeting was an uneasy one and seems to have decided the Chinese to take the initiative over the Fukien offshore islands and begin to bombard and blockade Chin-men (Quemoy) Island. The U.S.S.R. dutifully supported China's rights over Taiwan and these islands but it was clear it did not want a nuclear confrontation or any brinkmanship over the Taiwan Straits. It was a striking moment when China asserted its sovereignty at Soviet expense and the U.S.S.R. came away chastened and determined never to allow such a dangerous thing to happen over China again. From that moment on, the cracks on the surface of the Sino-Soviet friendship and alliance could not be totally repaired. There was no room in the Soviet framework for two centres of decision-making and the idea that there should always be only one centre was necessarily incompatible with the quality of independence

China was trying to achieve for itself.

Thus a major historical change had occurred in China. It was predictable that China should want to be truly sovereign. It was less expected that it would become so baulked over Taiwan, so humiliated at the United Nations and now dependent on a Soviet Union that was unworthy of the awesome Stalin. When this was combined with the remarkable success of China's foreign policies in 1954–8, and the speed in decolonisation, and the apparent dismantling of Western power in Asia and Africa, the time must have seemed right for China to demand to direct its own future. The Quemoy bombardments were not important in themselves, achieved nothing and revealed little of significance to the non-socialist world. They did, however, mark the moment when both Chinese and Soviet leaders recognised that China had changed and that their relationship could never be quite the same again. It has been suggested that both sides had already sensed some disenchantment when Khrushchev followed Chou En-lai so vigorously into south and south-east Asia in 1955, or when Mao Tse-tung had been unimpressed with Khruschev's 'Secret Speech' to the Twentieth Party Congress in 1956, or when Mao Tse-tung had become doubtful about the Soviet model for China in 1957. It seems likely that a gradual wariness with each other had begun some years before the Quemoy affair, but, following the events of August and September 1958, the acknowledgement of a major change could no longer be avoided.[15]

The impulse towards historical change, however, was not a function of Sino-Soviet relations or of the image which China wanted to project to the world. It hinged largely on what the Chinese leaders were able to do to their reorganised society and economy and for their millions of people and what the awakened multitudes wanted for themselves. Once the Party was in full control, once basic industrial and land reforms were completed and the education of illiterates and the re-education of the intellectuals had begun, the questions of what progress meant, what and how to modernise and at what speed to advance became central. The initial enthusiasm among most party leaders for adoption of the Soviet model was not diminished by Stalin's death or by the impatience to assert China's independence. At certain levels, the Soviet experience was unquestionably relevant. In any case, directly relevant or not, the slogan 'learn from the Soviet Union' was clearly meant to include learning from the U.S.S.R.'s mistakes as well as from Soviet successes. Mao Tse-tung summed this up crisply in March 1958, when he spoke of the Soviet 'dogmatism [that had] made its appearance both in economic and in cultural and educational work':[16]

In economic work dogmatism primarily manifested itself in heavy industry, planning, banking and statistics . . . Since we didn't understand these things and had absolutely no experience, all we could do in our ignorance was to import foreign methods. Our statistical work was practically a copy of Soviet work; in the educational field copying was also pretty bad . . . We did not even study our own experience in the Liberated Areas. The same applied to our public health work, with the result that I couldn't have eggs or chicken soup for three years because an article appeared in the Soviet Union which said that one shouldn't eat them. Later they said one could eat them. It didn't matter whether the article was correct or not, the Chinese listened all the same and respectfully obeyed. In short, the Soviet Union was tops.

But he did exempt the fields of military and agricultural work and, to some extent, the areas of commerce and light industry. In those areas, there is no evidence during the first four years that the Chinese would simply imitate what the Russians did and, as became evident later, the Chinese were possibly only too ready to evaluate Soviet methods and institutions critically and adapt what they wanted very selectively. The criteria used might be broadly described under the rubric of China's new perceptions of its national interests and the spirit of China's own revolution, but this does not say much about the difficulties experienced, the struggle to define what kind of progress was suitable for China and the fierce debates about what rates of progress to aim for.

Indeed, the theoretical questions were no less complex than the practical tasks of importing the key parts of the Soviet model. Marxist – Leninist theory had described a stage of socialism as rising out of the earlier stage of capitalism, the young shoots of socialism growing out of the class struggle or the internal contradictions within the capitalist system. Thus modernisation could be seen as the progress in capitalism which created the conditions for 'the building of socialism'. This made problems enough for the C.C.P. leaders, who had to contend with winning a revolutionary war in the 1930s and 1940s from an agricultural and non-capitalist base. But the success they achieved added another dimension to the vision of future progress. There was obviously no question of the revolution awaiting the full ripeness of capitalism when changes towards socialism would automatically follow. On the contrary, the conditions for victory could be induced and created by a high level of political consciousness accompanied by extraordinary efforts at mobilisation. This had been the chief lesson of the Chinese revolution and clearly was a different experience from that of Lenin's victory in the October Revolution in 1917.

The next question was whether the modernisation of China would have to follow the example of the U.S.S.R. since 1917. Was it simply a question of the Soviet 'short-cut', learning quickly and thus telescoping the Soviet experience by deliberate effort, or were there greater differences in China which would require that a *Chinese* way to socialism be developed? These questions had not surfaced during the first four years, even though it was obvious that non-C.C.P. intellectuals and politicians were reluctant to accept the easy road of the Soviet 'short-cut'. The mammoth task of establishing order, passing new legislation, liquidating enemies, reorganising industrial management and consumers' and producers' co-operatives, raising productivity and creating financial stability – and, above all, supporting the war in Korea and moulding a new pro-Soviet anti-American national identity – absorbed the energies of everyone. But from 1953 onwards, for the next five years, with the most important matters falling into place, there was more time to review the progress made so far.

At this stage, five major groups of protagonists may be distinguished. The most powerful obviously comprised the leading cadres of the C.C.P. and the P.L.A. and their representatives in the central and provincial governments. Still prominent were small groups of non-C.C.P. politicians and intellectuals who sought to play a role somewhat similar to that of a loyal opposition. A third and more silent group were the 'patriotic national bourgeoisie', consisting mainly of capitalists, industrial managers, technicians, middle-ranking government officials and rich and middle peasants. Although silent, they were still in positions which could either assist the rate of modernisation or slow it down. The fourth and fifth groups were far more numerous and in the course of becoming better organised and more articulate. One group consisted of the growing urban proletariat and the trade unions they joined, and the handicraft artisans who organised their own co-operatives. The other was made up of the poor and lower middle peasants who had been progressively introduced to collective living through mutual aid teams and agricultural producers' co-operatives.

Each of the five groups had distinguishable ideas of what was modern and progressive. Only one, of course, was in a position to determine over-all goals for China as a whole, and this was the first group. It was this group which had called for the country to learn from the Soviet model and it was this group which had to ensure that Soviet plans and styles of work would be carried out. As for the other four, only the fourth group, especially the urban proletariat under the trade unions, may be said to have responded readily to the decision to go the Soviet way. The others were obviously less easily persuaded, and the main reason for this was that they held ideas about being modern and progressive which were not always compatible with those of the U.S.S.R. The major task of the five years after 1953 was to change the assumptions and attitudes of those who resisted the imported model, if necessary by force.

The most persuasive argument apart from the use of coercion would be if the model was followed by obvious success, and the most visible examples of success would be, as in most underdeveloped countries in the world, the rapid growth of heavy industry and improved speed in all kinds of communications. And these were precisely the areas where Soviet aid and the use of Soviet blueprints and expertise were best equipped to register success. It was therefore understandable that no one questioned the Soviet model here. The figures of new plants opened, the production figures of these plants, the number of radio and television stations opened and the miles of new roads and railway tracks built were all invariably impressive.[17] The only questions asked concerned the quality of some of the early products, and steps were quickly taken to remedy the faults discovered. In fields where China was indeed 'poor and blank', success came easily and the Soviet model was entirely justified. In particular, advances in the munitions industry were pleasing to the armed forces. It was not long before the Chinese became confident that they could eventually produce all the artillery and small arms, all the planes and ships, all the tanks and trucks and all the telecommunications systems they would need for their own defence. By 1956, only nuclear weapons were still beyond their own capacity to produce. It is not surprising that when the U.S.S.R. baulked at providing this kind of expertise quickly, the Chinese were disappointed. But however disappointed they were there were no doubts about the Soviet model itself. From better guns to the bomb, there was no disagreement about what was modern, which direction was that of progress.[18] From the P.L.A. generals down to the poorest peasant, there was no lack of unanimity on such matters. No more universal criterion could be found for modernity than in the production of more and better weapons, and whatever else the new heavy industry did this was the contribution everyone agreed about.

Thus the non-C.C.P. men of eminence approved, the national bourgeoisie were prepared to adapt their administrative and technical skills for the new industries, the workers worked harder and the peasantry were persuaded to produce more in order to pay for the great advances. The implications of the policy emphasising heavy industry were reasonably clear. Sacrifices had to be made in equipping light industry and manufacturing consumer goods and in mechanising agriculture in order to increase productivity. Thus rises in the standard of living had to be slow, if not postponed, until the new plants were well off the ground. Again, there was little disagreement about the priorities at this early stage. The only source of debate was over the nature and volume of foreign trade. Consumer goods and agricultural produce would have to be sold abroad as much as possible to earn the foreign currency needed to pay for the equipment, materials and skilled manpower which China had to buy from the U.S.S.R. and its East European allies. The benefits were measurable in economic terms, exchanging known quantities of what China could afford for known quantities of what China could not produce. The foreign trade for political gains with 'neutralist' non-communist countries was not so easily quantifiable and direct grants and interest-free or low-interest loans to Asian neighbours which soon followed were something else again. Of course, if these were conducted to improve China's security and added to China's international status, all groups could be persuaded to make further sacrifices. If this was the price of modernisation, a vital index of a great nation's progress, there was certainly no notable dissent. There were probably disputes over details concerning which non-communist countries China should trade with, the amount of aid to send to developing countries, the extent to which China should be dependent on Hong Kong and overseas Chinese trade and remittances and similar issues, but the general policy was not in question. Indeed it became increasingly important to challenge the hostile U.S. embargo on strategic goods for China. And thus, for both economic and political reasons which all groups could support, trade with the developed but anti-communist countries like Japan, Britain, France and Italy was deliberately sought. And there seems to have been a consensus that the technology of such capitalist countries was clearly in advance of China's and, on several occasions, C.C.P. leaders like Chou En-lai and Liu Shao-ch'i spoke openly of catching up with these industralised countries.[19]

The equation of modernisation with industrial development was so complete at this stage that it would be easy to conclude that all groups in China really agreed and had no divergent views about the progress they all wanted for the country. And so much was published on this theme, and especially so much Soviet writing on industrial, technical, economic and administrative subjects was translated and studied between 1953 and 1958, that it would have been hard for any other view of progress to be heard. Yet other ideas of progress were evident. Among the non-C.C.P. politicians and intellectuals, there were continual discussions about greater freedom, more open centres of culture and higher learning and more funds to encourage humanistic as well as scientific specialisation. Among the 'national bourgeoisie', there were less articulate but no less persistent demands for material incentives and more efficient individual enterprise as well as for a freer system of marketing and distribution. The urban proletariat agreed more wholeheartedly with the goal of building socialism, but they were not unmoved by the idea that material incentives helped production. As for the poor peasants in their co-operatives, they needed time to get used to the idea that, on the one hand, land reform and the old slogan of 'the tiller should own his land' was but a stage towards collective ownership and that, on the other, they were not to drift into the cities in search of a higher standard of living but must remain where they were to improve their standards collectively. In short, even after they had all agreed that industrialisation was the key index to progress, the four different groups also expected modernisation either to improve their quality of life or to raise their standard of living more rapidly.

The power and authority of the C.C.P. leadership were never seriously threatened on their modernisation priorities. Certainly the two more numerous groups, the proletariat and the peasantry, could be counted as on their side, and the urban proletariat in particular could be trusted to give them their fullest support. It was largely a matter of asking for patience and sacrifice ultimately for their own benefit, and determined efforts were made especially to educate the rural party cadres to orientate the poor peasantry towards a better appreciation of national policy. Of course, the national bourgeoisie were relatively vulnerable. While some of the capitalists, bankers and financiers and some of the managerial and technical groups were still essential during the first decade, they were considered dispensable in the long run. They were all seen as members of a dying social class which would soon recognise that there was no alternative to the new social order and come to terms with its egalitarian and collective goals. During the 1953–8 period, progress for this class was towards reduced interest for their capital, greater worker participation in their units and closer party and state supervision, and by 1957 all private industrial and commercial enterprises had become joint state – private enterprises. At the same time, the state had taken full control over the distribution of basic commodities like grain and cotton cloth, and consumers' co-operatives handled more and more of the country's marketing channels. Step by step the government whittled away all the key symbols of capitalist activity, less ruthlessly than it had destroyed landed power in the countryside during the first four years, but no less effectively.[20] In fact, it would appear in 1956 as if the only remaining obstacles to a total unification of the nation's socialist vision were the non-C.C.P. intellectuals who worked in the cultural and educational institutions of the country.

These did not, of course, represent all the intellectual groups of China. Large numbers had left China for Taiwan, Hong Kong and elsewhere by 1949 or were to do so soon after, and many others had withdrawn from cultural and educational work or had been removed from it by 1953. Those remaining in 1956 were the ones who had indicated their willingness to serve the 'New Democracy' through self-criticism of their past errors and through the intensive study of the Marxist – Leninist classics and the writings of Mao Tse-tung.[21] Yet, as became clear in 1956 – 7, among these supporters of the regime there was growing discontent with what they thought was a narrowing down of modernisation goals, in particular, with the apparent rigidities of the Soviet model when applied to culture and education, with the uses of Marxist – Leninist categories to stifle thought and expression, with the potential damage such strait-jackets could do to all fields of research and discovery, but especially in the field of the humanities and the social sciences.

It is not possible to identify the backgrounds of all the critics and dissenters who were encouraged to speak up in 1957 during the period of the 'Hundred Flowers Blooming and Contending'. The well-known figures were university professors and lecturers, high-school teachers and some journalists. There were also some students. Not a few of them were activists from the main non-C.C.P. political parties, especially the China Democratic League, or were at least members of their local or campus branches. But whether or not their dissent had anything to do with their party affiliations, the dissent was seen by the C.C.P. leaders as a political act.[22] It reminded them that, when a regime made compromises with weak or defeated parties of an earlier era and tried to sustain a 'united front' for a period of transition, certain political goals from the past would be carried forward, especially goals pertaining to the definition of progress. It confirmed the C.C.P.'s distrust of all non-party intellectuals and it was a grievous disappointment for Mao Tse-tung personally, who had hoped that the initial successes of the P.R.C. would have convinced such intellectuals of the fundamental correctness of the chosen road to socialist modernisation. From the serious discontent revealed in 1956–7, after several years of the P.R.C.'s successes since 1949, the party could see that much more effort was needed to equate modernisation not merely with industrialisation but also with socialism. It also became evident that, however rapidly the economic base was being changed, it was premature to assume that the superstructure would change accordingly and just as rapidly. What was even more significant was a new awareness that, when the base was only beginning to change, it was dangerous to relax controls over a superstructure which was largely inherited from a previous era and which naturally retained many of the social and political values attached to an earlier economic stage. Historical change did not come that quickly. There was a strong underlying conflict between the conscious desire for change and the unconscious resistance to the new and the unknown. This was one of the lessons of the urge to modernise. However strong the urge to do so, it must be recognised that the cumulative forces of tradition, vested interests and earlier stages of history formed a strong barrier. To overcome such forces required greater and more determined and sustained force.

It was possibly coincidence that this lesson was learned so soon after the shock of Khrushchev's 'Secret Speech' at the Twentieth Party Congress and the unexpected revolt in Hungary.[23] Taken together with these two events the impact of the Hundred Flowers campaign on the C.C.P. and especially on Mao Tse-tung and his closest supporters was considerable. It certainly confirmed Mao Tse-tung's fears that the initial successes of the P.R.C., the satisfaction with the transplanted Soviet model in several areas and the apparent caution and timidity of those leaders in fields where there was no Soviet model to follow, would not merely slow down the urge to modernise and build socialism but also dampen the revolutionary spirit itself. The fears had first arisen in the bitter debates over collectivisation in 1955, over the speed at which all rural households should be brought into the larger agricultural producers' co-operatives.[24] It became ever more necessary to inject a new sense of urgency into the country, and even to ask fundamental questions about where the revolution was going and when and how the revolution was to be completed.

It is still not clear who else apart from Mao Tse-tung was engaged in thinking about the future course of the revolution in 1953 and the years immediately after that. In many respects, there would appear to have been no cause for serious rethinking. If revolution was a universal phenomenon and the one China was undergoing could have its lineal descent traced back to the October Revolution, then the future was assured. The Soviet experience provided the landmarks and what China had to do was to study the road closely, and this the Chinese had started seriously to do at Yenan and begun to adapt for Chinese conditions during the first four years after the C.C.P. victory. It was recognised that Chinese traditions were different, that the incomplete efforts at revolution during the 1912–49 period needed to be taken into account. Therefore, the specific difficulties in putting the Chinese people on the right path would need special care. But the confirmed successes of Stalin's Russia provided the inspiration and China could look forward to rapid advances towards the same goals. What did not become obvious until after Stalin's death was that the next generation of Soviet leaders might come to believe that the revolution *within* the U.S.S.R. was essentially completed and, what was worse, that it had in some ways gone too far. This Mao Tse-tung saw as at least a lapse from historical understanding because the element of class struggle would thus have been diluted and the fervour of those who believed in the dynamics of revolutionary change would also have been dampened down.

It is known from the texts of some of Mao Tse-tung's writings, speeches and notes of the period 1955–60 that he had, in fact, begun to worry early on about the heritage of Stalin.[25] Apart from reading critically some of Stalin's key doctrinal works on political and economic developments, Mao Tse-tung paid special attention to some of the long-term implications of Soviet achievements and especially to the implications for China if the Soviet model were followed. Presumably he shared some of his thoughts with the comrades who led the Chinese party. His doubts probably contributed to the first split within the party after victory and to the clash with Kao Kang, the most successful of those who administered the Sovietisation of government and industry in the north east. The purge of Kao Kang and Jao Shu-shih (*c.* 1901 –?) was probably the result of a power struggle rather than of a disagreement about Sovietisation. But it is relevant that it occurred not long after Stalin's death and was followed soon afterwards by a considerable debate about accelerating the rate of collectivisation in the countryside. Although the latter did lead in July 1955 to Mao Tse-tung's new directive to speed up the establishment of Higher Agricultural Producers' Co-operatives which produced spectacular results by the end of 1956, Mao Tse-tung's claim that China had undergone 'fundamental change' did not represent a departure from the Soviet model.[26] The goals of increasing agricultural production to pay for industrialisation as well as destroying private farming on the road to socialism conformed to the Soviet experience. The differences were mainly those of method, of better organisational skill and a keener sense of urgency.

The most significant development, however, was something less tangible, which may be described as a qualitative change in Mao Tse-tung's faith in China's revolutionary prowess. The unprecedented speed of change in the countryside convinced him that it was not too early to think of how and when the revolution might be completed and the ultimate goal of the Communist society realised. It was with this bold vision in mind that he began in 1956–7 to re-examine the stage that the U.S.S.R. had reached and the quality of the new Soviet leadership.[27] Mao Tse-tung's motives for so doing have been the subject of much speculation. It has been pointed out that he had been ambitious for China to provide the model for future revolutions in Asia as early as 1949 and resented Soviet moves to play this down. It has also been argued that he had hoped to don the mantle of Stalin when Stalin died, being the most senior and the most successful revolutionary leader around, and hoped to be acknowledged as the dominant figure in world communism. And this did seem attainable when he was set beside the brief and unconvincing leadership of Malenkov. Also, by 1953, there was no party leader alive apart from him who had produced a body of writings which contained so much evidence of infallibility and vision. Certainly there was no comparison between his manifold achievements and those of party *apparatchik* like Khrushchev and Bulganin, and it would not have been surprising if he thought it was his responsibility to provide fresh leadership for the world revolution. If he had any doubt that something had to be done, Khrushchev's 'Secret Speech' would have gone far to persuade him that the revolution was at a critical stage. What was more, if Stalin had made as many mistakes as Khrushchev had claimed, he might have made even more fundamental errors to have produced successors like Malenkov and Khrushchev so soon after his death. Stalin's whole record would also need to be re-examined to see what had really gone wrong.

Whether ambition, national interest or revolutionary faith motivated him most, Mao Tse-tung recognised in 1956 that a turning-point was near for China. Following the first careful response to Khrushchev's speech, published as an article in *People's Daily* early in April, Mao Tse-tung delivered his famous speech to an enlarged meeting of the Politburo, 'On the Ten Great Relationships'.[28] This was also just before he confirmed that there would be a relaxation of cultural policy in line with developments in the U.S.S.R. and that intellectuals would be permitted to 'bloom and contend'. The Politburo speech, however, went deeper into the problems of contradiction and really marked the beginnings of a series of debates leading to one of Mao Tse-tung's most important speeches, which he delivered to a Supreme State Conference in February 1957 called 'On the Correct Handling of Contradictions among the People',[29] and ultimately to the readiness to start 'building communism' and the mobilisation of the whole country in People's Communes in 1958. Events moved very quickly from theory to practice. Even as the C.C.P. was organising the Eighth Party Congress in September 1956 to register the great achievements of the last seven years, the ground had begun to move towards a testing of its new Central Committee and its cadres. Were they alert to the new needs of the people? Were they quick to respond to fresh calls for radical change? Had they kept their revolutionary flexibility? In particular, if Mao Tse-tung was right in thinking that the first stage in the *socialist* transformation of China was completed, would they be ready to launch the next bold step in 'the transition to communism'?

This 'transition to communism' was the main thrust to revolution, breaking free from both the pace and the framework of the Soviet model. It had begun with the decision to raise agriculture to equal importance with industry in September 1957. This was followed by the first push early in 1958 to develop local industry to support rural development more directly. By April 1958, an experimental merger of co-operatives, soon to be called a People's Commune, had been started in Honan province.[30] This brought together twenty-seven agricultural producers' co-operatives of four townships into one unit and came to be characterised by the following:

1) the merging of the grass-roots local government administration and the farm co-operatives into one entity;

2) the close co-ordination of agriculture, forestry, livestock breeding, fishery and subsidiary occupations;

3) the integration of industry, agriculture, trade, education and military affairs.

The People's Commune was not a necessary outcome of the Great Leap Forward campaign but a direct product of Mao Tse-tung's personal intervention in the countryside, and was intended to be the foundation for 'the basic units of Communist Society'. By September 1958 success was reported everywhere and it would appear that the Party and its cadres had not only proved that it had superhuman organisational skill but also that it was quick to stand in the forefront of a revolutionary leap into the unknown.

The spur to this dramatic push in China was what Mao Tse-tung perceived to have been the failure of the revolutionary spirit in the U.S.S.R. But in seeking to save China from failing in the same way he had in effect to revise considerably one of the key ideas about the road to socialism. It had always been firmly stated from Marx to Stalin that industrialisation was a prerequisite for socialist transformation, and this had been understood to mean that communism would only follow from a highly industrialised economic base. The new faith placed in the extensive development of a low level of industry in the rural countryside seemed to offer a new kind of goal: a communism of underdevelopment. This would have vital consequences in the years to come on the understanding of what revolution was all about and how and when the revolution was to be completed. These consequences will be examined in later chapters.

Surveying the five years from 1953 to 1958, what were the historical changes that did come about? China had become an independent agent which chose to continue within the framework of socialist countries. It had begun to industrialise on a large scale. It had restructured agricultural production and distribution. It had started to change the economic base even more radically with the People's Communes. Private property had become so circumscribed that it no longer wielded power. The C.C.P. had become all-powerful and non-party intellectuals had been converted, cowed or crushed. All this had been achieved at great speed by organisation, mass mobilisation, with a totally new sense of purpose that few would have thought possible for so many Chinese to have. It was certainly a time when nothing seemed impossible.

Yet amidst these changes, there were already features which appeared to go against the very nature of historical change. Could the new independence be freed from the fetters of traditional boundaries and a deep-seated sense of cultural ethnicism? Could rapid industrialisation be reconciled with a vast agricultural population which was being asked to 'modernise' at an even faster rate? Could sheer revolutionary fervour demolish two thousand years of social and cultural values or would the take-off in vision and rhetoric come thudding to the ground when their links with reality became too thin? The great irony in the changes of these five years was that they occurred under the leadership of men who had a keen sense of history and then led the same men to the dream of unlocking themselves from that history. The will to change had appeared to replace the very laws of change that their faith in historical materialism had firmly laid down.

5 Facing the Storms, 1958 – 66: Part I

THERE are many examples in history of newly unified countries led by a fresh set of leaders achieving remarkable successes during the first years. China itself has had several examples of the founders of new dynasties restructuring governments and re-establishing social and economic order not only at great speed but also to last for centuries. And the three modern revolutions which China had acknowledged, the English, the French and the Russian, brought spectacular changes quickly, although unlike some great Chinese dynasties and some new nation-states, the revolutions did not all survive the violence of their early changes. Only the Russian Revolution was an exception and hence the U.S.S.R. was a safe and worthy model to follow. Even more than most peoples, the Chinese are prone to make historical analogies, and in any comparison with the first nine years of the October Revolution the Chinese would appear to have fared much better. It had learnt directly from Russian mistakes, it received active help from the U.S.S.R., and it looked as if it could telescope the forty years of Soviet experience into some fifteen or twenty years. Certainly towards the end of 1958, nothing could have seemed more sure than that the worst was over. China had not only 'stood up', but had begun to move increasingly freely in world politics; its industries had mushroomed everywhere and the pace of modernisation had started to quicken; the revolution was poised to take off and produce an ingenious socialist transition to communism. Yet, rather unexpectedly not only for the outside world but also for many of China's leaders themselves, the storms began to blow within months of China's assertion of independence in all its fields of development: in its foreign policies, in its domestic 'great leap' and in its ideological pronouncements. This chapter and the following one examine these changes during the eight years from the 'Great Leap' to the eve of the Great Proletarian Cultural Revolution: in terms of China's obsession with its independence (in this chapter), and of the manifold contradictions between the criteria for modernisation and the goals of revolution (in the next).

China in 1958 had taken a quick step from its dependence on the U.S.S.R. to an independence which was still assured of socialist allies. The consequences of this did not appear to have been foreseen. The first step was the decision in August to bombard Chin-men (Quemoy). It was almost an act of defiance with regard to the U.S.S.R., because Khrushchev had been in Peking only a few weeks before and did not seem either to have been told about the plan or to have wanted to support anything like it. Indeed, the bombardment was probably more a declaration of independence than a challenge to go to war because there is no evidence of any plan to liberate the offshore islands, least of all Taiwan itself. Indeed, it is likely that the brinkmanship involved in provoking a hard U.S. response was a kind of test of Soviet mettle. There had been some disagreement about strategy a little earlier when the Chinese had expected the U.S.S.R. to oppose more forcibly the sending of American and British troops to the Lebanon and Jordan and the threat to the new government of Iraq. The Chinese thought the Russians were militarily strong enough to do so, and urged them to go to the brink. The Russians, however, were convinced of the danger of general war if they mistimed their challenge to American interests, and acted with extreme caution. The test for the U.S.S.R. in the Taiwan Straits, therefore, was what it would do if the U.S.A. went to war on behalf of Taiwan. Significantly, the Russians continued to be cautious and only reluctantly and belatedly announced that they would retaliate with nuclear weapons if the U.S.A. launched a nuclear attack on China. It soon became clear to the Chinese that the U.S.S.R. was offering only to defend the *status quo* but did not in effect take seriously China's sovereign rights over Taiwan and was, therefore, not prepared to help China eject American forces from Chinese territory.

Of course, it could have been argued that the U.S.A. was also merely defending the *status quo* and did not support any attack on the Chinese mainland. But the Chinese would stress that this was an incorrect analogy. The island of Taiwan could have had no sovereign rights over the whole mainland and, in any case, there was no Soviet fleet in the Taiwan Straits and no Soviet forces on Chinese territory. For the U.S.S.R. to join with the U.S.A. to maintain the *status quo* was an ominous sign. Thus would Mao Tse-tung begin to perceive that, the more like a Super Power the U.S.S.R. became, the less willing it would be to take risks on behalf of a socialist ally, even when the cause was just and self-evident. The reason Khrushchev gave, and this was to be more fully and formally elaborated during the next two years, was that a different strategy was needed for a nuclear age.[1] But if the price of this new strategy was the indefinite postponement of China's liberation of Taiwan and ultimate unification, it would be fatal to China's self-image as an independent sovereign nation. It had been humbling enough to depend on an ally's nuclear support to do what China wanted for itself. It was all the more chastening to have it confirmed that, without its own nuclear weaponry, its own independence had become very obviously vulnerable, uncertain, even hollow. In short, what seemed to have begun merely as disagreements over strategy was found to have profound implications. Taken any further, these would open up questions about Soviet leadership of the socialist world.

If China valued its independence as much as it claimed to and continued to think that its ultimate independence at all levels was a non-negotiable position, this must sooner or later raise great storms not only among its enemies and rivals but also among its friends. It was a considerable step for China to move from its dependence on one major power to a position of independence supported by strong allies. But it was only a short step from the latter to one of independence without reliable friends. And the short step seems to have followed, almost imperceptibly, when Soviet support became hedged and conditional in 1958.

The central issue of China's independence remained tied to the question of its sovereignty over the territories and peoples it inherited. The most immediate was certainly Taiwan, but the failure to elicit Soviet help in the Taiwan Straits resolved the Chinese to find a new longer-term strategy. Attention was shifted towards winning support from the newly independent members of the United Nations towards efforts to isolate Taiwan. This strategy was to draw China more and more into an active role in the Afro-Asian world and into global politics which brought it into conflict not only with the U.S.A. and its allies but also with the U.S.S.R.

The results in the United Nations were not remarkable. From the end of 1958 to 1965, the following nations established diplomatic relations with China:

Sep–Dec 1958	Morocco, Algeria (Provisional Government)
1959	Sudan, Guinea
1960	Ghana (to 1966), Cuba, Mali, Somalia
1961	Congo (Leopoldville) (for 7 months), Tanganyika (later Tanzania)

1962   Laos, Uganda
1963   Zanzibar (to 1964), Kenya, Burundi (to early
        1965)
1964   France, Tunisia (to 1967), Congo (Braz-
        zaville), Central African Republic (to 1966),
        Zambia, Dahomey (to 1966)
1965   Mauritania

With three exceptions, all of them were in Africa. Those in Africa were important, but in terms of numbers almost as many chose not to recognise the P.R.C. or recognised the government in Taiwan.[2] In different ways, the three not in Africa were more significant.[3] Cuba was the first opening in the Americas, its first uneasy foothold. Laos was the last link in the land frontiers around China; its recognition closed a vital gap on the eve of the American escalation of the Vietnam War. As for France, it was perhaps the most meaningful for China's position in world politics as it meant a break in solidarity in the North Atlantic Treaty Organisation (no NATO country had recognised China since 1950, before the outbreak of the Korean War); it was the third permanent member of the U.N. Security Council and its defection emphasised the isolation of the U.S.A. and its Taiwan 'puppet'. But where U.N. voting on the China question was concerned, the change in voting in favour of China was very slow, and it was not until 1965 that the figures for and against China became equal (47 each, 20 abstentions). Thus the long-term strategy had little effect on the isolation of Taiwan. Its main effect was to exacerbate Sino-Soviet rivalry and China's relations with the Third World in the years from 1963 to 1965.

In the meantime, other questions concerning China's sovereignty became more urgent. The most notable of these arose out of the revolt in Tibet in March 1959.[4] The local government under the Dalai Lama had been under pressure to democratise since 1956 when a Preparatory Committee for the Tibet Autonomous Region had been established. The traditional élites saw that their power would be undermined by the reforms being proposed and, encouraged by external support which Tibetans abroad had been led to believe was forthcoming, began to resist. By mid-1958, the leaders of the Khambas of eastern Tibet had revolted openly. The suppression of the revolt placed additional strains on the leaders in Lhasa. Furthermore, the land-reform policies of the central government, which had been gradually extended to cover the territories of the minority peoples, had reached the stage of collective ownership and the land-owning élites of Tibet could see what was in store for them. In March 1959, several of the senior officials of the local government persuaded the Dalai Lama to leave Lhasa before the revolt was launched. A few others refused to join the revolt and helped the central authorities to crush the rebellion swiftly. By April, Chou En-lai was able to report that the situation in Tibet was completely under control and the Preparatory Committee had begun to assume the functions and powers of local government under its acting Chairman, the Panchen Lama. The points emphasised in the statements that followed were that 'the backward social system in Tibet must be reformed', that the traditional élites wanted to 'preserve a backward, dark, reactionary and cruel serfdom in Tibet' and 'did not want at all to put into effect a democratic local autonomy with the participation of the people'. The key point, however, which was repeated again and again, was that 'Tibet is China's territory, and the rebellion of the Tibetan reactionaries and its suppression are China's internal affairs'. And it was a statement that did indeed have to be made.

The Dalai Lama had escaped to India and was given political asylum by the Indian government. He made a large number of accusations against China's policies in Tibet since 1956 and eventually brought the issue to the attention of the United Nations. The Indian government showed increasing sympathy for the Dalai Lama's cause, so much so that the Chinese accused India of interfering in China's internal affairs. Eventually, the strain on Sino-Indian relations opened up wider issues concerning the long border between the two countries:[5] chiefly the so-called McMahon Line in the Indian north-east region and the Aksai-Chin plateau in the disputed regions of Ladakh. There were several questions to be resolved, of which, despite its tragic features, the future of the Dalai Lama and his Tibetan followers was possibly the least important. More at stake were the threat to China's sovereignty over Tibet, the major boundary dispute with an Asian neighbour and China's image as a potential leader of the colonial and anti-imperialist countries of the world.

Superficially, the question of China's sovereignty had been resolved. This had been acknowledged by India when the P.L.A. marched into Tibet in October 1950, and confirmed when Indian troops and certain residual rights there were withdrawn according to the Agreement of April 1954. The Dalai Lama and his officials also accepted that, while Tibet was autonomous, it was part of China. But once the Dalai Lama had led the rebellion and accused China of virtual genocide, more complex issues were brought to the surface.[6] They were issues which embarrassed not only China, but all those other countries which were quick to condemn China and encourage the Dalai Lama without understanding or conviction. After their expressions of open hostility towards China in the United Nations, they implicitly challenged China's rights in Tibet, but this was confounded by the legalistic hair-splitting in the U.N., which recognised the rump island as China instead of the victors in a civil war on the mainland. The tone of moral condemnation sat uneasily with the power manipulations which denied China its rightful place in that body. China was quick to exploit the contradiction. This was probably the only time when the injustice of keeping China out of the U.N. actually saved it from further embarrassment. Without moral authority, the U.N. resolution meant little and the Tibetan revolt soon became a matter of social revolution or bad management, depending on from which side the problem was looked at. But the threat to China did remain. Tibetans were ethnically and culturally different from Han Chinese. Most of their leaders had rebelled, the others could be subverted by foreign powers on Tibet's borders, the territory was large and inhospitable and, while it was not vulnerable to attack from outside, it was difficult to control from Peking. The only reliable answer was to win over the Tibetans to the social revolution and integrate them with the ideals of the rest of China.[7] This the Chinese proceeded to do, with the P.L.A. defending the borders with India and political and administrative cadres training a new generation of Tibetans.

As for the Sino-Indian borders, the dispute dragged on for another three years and reached a climax with a war neither side really wanted. It was an unnecessary war.[8] The Indians were firm about what they thought were clearly established borders which they had inherited from the British. The Chinese were uncompromising that all borders drawn by imperialist powers like Britain should be renegotiated by the new national governments. Before the Tibetan revolt, the Chinese had built a road through western Tibet over the Aksai-Chin plateau, which India claimed was part of Ladakh. After the revolt, Indian troops were sent into areas across the western and the north-eastern 'frontiers' which the Chinese disputed. The minor incidents that had begun as early as 1955 became increasingly serious after 1959 and also more frequent. What had begun mainly as an affair of diplomatic notes could remain secret no longer after the Tibetan revolt had focused world attention on the affair, and the Indian parliament clamoured for a demonstration of toughness which left no room for Indian and Chinese leaders to manœuvre. At the same time, the Chinese reinforced their border forces as they became more alarmed at the possibility of outside support for more Tibetan unrest. Also, the Chinese increased the political pressure on India to negotiate new boundaries by acting quickly in 1960–1 to complete border treaties with Burma and Nepal. When these negotiations did not lead to much progress with India, additional pressure was put on when China opened boundary negotiations with Pakistan.[9] This was provocative and probably counter-productive and serious talks soon became impossible. From March to October 1962 one incident after another and the exchange of strong protest notes led inexorably to open war.

The background to the war has been told in some detail on the Indian side, but there has been nothing comparable written about the Chinese position apart from Chinese officially published statements and what the Indians have revealed about China's contacts with them. All that is known, however, confirms that China really wanted genuine negotiations and did not want a border conflict, but was determined not to allow Indian troops to advance into disputed areas while India insisted that there was nothing to negotiate. The last straw was the Indian military moves on the western edge of the McMahon Line in September and early October 1962. Here the Chinese saw that the Indian troops had crossed the Line itself and were preparing to move further into Tibet, despite several Chinese warnings about the consequences of such actions. On 20 October, the Chinese attacked the Indian forward positions along both the western and eastern sectors. The attacks were entirely successful and Indian troops fell back. In just over a month, the Chinese were satisfied and unilaterally announced a ceasefire and a plan to withdraw their troops to positions twenty kilometres away from what they called 'the line of actual control which existed between China and India on 7 November 1959'. So ended the unnecessary war.

But the bitterness created in India was too deep for any settlement to follow; the borders remained undefined and small border incidents continued for years afterwards. What the Chinese did achieve was a greater security for their control over Tibet. The war showed that they were prepared to fight to affirm their sovereignty over a region which several countries had questioned their right to have. But the cost was also high. They lost a chance to play a more positive role in south Asia and allowed anti-Chinese feelings to play on the issue of Chinese aggressiveness for several years longer.

Of greater long-term interest was whether the Sino-Indian troubles of 1959–62 affected China's image as a potential leader of the colonial and anti-imperialist countries in Asia and Africa. The picture of belligerence in the United Nations ever since the Korean War had been much softened at Geneva and Bandung in 1954–5. This had sharpened again following the suppression of the Tibetan revolt in 1959. But that was recognised by most nations as an internal affair which was unfortunate but did not threaten the prospects for peace outside China's boundaries. The war with India, however, was ambiguous. Whatever the rights and wrongs of the case, the question was who had started the shooting and wanted to change international boundaries by force. The Chinese victories were taken as proof that the Chinese were more ready to fight than the Indians, and a world-wide campaign was organised to brand the Chinese as aggressors. It took several years for contrary evidence to appear which showed also the extent to which India had been responsible for the war.[10] In the meantime, while doubts remained, China acted quickly to counter the propaganda against it and mend its fences with other Afro-Asian nations. It pointed repeatedly to its reasonableness and fairness in settling border questions with Burma, Nepal and Pakistan. It insisted that the war had been forced on it by the steady advances of Indian border troops while efforts were still being made to settle matters at the negotiating table. And most of all it reiterated its view that renegotiating borders laid down by imperialist powers was not only legitimate but also symbolically necessary to affirm a country's independence and mark the end of the imperialist era. Logical though it appeared, this was the least persuasive of the Chinese arguments. It was an uncomfortable, and even dangerous, approach for most of the new nations, and especially for the newest African nations south of the Sahara, where post-imperial boundaries had drawn artificial lines through numerous tribes and where any renegotiation would have opened up Pandora's box and raised far more questions than could ever be solved. Fortunately, there were other factors which helped China's image. China's unilateral withdrawal of troops was a striking gesture. India's invasion of Goa a few months before the China war made its position about the use of force a little ambiguous, as did the inconclusive war it fought with Pakistan three years later. Also, although quite unintentionally, the war with India caused China's open quarrel with the U.S.S.R. to reach such serious proportions by the end of 1962 that China's image abroad began to develop new dimensions. China's complete independence from the U.S.S.R. was no longer in question. It had shown that it could free itself from the communist 'monolith' which so many neutralist new nations feared. It gave China a better chance to outflank the 'Cold War neutralist' nations and press for the second coloured regionalist Afro-Asian conference which had been promised ever since the first successful meeting in Bandung.[11]

Thus the events of 1959–62 north of the Himalayas did little damage to China's international image apart from losing it the friendship of India. This would have serious repercussions a decade later, but it would appear that China was satisfied with the most immediate gain: the firm reassertion of what it regarded as its traditional sovereignty over Tibet. At least, in contrast with its frustrations over Taiwan in 1958, the revolt in remote Tibet and a brief border war did not attract the intervention of major powers. The situation was not to be as simple further east on its borders with the Indo-Chinese states of Vietnam, Laos and Cambodia. The Geneva Conference in 1954 had, in effect, created two Vietnams and South Vietnam obviously had no intention of holding elections to determine whether the two should become united as a single Vietnamese state. In itself, the Vietnam question did not trouble China. North Vietnam under the leadership of Ho Chi Minh was clearly capable of looking after itself and, in any case, it was a socialist country and in the vanguard of revolution in south-east Asia. Also, by 1958, Prince Sihanouk of Cambodia had recognised China, and this was a useful neutralist wedge between the American-supported regime of Ngo Dinh Diem in South Vietnam and SEATO headquarters in Thailand. But by 1959, there was growing unease about the instability in Laos.[12] On the one hand, the Pathet Lao with North Vietnamese support was gaining territory and challenging the government in Vientiane. On the other, this was being interpreted by the U.S.A. as evidence of outside interference and thus served to attract American activity in turn. And increased American activity in a country which had a common land border with China was clearly something China had to stop. China could hardly fail to note that, by 1959, nine of the ten countries which had a land border with China were under the control of socialist or more or less neutralist countries which recognised the P.R.C. Only Laos remained uncertain and this Chou En-lai and the new Foreign Minister, Ch'en Yi, began to try and remedy.

The issue of the Indo-Chinese states was soon to be raised to a titanic struggle between what looked like the proxies of the U.S.A. on the one hand and the U.S.S.R. and China on the other. Whether this was avoidable or not, such a simple view would not do justice to the urge to national unity of the bulk of the Vietnamese people. From the point of view of China, this was the central point, the unification and independence of Vietnam, and it was certainly fully committed to support Vietnamese victory. But was unification and independence the only question in Indo-China? Was the U.S.A. right in believing that this was but a smoke screen for Chinese dominance, and but the first step in China's ambition to spread revolution throughout south-east Asia and eventually turn all the new states in the region into satellite states analogous to those of the U.S.S.R. in Eastern Europe? The question remains a difficult one, but in its consistent rejection of China's repeated support for Indo-China's independence from foreign interference, the U.S.A. was clearly obsessive about China's ultimate ambitions.[13] It was a dangerous obsession which led to greater intervention in the Indo-Chinese states than anyone expected and to unnecessary defeat. The American interventions, however, helped to confirm the Chinese view that imperialism was still very much alive and that no independence was possible for any of the underdeveloped new nations as long as that was so.

It is not obvious when a country's concern for its own independence justifiably leads it to anxiety about the independence of others. At the level of theory, Leninist ideas about imperialism are global, and revolutionaries are expected to be vigilant and militant until the economic system that produced it is destroyed. In its broad utterances, China insisted on its Leninist heritage and there was no reason to believe that its leaders did not take that duty seriously. Towards that end, the first practical steps were to protect its own independence and to ensure that of its immediate neighbours. And at an even more mundane level, China certainly held that a country's security was still largely determined by success in keeping powerful enemies as far away from its borders as possible. And there was no question that the U.S.A. was its immediate enemy. U.S. policies in Taiwan and the Straits were the only obstacles to China's unification. Thus the advent of American military advisers in South Vietnam and then Laos aroused the greatest alarm. The Chinese had hoped, after the Geneva agreements in 1954, that the French withdrawal was the beginning of the end of imperialist power on its borders. While they were worried about increased U.S. involvement, they did not seem to have anticipated (and who could have in 1959?) the developments which led eventually to American bombing of North Vietnam and the sending of half a million troops to South Vietnam.

In 1959, even before the Dalai Lama reached India, the question before China was Laos. Ho Chi Minh had been through Peking in January and outlined the ineffectiveness of the International Control Commission in preventing further American involvement in Laos. It was not an auspicious time for China. Within months, the Chinese were immersed in an open quarrel with India and in preparations to defend its disputed borders in Tibet and, at the same time, in a secret but more fundamental disagreement over revolutionary strategy with the Russians after Khrushchev's meeting with Eisenhower. It was a time when relations with North Vietnam had begun to be delicate. How could the Chinese give full support to the Vietnamese urge to unification without further arousing American fears that China was out to dominate the region? The more such fears were aroused, the greater the American commitment and the harder it would become for the Vietnamese to unify. Only the guaranteed neutrality of Laos could advance the cause of Chinese security without hindering the Vietnamese goals. This the Chinese then actively sought by pressing for a return to Geneva, and this they succeeded in gaining in 1961.[14] Even more satisfying was their success in getting the Laotian premier to visit China before the Geneva meetings started. A satisfactory conclusion was reached when a new set of agreements was signed in July 1962 and Laos officially established diplomatic relations with China later that year. The problem of Vietnamese unification was, of course, far from resolved, but China was relieved of having to confront the U.S.A. directly on its border with Laos and was, in any case, confident that North Vietnam was now better placed to assert its claims more independently than ever before.

But the relief was only partial. China's relations with its southern neighbours remained complex. Despite its frequent assertions to the contrary, China could not escape from the residual image of Chinese traditional hegemony in south-east Asia. And with its new assertiveness and as a potential Great Power, it could not assuage the fears that its enemies kept alive among the leaders of the countries in the region. And, to add to China's difficulties, there were more than ten million Chinese living in various countries there whose loyalty to the new states was at best still untested and suspect. This question of the overseas Chinese continued to be an embarrassment to China and was always an easy topic for anti-Chinese elements to raise whenever China seemed to be making progress in making the region less hostile.

China's perceptions of south-east Asia did undergo a change during the 1950s. It had had a bad start because it had not understood the changing status of the countries in the region. The C.C.P. had accepted the Sun Yat-sen connection with patriotic overseas Chinese without question. It had agreed to shoulder the responsibilities which the Nationalist government had undertaken in the hope of winning support from these Chinese overseas away from the K.M.T. government in Taiwan. The C.C.P. had won the admiration of several overseas Chinese leaders during the war and some of the best-known, like Tan Kah Kee (Ch'en Chia-keng, 1874–1961) of Singapore, had declared allegiance to the P.R.C. early and persuaded many Chinese abroad to acknowledge the legitimacy of the Peking government. In the first flush of victory, it welcomed many such Chinese to serve in the new administration, and these men brought with them many outdated views about conditions in south-east Asia. With these returned Chinese providing advice at high levels of policy-making, there were rigidities in their views which delayed a clearer understanding of China's long-term interests in the region. It was, therefore, not until the Bandung conference in 1955 that leaders with experience in foreign affairs like Chou En-lai began to modify the cruder ideas adopted in 1949. Only then did they realise that, by openly competing with the Nationalists in Taiwan for influence with the 'Nanyang Chinese', they were playing into the hands of those who argued that China had imperialist aims in south-east Asia and were using the Chinese there as a 'fifth column' for eventual domination. By that time, in many ways the damage had already been done. There had been commitments to encourage the overseas Chinese to invest in China and send remittances to their families. Special arrangements had been made for returned Chinese to enjoy better standards of living if they were receiving remittances from their relatives abroad. More seriously, the impression had been widely given that China would protect the Chinese overseas, especially if they supported the new regime.

The great change for which the P.R.C. government was ill-prepared was the rapid decolonisation of the region and its impact on the Chinese residents in the newly independent countries.[15] This was partly because it was too busy over the Korean War and Taiwan and in its efforts at reconstruction. There was so much to engage its leaders' attention that it had let the returned Chinese determine priorities and the emphasis therefore was on the protection of overseas Chinese whether they lived under colonial rule or under indigenous governments. The lack of distinction was justified on the grounds that the nationalist leaders of the new nations, especially those of the Philippines who welcomed American bases and those of Malaya who were not only anti-communist but actually anti-China, were the puppets of imperialist forces. This in turn was reinforced by revolutionary rhetoric which tended to advocate support for all left-wing forces who continued to oppose the nationalist leaders. But no less important was an underlying urge to patronise indigenous and 'unprogressive' peoples and to underestimate their leaders' capacity to organise viable and effective nation-states. Despite the skilful diplomacy at Bandung, China was still apt to see the south-east Asian scene in terms of Thais, Filipinos and Malays being manipulated by the Americans and their British allies.

Of course, there had been reassuring gains in the friendship of North Vietnam and Burma, both significantly countries with no serious overseas Chinese problems, and in 1955 the treaty with Indonesia was specially designed to solve the overseas Chinese question once and for all. Unfortunately, it was still not fully appreciated that this was not a question that could be solved merely by a piece of paper and by the goodwill of a few leaders. Overseas Chinese in China and their families in south-east Asia continued to expect protection, guarantees and privileges as their right as late as 1958, as can be seen in the deliberations of the National Conference on Overseas Chinese held in November and December of that year.[16] The various indigenous peoples had historic grievances against the Chinese in their respective countries which were not resolved by having some of these Chinese placed under P.R.C. jurisdiction. Indonesia was a specially difficult case, where the three million Chinese were divided almost equally into three parts: one seeking local citizenship and national integration, one seeking P.R.C. nationality and the protection which that was supposed to promise, and the reminining third in a stateless limbo in which they sought some unofficial help from Taiwan, adopted a low posture, minded their own business and hoped that no one would notice them. Under such conditions, the treaty of 1955 was most difficult to implement.[17] The distinctions were unclear, even confusing, and anti-Chinese groups were able to exploit the conditions to their benefit. The Indonesian government was forced to acknowledge that, even with its mishandling of the economy, Chinese businesses appeared to have done better than ever and local enterprise was unable to get off the ground. It seemed an appropriate time to take drastic measures to show official concern. Hence the law against alien retail trading in 1959 which fell heavily on Chinese citizens who were widely distributed throughout the Indonesian countryside.

The Chinese officials both in Peking and in Jakarta were taken by surprise by the acts of violence which followed.[18] All at once, the protection the P.R.C. had offered its citizens abroad was severely tested, and this by a government China was very keen to have on its side. It was a most difficult position from which to extricate itself, and it could not have come at a worse time. The Tibetan question in the United Nations, the bitter quarrel with India, the efforts at Geneva to solve the Laos problem, the urgent need to demonstrate goodwill and restraint towards the governments of Burma, Nepal, Pakistan and Cambodia and impress the still open-minded new nations of Africa all came together, while some of the overseas Chinese leaders in China and in Indonesia clamoured for justice and action on their behalf. Not least, the failure of the Great Leap Forward campaigns and the severe droughts that cut production down throughout China put on even greater pressure to perform well abroad, especially on behalf of Chinese citizens who had placed their faith in the P.R.C. Fortunately, this was also a time when the new guided democracy of President Sukarno of Indonesia needed all the international help it could get and its campaign to recover West Irian from the Dutch had always received China's support. Both governments were desirous of friendly relations. Even then, the Chinese 'aliens' issue in Indonesia dragged on for a year and a half, with both governments trying their utmost to prevent it from getting worse, and there was great relief on both sides when a treaty of friendship was finally signed in March 1961 and Mao Tse-tung was able to entertain Sukarno in Peking after its ratification three months later.

By this time, the Chinese had clearly seen the light about the overseas Chinese question. There could no longer be any equivocation. The P.R.C. government must come down firmly against enthusiasts both within and outside China who failed to appreciate the country's wider foreign-policy interests, especially in south-east Asia. The Chinese overseas must also make up their minds either to take up foreign citizenship and give their loyalty to their country of adoption or to become P.R.C. citizens and observe all foreign laws while living abroad. China could not afford more troubles of the kind that took place in 1959–60 in Indonesia. To leave the question of citizenship and allegiance ambiguous was embarrassing if not actually dangerous to

China's foreign relations. Also, it became clear that the large majority of overseas Chinese were petty merchants who aspired to be capitalists and seemed to flourish and to perform for south-east Asia what could be considered progressive roles. It was certainly not in China's interest to encourage them to return to China where they would not fit easily into a socialist framework. In effect then, largely for reasons of state and with some ideological rationalisation, a major break with traditional attitudes about being and acting like Chinese had occurred. This was not, in fact, adequate to convince either south-east Asian governments or all of the Chinese abroad that the P.R.C. would not return to older ways of thought, but it was an important beginning.

Relations with south-east Asia remained difficult even after the Indonesian treaty of 1961. Whether the Chinese liked it or not, China's enemies persisted in regarding all regional questions as having global implications involving the Free World against communism. While this was not entirely unjustified, this point of view did mean that China could not hope to isolate the questions and try and solve them either bilaterally with each of the countries concerned or regionally without the participation of major powers like the U.S.A. and Britain. Thus, despite its successes with neutralist countries like Burma, Indonesia and Cambodia and then with Laos, China found itself faced with increasing U.S. military involvement in South Vietnam (with allies in Thailand and the Philippines) and with the remnants of British power in Malaya, Singapore and the Northern Borneo territories of Sarawak, Sabah and Brunei. With the birth of the idea of a federation of the latter states in a new state of Malaysia in 1961, China found itself on the side of Indonesia, in opposition. For the next four years, until the abortive coup in Indonesia in September – October 1965, China opposed the Malaysian Federation with growing vehemence.[19] Precisely why it did so is not clear. It suited the Chinese to support 'progressive' Indonesia and progressive forces in the Malaysian territories against what it claimed was a 'neo-colonial' plot to prolong British power in the region. It was probably also convenient to try and stop the British as a means of further isolating the U.S.A. in south-east Asia, tactically picking on the power that was weaker and whose bases were further away from China. But the Malaysia issue was far from a single one of being progressive or not. It also became entangled with the ethnic issue of uniting the Malay races of Indonesia, the Philippines and the Malaysian territories (Maphilindo) in order to weaken the economic power and influence of their respective local Chinese and ultimately strengthen defence against

Chinese expansion. Maphilindo was not a practical proposition at the time and the Chinese probably knew it. Certainly one way of ensuring that Maphilindo did not become a reality was by supporting Indonesia against the creation of Malaysia. By emphasising the most radical and ideological aspects of Indonesian opposition China could be sure of keeping Indonesia away from a close association simultaneously with the U.S.A.'s closest ally and Britain's closest ally in the region. Thus siding with Indonesia despite some of the anti-Chinese features of its 'Crush Malaysia' campaign could both keep an anti-Chinese 'grand confederation' from emerging and demonstrate China's lack of interest in those Chinese in the region who should be owing loyalty to their adopted countries, and in this way emphasise China's rejection of traditional ethnic ties.

Whatever the reasons for China's support for Indonesia, the result was not a happy one for China.[20] It encouraged Indonesia to go much further than was wise, it exposed the Indonesian armed forces as being inept and disunited, it attracted more British and Commonwealth forces into the region than either Indonesia or China wanted, it led to Sukarno's frustration and dubious decision to walk out of the United Nations, it divided the Afro-Asian world when China desired its unity and co-operation more than ever, and it probably strengthened American resolve to intervene more forcibly in Vietnam. Ultimately it contributed to the tensions within Indonesia that made both the Indonesian Communist Party and its allies and the anti-communist generals of the armed forces more desperate for a showdown. China's deep involvement with Sukarno and his grandiloquent gestures, with the Communist Party of Indonesia and its leader D. N. Aidit, and with what looked like the 'high tide' of revolution, left it with no room to manœuvre when in 1965 Sukarno fell, Aidit was killed and the revolution faded away. This was a political disaster for China and one that set it back very badly in its efforts to remove Western power from south-east Asia and made an implacable enemy of the new Indonesian government. Even if China had not been in any way responsible for the abortive coup, it could not, in the short run, escape the odium of having befriended those who had failed disastrously.

China's concerns in south and south-east Asia were, of course, only part of its efforts to take the initiative in asserting itself in world affairs. They were, however, the most vital not only because they were matters of security but also because they tested China's capacity to define a new peaceful image in areas where China had had complex and ambiguous traditional roles.[21] That the latter was not more successful was not all China's fault. Its neighbours were suspicious and its enemies who had interests in the region were skilful and determined to make China out to be expansionist. But China did contribute to its lack of success in this respect. It could not merely concern itself with its own borders and neighbours. Its size and its history ensured that it would be confronted by Great Powers who would seek to contain it. Its quest for independence could not be satisfied simply by the freedom to manoeuvre in international politics; independence had to be equated with being on a par in some key areas with other great powers. And its commitment to world revolution required that it be in the vanguard inspiring all other countries to follow suit, if only in their own individual ways. It did not, therefore, matter whether China planned from the beginning to become a Great Power. For its neighbours, it mattered even less whether this was for a good revolutionary cause or merely in order to restore itself to its historic central place in the world. Nor did it matter if China was only compelled step by step by 'the forces of history' to play the Great Power. The fact is that large and potentially powerful countries are alarming and it was useless for China to protest its innocence and friendliness and hope that its neighbours would lower their guard. Even the most powerful country tries to check the power of others and it must therefore expect others to try and check its power in return.

Until 1958, China could believably insist that it was forced into Great Power activity by events largely beyond its control. After 1958, it unmistakably took the initiative more and more often and seemed resigned to the fact that it could escape neither its own past nor the revolutionary demands of its future. This was particularly true in two areas: China's initiatives among the socialist countries, and especially the U.S.S.R., and its initiatives in Afro-Asia. The former will be considered in the next chapter. The rest of this chapter will briefly survey China's successes and failures in the Middle East and Black Africa.

Early in the chapter, it was shown that China adopted a long-term strategy to isolate Taiwan and eventually win its rightful place in the U.N. by wooing newly independent nations. The policy was a practical one, even though the results in the U.N. were disappointing until 1965. What was more significant, however, was the effective leap into global politics that this policy represented. It had, in fact, begun with the Afro-Asian conference in Bandung, followed the next year by the diplomatic relations established with Egypt, Syria and Yemen. The logic of the policy was to advance wherever the government in Taiwan had gone and anticipate Taiwan's moves where new nations were concerned. But each step had meant greater involvement.[22] The competition was not only with Taiwan but also with the U.S.A., which held its smaller allies to support Taiwan as long as possible and helped Taiwan in many other ways. Thus as Taiwan offered aid and advantageous trading terms China had to offer similar if not better terms of aid and trade. More often than not, American aid was decisive and recipients of U.S. aid were reluctant to deal with China. But as the involvement increased, the question of Taiwan became less important. China was reaching further into areas which were unrelated to security, its U.N. seat or to normal trade, and which were unquestionably matters of great power politics. Competition with the U.S.A. was unavoidable, but as the Sino-Soviet quarrel came into the open by early 1962, it also became clear that there was competition with the U.S.S.R. in Asia and Africa as well. In retrospect, it would appear that an underlying tension had crept into Sino-Soviet policies regarding newly independent nations ever since Khrushchev's visit to the U.S.A. in 1959. After that, the U.S.S.R. began to wonder about the wider ramifications of Chinese diplomatic activities in Africa and the Middle East. On the surface, relations between Soviet and Chinese diplomats in these regions where they were both present remained fraternal and Soviet activities in their various embassies appeared to support China in the quarrels with India between 1959 and 1962. What became clear after that was the intense rivalry between the two which reached its climax when Chou En-lai and Ch'en Yi started their extensive tour of North Africa and then sub-Saharan Africa in December 1963. This was an astonishing development. The two had gone first to Egypt, Algeria and Morocco. Then, after a break in Albania, they had gone on to Tunisia, Ghana, Mali, Guinea, Sudan, Ethiopia and Somalia. The total was ten African states in the course of eight weeks. It would have been even more spectacular if they had visited Uganda, Kenya and Tanganyika, but army mutinies in these countries and the use of British troops to suppress them made such a visit embarrassing to the Chinese and they changed their minds. The trip was spectacular enough. It was quite unprecedented and the global implications of Chinese policy were unmistakable.

Despite the revolutionary overtones of some of Chou En-lai's speeches, the African tour was not directed at encouraging revolution.[23] It included countries like Morocco and Tunisia and even an ancient feudal monarchy like that of Ethiopia which had not even recognised China. More immediately important was China's concern to hold the second Afro-Asian Conference, if possible on the tenth anniversary of Bandung. This they were to find was no longer the simple affair that had been quickly organised at Bandung. There were now many more new countries, there had been serious conflicts between old Bandung members like China and India, there had been successful meetings of non-aligned countries led by Yugolsavia, India and Egypt which had kept China out, and most serious of all, the U.S.S.R. had now decided that it was also an Asian power and wanted to participate. Perhaps no less relevant, objections were raised against China's participation when in October 1964 it detonated its first atomic bomb and became a nuclear power.

But the Chinese pressed on. Algeria was to be the site and July 1965 the date. There was strong support from the Indonesians and the Ghanaians. There was even speculation that this conference would lead to a rival U.N. which Indonesia would join together with China (Indonesia had withdrawn from the U.N. following its quarrel with Malaysia). Again, Chou En-lai and Ch'en Yi did their rounds, this time separately, in March – April 1965. Then the conference plans began to go wrong. Chou En-lai's visit to Africa in early June was cut short. Ben Bella of Algeria was deposed ten days before the conference was to meet and the Chinese were forced to agree that the conference had to be postponed. Yet more troubles were to follow. Even as Ch'en Yi went on yet another African tour to prepare the ground for the postponed conference, war broke out between India and Pakistan. A few weeks after that, on September 30, the GESTAPU abortive coup took place in Indonesia and that led quickly to a breakdown in Sino-Indonesian relations. Finally, the Chinese saw the warning light and decided not to pursue the Afro-Asian conference they had worked so hard to set up.[24] As Ch'en Yi saw it, some developing countries would not openly denounce U.S. imperialism 'because of their need for U.S. aid to solve the bread question', while others believed that 'there will be no sense in convening the conference' if it was not to denounce U.S. imperialism. But certainly no less important were the indications that several countries were in favour of inviting the U.S.S.R. to the Conference: 'the Chinese government is firmly opposed to it. Whether historically or politically, the Soviet Union is by tradition a European country, and there is no reason for its participation.' In short, when it became clear that there was no assurance that the Conference would be a success in

Chinese terms, the Chinese preferred 'to wait till the conditions are ripe'.

Contemporary accounts in 1963–5 have emphasised China's revolutionary aims in explaining its early successes and its disastrous failures. China was described as trying to challenge the slowness of Soviet strategy by putting the greatest possible pressures on the few progressive Afro-Asian leaders they could find, feeding their vanity and impatience, so that revolutionary conditions could be produced and Soviet timidity could be exposed. This would make Chinese policies during this period mainly a function of the Sino-Soviet ideological struggle. As will be shown in the following chapter, there was some truth in the interpretation. But it would be misleading to neglect the other historical factors which moved the Chinese to such a frenzy of activity. The first of these would be the obvious independence of Chinese foreign policies which began in 1958 and became quite obvious by the second Geneva conference in 1961. From the early successes of this period, especially with Indonesia and Pakistan, grew a confidence in diplomatic activity among African nations which was not justified. This is particularly true when Chinese knowledge and experience of Africa are looked at more closely. Unlike Asia, where there had been a growing literature on all aspects of south Asian and south-east Asian histories and cultures, where Chinese understanding of countries like Korea, Vietnam and Burma was acute, where there have long been Chinese Muslim scholars in touch with opinions and policies in the Arab Muslim world, there simply was no one who could write or speak authoritatively on any aspect of sub-Saharan Africa.[25] When interest began after 1958, diplomats and other experts were totally dependent on the few English and French secondary works they could find. A few less suspect ones were translated, but at a time of economic disasters in China during the three years 1959–61, hardly any of the translations were published and it was not until 1963 that a serious book on African history appeared. All other current writings were hastily compiled from the handbooks which some of the new nations produced together with reference works published by various U.N. and other international agencies. When it is borne in mind that, even with the expert advice of returned Indonesian Chinese, China made many mistakes in its relations with Indonesia, and despite the large number of books and articles on the Indian nationalist movements available in Chinese, the Chinese underestimated the deep sense of national outrage which their actions produced in India, the situation where Africa was concerned could be described as pathetic. It is quite astonishing how bold and reckless the Chinese were in expecting diplomatic responses which could change the course of history. The Chinese miscalculations about African solidarity with Asians, for example, would suggest a great lack of respect for African intelligence were it not for the more likely explanation that the Chinese were simply still ignorant of African affairs. It is in this context that one can explain why the Chinese confidently believed that the example of their newly won independence could help the Africans assert theirs.

The second factor is related to the first. The Bandung conference did not involve any independent black African state. Thus Afro-Asian solidarity looked far more straightforward than it turned out to be. Also, Bandung was held when there were still some forty countries yet to be independent and the atmosphere of anti-colonialism and the need for anti-imperialist solidarity seemed obvious. By 1963–5, the process of decolonisation had speeded up so much that most of the new national élites were concerned more with trade and development than with issues like American imperialism in Vietnam, the illegitimacy of the U.N., tensions in the Indo-Pakistan sub-continent and a Chinese style in revolution.[26] China's anger against U.S. Far-Eastern policy, its obsession with a U.N. that rejected China in favour of Taiwan and its anxieties about the balance of power in south Asia were non-issues for most of Africa and the Middle East. In particular, knocking the U.N. was clearly misguided as these new nations realised that the Afro-Asian members made up more than half the U.N. membership. In short, China's growing frustration at its exclusion from the U.N. and other major international bodies provoked the impatience and the hopeless sense of timing that led to the failure of the Afro-Asian conference.

Finally, the domestic scene in China was also relevant. The failures in production in 1959–61 had led to a reversal of certain key re-volutionary measures and the restoration of more moderate economic institutions and these were beginning to take effect in 1962–3. At the same time, Mao Tse-tung was leading the fight against Khrushchev's 'revisionism' and proposing bolder steps in world affairs. (See following chapter.) Having successfully modified Mao's domestic programmes and not wanting to give in on these modifications, some of his colleagues might have found it expedient to let Mao have his way in foreign policy. After all, in October 1964, the first Chinese atomic bomb was accompanied by Khrushchev's fall from power. The time seemed ripe to push Mao's demand for Afro-Asian action to the hilt. Hence the air of desperation when it seemed clear that no amount of pressure could produce quite the conference that Mao had predicted and wanted. Thus the failures in 1965–6 were not merely errors in revolutionary theory, they were also due to a combination of ignorance and over-confidence, impatience and bad timing and a degree of cynicism about domestic politics which was soon to bring China itself to the brink of disaster.

6 Facing the Storms, 1958–66: Part II

THE C.C.P. leadership has always insisted on the close relationship between theory and practice. And as long as it advocated learning from the U.S.S.R., Marxist–Leninist theory was broadly related to Soviet practice and the goals of revolution were expected to be achieved through the modernity on which Soviet achievements were based. Thus until 1958, it would appear that modernity was a necessary stage in revolution, the communist one being the most modern and progressive revolution in history. Even when from time to time doubts were expressed about whether the Soviet experience was directly helpful to China, even when Soviet methods were greatly modified to fit Chinese circumstances, there was no question but that modernity had to come and that it would be something like that of the U.S.S.R. A break in this confidence came when the Chinese began to find the U.S.S.R. wanting in several different ways simultaneously, most notably in its socialist leadership in international affairs but perhaps no less important in its policies concerning revolution. The consequences of the first inadequacy have been surveyed in Chapter 4 and those of the second will follow later in this chapter. Before going into the problems of revolutionary policy, it may well be best to begin with an area where the U.S.S.R. never ceased to provide valuable examples, the area of Soviet modernity.

We have already noted the enthusiasm with which the Russian language was studied, and Russian writings in almost all fields were being translated into Chinese right up to 1958. Many organs of government, especially those dealing with law and public order, economic planning and scientific and technological administration, benefited greatly from the Soviet experience and this was frequently acknowledged. And everyone could see the Soviet debt in the new buildings, factories, machine designs, and then trucks, ships, aircraft and the weaponry of the P.L.A. Even in the fields of modern art, drama, music and literature, Soviet styles and motifs were competing with what was popular and traditional Chinese, and other Western influences were quickly diluted. Less visible but no less important was the Soviet model in socialist education, in advanced technical training, in scientific research. Even the Soviet outlook on the world and Soviet writings on world history were receiving serious attention. And most striking of all, of course, were the developments in heavy industry where Soviet technicians and engineers directly helped in planning and construction. All these were still symbols of modernity even after 1958.

The first challenge to Soviet modernity originated not in dissatisfaction with Soviet theory or with Soviet practice in the areas noted above. The roots lay on the one hand in the size and nature of China's rural population and on the other in the personality and temperament of Mao Tse-tung. The two were related and it would be hard to determine which was more decisive in the change of course to follow. The large number of households dependent on agriculture was a basic fact, but the speedy transformation of traditional villages into producers' co-operatives was the result of lessons learnt by Mao Tse-tung during the revolutionary struggle before 1949. This first stage in collectivisation in 1955–6 had been so successful that it soon became urgent to ask what was to follow. Soviet experience had shown that the emphasis on heavy industry meant relatively gradual and slow developments in light industry and agriculture.[1] If the Soviet model was followed, it would obviously take a long time before consumer needs could be satisfied and rural productivity, especially mechanised agriculture, raised to any great extent. In addition, if that productivity was slow to rise, national accumulation of capital to speed up industrial growth would be affected. This would then in turn delay the growth of consumer-goods industries and mechanised agriculture. A vicious productivity circle of this magnitude would delay the whole course of socialist transformation. The transformation would become so gradual that the spirit of the revolution itself could be threatened. And this Mao Tse-tung was not prepared to see happen.

In other words, modernisation in the Soviet way in China could lead to a fast-growing gap between industrial cities and the agricultural countryside. The uneven rates of progress would lead to unacceptable differences among the Chinese peoples and a whole range of economic and ultimately social, cultural and political contradictions could flow from such differences. The Party was obviously not willing to slow down the rate of industrialisation. This was vital to modernity and modernity was still essential to the building of socialism. Something therefore had to be done to make sure that the Chinese peasantry did not fall further behind in technology. In Chapter 4, Mao Tse-tung's theoretical writings on this problem have been mentioned; also the first steps in trying to restructure the countryside into People's Communes have been outlined. It remains to be shown what happened when the restructuring took place and how the translation of theory into practice was to bring about something of a challenge to accepted ideas of modernity.

Firstly, the People's Communes formed the spearhead of a Great Leap Forward from economic units like the Lower and Higher Agricultural Producers' Co-operatives to the larger general administrative unit which was expected to lead to rapid rural industrialisation and the vastly increased productivity that was to follow.[2] If the units of production were changed and the means of production modernised, a new social framework representing the next historical stage would surely begin to appear. This was the essence of the phrase, 'the basic units of communist society', which presaged the coming of that next stage of history. These communes were large units of collective ownership, large enough for the necessary specialisation of skills to support some local light industry and with a large enough demand for the consumer goods and small machines which that industry would supply. Mao Tse-tung went even further and expected some of the communes to produce steel and other materials for their own industries and thus not make calls on the national supply needed for the great centres of heavy industry. These communes were not expected to become industrial units. The few in the cities which were based on big factories quickly failed and were abandoned. What was significant was the idea that the rural communes would become self-reliant social units which would be in a better position to keep pace with urban developments and raise the level of education and culture in the countryside to conform with new standards of modernity.

The initial enthusiasm of party cadres throughout the country to organise everybody into communes was breathtaking. Within a month of the Central Committee Resolution agreeing to establish such communes – that is, by September 1958 – it was announced that 90 per cent of all peasant households had joined communes.[3] The average size of each of these was about 4800 households and there were 23,384 of them in the country. And by the end of the year, more than 99 per cent had joined. The implications of this for the central government were enormous in the area of trade and finance, but there was great hope that with decentralisation, the communes would be more efficient and productive, far less wasteful, and if they substantially increased the tax receipts for national use, the complex administrative changes necessary would be most worthwhile. But enthusiasm was not enough.[4] There simply had not been adequate planning for such a radical step on such a large scale. The competition to succeed had led many of the cadres to value speed over care and eventually to dishonest reporting and various other errors. In fact, none of the communes were really ready to be tested when, in the spring of 1959, China was hit by one of the worst droughts in its modern history. Despite modifications and adjustments, the new untried structures failed disastrously to cope with the challenge, and agricultural production dropped very quickly. Thus plans had to be further redrawn and more realistic targets were set. More central control of production methods was introduced while more private plots were permitted. So seriously had morale been affected that Liu Shao-ch'i had to defend the communes publicly against growing criticism. Within the Party itself, so serious was the opposition by a senior general like P'eng Te-huai (b. 1899) that Mao Tse-tung demanded P'eng's removal with several others. At the Eighth Plenum held in Lushan, Kiangsi, in August 1959, he persuaded the Central Committee that 'the principal danger now facing the achievement of a continued leap forward this year is the emergence of Right opportunist ideas among some cadres'. The resolution on the 'anti-Party clique' was then passed.[5] This referred in particular to a letter which P'eng Te-huai wrote to Mao on 14 July 1959, and went on to say that P'eng

negates the victory of the general line and the achievements of the great leap forward, and is opposed to the high-speed development of the national economy, to the movement for high yields on the agricultural front, to the mass movement to make iron and steel, to the people's commune movement, to the mass movements in economic construction, and to Party leadership in socialist construction, that is to 'putting politics in command'. In his letter he brazenly slandered as 'petty-bourgeois fanaticism' the revolutionary zeal of the Party and of hundreds of millions of people.

Particularly galling to Mao was the last remark about 'petty-bourgeois fanaticism' which echoed the sentiments already known to have been expressed by Khrushchev and other Soviet theoreticians.

The communes in their original form in 1958 could not have been really successful. Events had moved too fast and most rural cadres were not experienced enough to take so much responsibility for these new units. But the droughts, floods and pests of 1959–61 made sure that they could not survive even as experiments. Drastic steps had to be taken to reform these structures, especially to improve incentives for the peasants to increase productivity. During the three crisis years, the chief preoccupation became the saving of the national economy.[6] All thoughts about 'the transition to communism' had to be set aside. By the end of the period, when the economy was recovering, the People's Communes survived largely in name. The effective accounting unit had become the production team of some 20 to 40 households, or at best the production brigade of about 170 households. The production teams were certainly manageable by local cadres. They had less autonomy and were far more amenable to bureaucratic control by the centre. This was essentially a return to the small agricultural producers' co-operatives, the units where ownership of land and implements were located after the major set of land reforms in 1954–6.

The failure of the Great Leap Forward Campaign and the disastrous famine years of 1959–61 did have one positive result. They confirmed that the size of China's population and its density even in the countryside required that far greater attention had to be paid to agriculture than was thought necessary in the 1950s. If there were to be more even rates of development, it was not a question of pressurising the countryside to 'industrialise', but of moderating the growth of urban and industrial centres so that agricultural areas could keep pace, not merely economically but also culturally and politically. This would appear to be a realistic appraisal of what was or was not possible, but it was much more than that. It amounted almost to a rejection of the standards of modernity that China had first accepted from the U.S.S.R.

The full implications were not immediately obvious. There were many ambiguities. On the surface, modernisation still meant the overthrow of feudal and capitalist modes of production and the maintenance of the dictatorship of the proletariat. The structure of the central and provincial government and the nature of the C.C.P. and all its branches, organs and functions remained essentially unchanged. Law and order was maintained on Soviet lines. The industrial economy and society were still regarded as desirable and inevitable. Science and technology were still the keys to progress and collective ownership the prelude to socialism. Superficially, it was all rather simple and only a matter of time and determination plus vigorous organisation. But the experience of the Great Leap Forward and the painful trials and errors to raise agricultural production, as well as to transform rural Chinese men and women into self-confident socialists, began to raise doubts about what the accepted ideas of modernity might do to Chinese society. The experiments had revealed that changes which were too rapid might release great productive energies, but they might also expose tensions which were not foreseen.

Under these circumstances, it was natural that the C.C.P. leaders began to divide among themselves about what precisely to do next. Despite Mao Tse-tung's poor judgements about collectivisation, his position as leader was not seriously challenged. Although he gave up his position as head of state of the P.R.C., after the sixth Plenum in November—December 1958, this was not a matter of being pushed out of power.[7] The Central Committee took great pains to explain why this would enable him 'all the better to concentrate his energies on dealing with questions of the direction, policy and line of the Party and the state; he may also be enabled to set aside more time for Marxist—Leninist theoretical work, without affecting his continued leading role in the work of the state'. In fact, he had his way at the Sixth Plenum, actively investigated the serious problems about commune administration and the confusion over collective ownership and agreed to an overhauling of the rural communes. He still seemed to have been in full command at the Seventh Plenum in Shanghai five months later and it was not until the Eighth Plenum at Lushan in August 1959 that enough had gone wrong for him to back down from his earlier confident position.[8] From the details we now have that came out of the Cultural Revolution in 1966—7, this was a most important meeting, but even at the time it was realised that there had been a strategic retreat from the great revolutionary thrusts of 1957—8. P'eng Te-huai's replacement by Lin Piao (1907—71) as Minister of Defence, however, was not a defeat. On the contrary, it was a measure of Mao's ultimate victory over his critics and some of his unenthusiastic followers to have placed Lin Piao in this key position. Mao was not only unswayed by the enforced retreat; he remained most active in areas of dispute with the U.S.S.R. as well as in the areas where he had erred in 1958—9. And after three relatively quiet years while the country struggled through unprecedented natural disasters, Mao Tse-tung reasserted his authority in the Tenth Plenum held in Peking in September 1962.[9] They were years of grave anxiety in both international and domestic affairs and not least in fraternal socialist relations. On his reassessments of the socialist world and revolutionary theory, more later. What was more worrying at home was the undermining of Mao's infallibility begun by the fierce opposition of P'eng Te-huai before his removal.

The underlying question behind this opposition was one concerning modernity. Specifically, it arose from the growing needs of the modern armed forces that P'eng Te-huai wanted for China. Together with the drive to have its own bomb, these needs had always been seen as a necessary development for which sacrifices in other sectors of the economy would have to be made. More and more expensive resources would have to be set aside if there was to be any hope that China might catch up with the armed might of the world's strongest countries. Even to keep up and not fall too far behind the two powers engaged in a super arms race demanded higher and ever higher rates of modernisation and professionalism. The ramifications of the issue were great indeed: it touched on problems of China's independence and status as a power and on the relationship between modernity and revolution. Most directly, however, P'eng Te-huai's removal clarified one point. Expertise was not enough.[10] Officers and their men had to be 'Red' as well, that is to say, knowledgeable and sound in Marxist–Leninist theory and the Thought of Mao Tse-tung. And Lin Piao, who succeeded P'eng Te-huai, personally led the campaign to 'put politics in command', placing even greater weight on being 'Red' than 'Expert'. In Chinese terms, this did not mean a retreat from modernity. On the one hand, it was apparent that being political was being modern, especially as this was based on the most advanced revolutionary theory available. On the other, modernity in special areas must not be allowed to get too far ahead of the rest of the society; such a development would produce distortions if not also unnecessary contradictions.

There was another feature of P'eng Te-huai's removal which is still mysterious. P'eng Te-huai had possibly been indiscreet during his visit to Moscow in 1959. He might have been too admiring of the professional skills of Soviet officers, the technological sophistication of Soviet weaponry and the amount of resources devoted to research and innovation. There have been hints since his departure that he might not have been totally loyal, that the experience had made him pro-Soviet and blinded him to the growing reservations about the Soviet model. At the time he was being replaced, Khrushchev's growing irritation with Mao Tse-tung was obvious to the Chinese. His claims to have corrected Stalin's errors and completed the socialism of the U.S.S.R. certainly aroused Mao's gravest doubts. The strains on both sides had begun to be unbearable and by August 1960 the disagreement had reached the point when Soviet advisers, engineers and skilled workers were suddenly withdrawn and told to take their plans and blueprints with them out of China.[11] It is still not clear whether this Sino-Soviet break had occurred over theoretical or strategic disagreements. If the latter was significant, then it came not only because the two leaders had disagreed about international strategy but also because they placed quite different weight on the need for modernity as a prerequisite for socialist transformation. On this point, P'eng's dismissal as well as the withdrawal of Soviet experts were equally revealing.

Despite P'eng's removal and the increasingly strident call to put politics in command of every field of activity, there was no consensus about the degree of modernity China needed to build socialism. The broad agreement that equal importance should be attached to both heavy and light industry and to agriculture was a realistic readjustment of policy. Productivity in both had become closely linked. But as both had fallen sharply in 1959–61 and did not begin until 1962 to return to 1958 figures, there was no agreement as to what measures should be taken to speed up development. There had been a general reaction against dramatic and sudden moves; certainly no one had the stomach for radical changes the success of which could not be guaranteed. Thus most of the party leaders seemed to have settled for gradual recovery and cautious progress even while they conceded that more emphasis should be placed on being 'Red' than on being 'Expert'. Mao Tse-tung and others might have preferred a bolder approach, but they accepted the moderate lines adopted at the Ninth Plenum in 1961 and the meetings in 1962 of the People's Political Consultative Conference and the People's National Congress. It was not until recovery was more certain that Mao Tse-tung returned to a harder line and reminded the Party of the dangers of 'revisionism' and the 'restoration' of capitalism and of the long and complex struggles ahead.[12] By that time, there was a distinct lack of enthusiasm among those who had just experienced more than three years of uncertainty and hardship, a lack which Mao Tse-tung could hardly not notice. Although there was genuine exhilaration at having come through near-disaster and at having learnt to adjust and cope without Soviet assistance, the intensifying public quarrel with the U.S.S.R. since early 1962 promised more storms ahead. The critical question of what new 'Chinese' standards of modernity would support the revolution from now on had to be faced.

Modernity had, at least since 1900, been seen in China as coming from outside. It had long been associated with Western Europe and the U.S.A. Only the C.C.P. had believed in Soviet modernity and, in 1949, they had acted on this by denying the modernity of the West and hitching the country to that of the U.S.S.R. When many of the non-party intellectuals had, as late as 1957, shown that they still clung to Western standards of modernity, they were severely criticised by those who pointed to the uncorrupting and more directly valuable example of Soviet Russia. But since at least 1960 and possibly as early as 1958, a sort of liberation from foreign standards of modernity can be discerned.[13] By 1962, it would appear that new standards were called for. These would have to be constructed from selected parts of Western and Soviet modernity which suited Chinese conditions and given a new legitimacy by correct Chinese projections of the Marxist–Leninist vision of the future. It would be expected that such Chinese extensions of the vision would draw some of its inspiration from viable remnants of Chinese civilisation. But how these new standards were to be made consistent and coherent was far from clear.

As a result, the years 1962–6 saw no clear sense of direction. Even the Socialist Education campaign which was launched during this period seemed to have been enveloped by a pervasive uncertainty.[14] There is ample evidence of an uneasy freedom to write and publish, accompanied by strenuous efforts to determine which lines of development should be discouraged and which others severely criticised. It was obviously easier to say what was not than what was the correct road. Thus strong appeals were made by various C.C.P. leaders themselves to traditional China, from Confucius and other later philosophers to Tu Fu, 'the people's poet' and to the popular Peking opera. There were other more modern literary and philosophical debates about the place of Lu Hsun, the role of Soviet socialist realism and the Marxist implications of contradiction and harmony (e.g. Mao's 'One Dividing into Two' and a Khrushchevian 'Two Uniting in One'). And there were dogged disputes about the class struggle in traditional Chinese history, the applicability of Marxist categories for ancient China and the possibility of 'Good' emperors and ministers in the eyes of the Chinese people of pre-modern China. When someone had gone too far, he was stopped, as Wu Han (b. 1909), Teng T'o (b. 1911) and Liao Mo-sha (b. 1907) were stopped from publishing in the *Peking Daily* and Liu Chieh was asked to stop attacking historical materialism. Whenever it was possible, a campaign was launched, such as the one against Chou Ku-ch'eng (b. 1910) in 1963, against Yang Hsien-chen (b. 1899) in August 1964, against Feng Ting (*floruit* 1930–66) in October 1964, against Hsia Yen (b. 1900) and Mao Tun (Shen Yen-ping, b. 1896) in May 1965–and then, in November 1965, the campaign against Wu

Han, the historian and dramatist, which marked the first shot of the Great Proletarian Cultural Revolution.[15]

None of the above criticisms, counter-attacks and campaigns were specifically aimed at determining new standards of modernity for China. They did, however, reflect the lack of agreed standards, even within the Party itself. Liu Shao-ch'i, the President of the P.R.C. since 1959, seemed to have stood for order and gradualness within the established framework. He accepted the standards of higher productivity in both industry and agriculture which had pulled China out of the abyss of 1959–61 and entrusted the party cadres to get on with their jobs without rocking the boat. Consciously or not, he had allowed the Party, the government and the economy to be guided by basic material interests which became less differentiated from more familiar traditional Chinese or bourgeois pragmatism. Whatever worked for greater productivity was permitted. All varieties of socialist campaigns were taken in their stride but none of them with the enthusiasm which might have endangered the steady but certain pace of growth that was thought desirable. The country was expected to ride all storms, whether large or small, whether actual or potential, on a simple measure of effectiveness in industry and agriculture. Thus the heroic and radical sting was removed and a stabilising order placed under firm central and bureaucratic control. For Mao Tse-tung, this was intolerable, not only because such an order lacked revolutionary direction but also because it was reaching the point when even he could not move the cadres to revolutionary action. It was now no longer a question of modernity, but one of mindless growth and ideological stagnation. It was against this background that the Cultural Revolution was planned and staged in 1965–6.

One final word about the standards of modernity during the years 1962–6.[16] The indices of growth were conventional and easily understood. Industrial plants were maintained and extended, most of those the Soviets left unfinished were completed and put into production, more railway lines and roads were built, so were new communications units and new public housing. Several new machine-building and chemical fertiliser plants were purchased from abroad, also smaller units of refineries and the beginnings of an electronics industry. And not least, nuclear research advanced rapidly and in 1964, China had its own bomb. In the countryside, light industry was encouraged to develop nearer sources of raw materials; also considerable central assistance was given to local production of generators and other farming machinery and all kinds of agricultural implements. A beginning had been made in rural self-sufficiency. Only in the area of grain production and textiles did shortages continue as they failed to keep up with the steady rise in population. Foreign imports of grain had been necessary since 1960 and this had to continue. But the general improvement in living standards, in the quality of goods exported and generally in the successful shift in foreign trade from the socialist countries to various Western countries was unmistakable. Economic growth was matched by higher educational and technical standards in the universities, specialised colleges and the central and provincial research institutes which continued to proliferate during this period. Not least significant was the decline in Russian language studies and the rapid growth in English language teaching and the teaching of other Western, Asian and African languages. Much of the new development was achieved with an eye to rapid growth and much less attention to revolutionary ideals, but in broad terms, the developments would have satisfied basic Western, Soviet or for that matter, Chinese standards of modernity. And that was probably what condemned them in the eyes of Mao Tse-tung, for whom the very concept of modernity had become suspect.

At the beginning of the chapter, it was suggested that the storms had started to blow in China when the Chinese felt obliged to tamper with the Soviet model. Nothing was, of course, as serious as when Mao Tse-tung began to doubt the correctness of what Khrushchev was doing to the U.S.S.R. and proposing for its socialist allies to follow. The doubts had begun with Khrushchev's criticisms of Stalin and taken shape with Khrushchev's conduct and tactics in international affairs. Only later did the doubt spread to the more elusive subject of Soviet modernity. Finally, the alarming question of deviation and revision of Marxist – Leninist theory arose and thus the undermining of the very goals of revolution themselves.[17]

The importance of revolution for Mao Tse-tung and the C.C.P. has already been stressed. In some respects, it was the means to the goal of a communist society for which independence had to be assured and modernity attained. But it was one thing to believe that the road to revolution had already been built and another to find that the road led into deep jungle or, worse still, led all the way back and that a new road would have to be charted into unknown country. It appears that this was what Mao Tse-tung began to feel at the latest by 1959. Khrushchev had been preaching peaceful coexistence and had visited Eisenhower in the U.S.A. Although he also came to Peking afterwards to reassure the Chinese leaders, the doubt grew among the Chinese that Khrushchev was not merely making tactical errors but that the errors stemmed from something far more fundamental. The suspicion grew when Khrushchev seemed to have been willing to be reconciled with Tito's obvious revisionism. It was confirmed when the Soviet party theoreticians were encouraged to draw up a document that emphasised the completion of the socialist stage of the revolution and the emergence of 'the state of the whole people'. Mao Tse-tung seemed to have anticipated this in Khrushchev's 'Secret Speech' in 1956 and had begun in 1957 to warn his colleagues about the continuance of contradictions even within the socialist society. But he probably did not believe that a fundamental restatement implying the end of class struggle in the U.S.S.R. would really follow. Once such a statement appeared and the Chinese found it unacceptable, the question of what the Marxist–Leninist revolution was about was thrown wide open.

Mao Tse-tung had prepared for a more direct hand in ideological control within the Party when he arranged for the journal *Hsueh-hsi* to be discontinued and the new journal *Hung-ch'i (Red Flag)* to be started in May 1958 under the editorship of Ch'en Po-ta, his closest political assistant. Soon afterwards in 1959, he withdrew himself from the P.R.C. presidency to concentrate on theoretical work, and it has long been acknowledged that the theoretical articles in *Hung-ch'i* came under his close scrutiny and some might have been partly written by him. Certainly, when the Sino-Soviet quarrel came into the open, there was never any doubt that each of the statements and open letters that were published in the name of the Central Committee of the C.C.P. had his personal approval, if they had not been actually drafted by him to begin with.

The international ramifications of the Sino-Soviet conflict have been considered in Chapter 5. The remainder of this chapter will focus on the question of revolution and the difficulties this had created within the socialist bloc and within China itself. Where the bloc was concerned, the C.C.P. was initially hoping to persuade some of the Eastern European leaders to give it support to dissuade the U.S.S.R. from laying down the law for future revolutionary developments. The C.P.S.U., however, was in a far stronger position to insist that its socialist allies in Eastern Europe prefer its formulations over the Chinese objections. In any case, many of the Eastern European leaders seemed to have been genuinely convinced that C.P.S.U. was more advanced in both theory and practice than the C.C.P. Thus, in three critical meetings in 1960 in Moscow and Bucharest, the C.P.S.U. came away with majority support, while the C.C.P. was only able to gain unequivocal assent to its views from the Albanians.[18] But the tactics of the C.C.P. did seem to pay off. At the first meeting in Moscow, in February 1960, it had sent K'ang Sheng (1899–1975), a subtle man well known in Europe for his former Comintern connections. He spoke to the Warsaw Pact countries of the dangers of revisionism, but was politely ignored. At the second, in June at Bucharest, P'eng Chen (b. *c.* 1902) spoke more bluntly and drew more fire by openly disagreeing with Khrushchev. Preparations for this confrontation had been made earlier in April in a series of articles published in *Hung-ch'i* and *People's Daily* and a tough speech during the celebration of the ninetieth anniversary of Lenin's birth made by the C.C.P. Head of the Propaganda Department Lu Ting-i (b. *c.* 1901). By the time of the third meeting, the Moscow Conference of eighty-one communist parties in November, the C.C.P. was represented by Liu Shao-ch'i and he did succeed in modifying somewhat the statement the C.P.S.U. wanted to make. Although Khrushchev's main thesis, that peaceful co-operation with the West was in the interest of the communist movement and peaceful transition to communism was possible, was retained, he was made to sound harder in his opposition to imperialists and re-actionaries. More significantly, the statement confirmed that the communist parties were no longer led automatically by the C.P.S.U.: this reinforced the trend towards the bloc without a centre, without a head.

The Moscow Statement left too much unsettled and it became inevitable that the debate over who had the correct view about the nature of revolution would intensify and that the C.C.P. would be forced to challenge the C.P.S.U. more and more openly. As the debate continued, it became clear to the C.C.P. that the emphasis on 'peaceful coexistence', and in particular, 'peaceful transition' to communism had theoretical implications. It was a marked departure from the Marxist–Leninist principle that revolution could only succeed through violent class struggle. The view that conditions had changed, that nuclear technology had created a different kind of struggle and therefore adjustments in over-all strategy were necessary did not convince the C.C.P. leaders. They continued to speak of nuclear weapons and the imperialists as 'paper tigers' and questioned the need for what amounted to a revision in Marxist–Leninist theory. They also began to reject the idea that the new strategy depended on the unity of the socialist bloc, especially if the price of its unity was the C.C.P.'s submission to the leadership of the C.P.S.U. right or wrong. The C.C.P. did not, of course, reject the idea of solidarity *per se* and was willing to compromise at the formal level. It did not want the risk of isolation that might follow if it left the bloc or was expelled from it. It did, after all, still believe that the bloc was in the vanguard of world revolution.

The years 1959–62 were not good years for the C.C.P. to keep up a fierce dispute with the C.P.S.U. As has been shown above, the calamitous effect of bad harvests had been pervasive and food shortages had forced the Chinese to purchase grain from Canada and Australia. China had to crush the Tibetan revolts of 1959 and strengthen its defences of the Sino-Indian borders where the dispute had become increasingly serious. In 1961–2 the country was at its weakest point in terms of both revolutionary success and international prestige. Thus the pressure Khrushchev put on the C.C.P. when China's situation was at its worst could have led only to greater distrust, if not downright hatred. First, the U.S.S.R. had in 1959 reneged on its agreement to help China with the development of nuclear weaponry; in 1960 it had withdrawn all its experts; then began a series of indirect but obvious attacks on China's 'dogmatism' in various East-European capitals and openly in the Soviet press and radio, which culminated in Khrushchev's attack on Albania at the Twenty-second C.P.S.U. Congress in October 1961.[19] Albania was merely the proxy for China. This was so obvious that Chou En-lai, who had led the C.C.P. delegation to Moscow, was obliged to leave in protest before the Congress was over. The Chinese stood stubbornly against Khrushchev's tactics and wherever possible had begun to retaliate. By the end of 1962, when the U.S.S.R. seemed to side with India during the Sino-Indian war, along with the U.S.A. and all its allies, there was no longer a good reason to keep the conflict muted and indirect. This had also come soon after the Tenth Plenum of the C.C.P. Eighth Party Congress in October, a time of restored confidence after signs of economic recovery had been confirmed. Mao Tse-tung was in no mood for moderate resistance. He ordered a fresh counter-attack, beginning with Khrushchev's retreat from Cuba and extending in 1963 to a wide-ranging series of public statements and open letters which continued unabated until the fall of Khrushchev in October 1964.[20]

The immense caution of the years from 1959 to 1962 was now thrown to the winds. Despite protestations that it still wanted socialist bloc unity and despite the restraint that its delegates to the Moscow meeting with the C.P.S.U. in July 1963 were asked to show, the C.C.P. clearly indicated that it thought it had put up with enough and was ready to expose Khrushchev for what he obviously was. The most systematic examples of this campaign to undermine Khrushchev's authority may be found in the nine Open Letters published in *People's Daily* between September 1963 and July 1964.[21] They ranged in subject matter from Soviet violations of the Treaty of Alliance and Soviet fears and weaknesses about nuclear war to Soviet ambitions to share world power with the U.S.A., from Khrushchev's revision of Marxist–Leninist principles to his readiness to 'restore capitalism' in the U.S.S.R. The final letter suggested that Khrushchev must go. The C.P.S.U. did not take the counter-offensive lying down. It argued that the C.C.P. wished to split the communist movement and that its policies endangered world peace, that its leaders were dogmatic and fanatical, petty bourgeois, chauvinist, and even Trotskyite (though Mao Tse-tung was also accused of reviving Stalin's cult of personality), and seemed to wish to have the C.C.P. leaders overthrown. Mao Tse-tung had the satisfaction of seeing Khrushchev ousted, but this in fact changed nothing. Chou En-lai's visit to Moscow to meet the new Soviet leaders in November 1964 produced no change; nor was Kosygin's visit to Peking helpful. The end of Khrushchev had stopped the most vituperative outbursts and, thanks to the full-scale U.S. intervention in Vietnam, which forced a degree of Sino-Soviet co-operation to assist a fraternal socialist state, the polemics which continued were not to reach the dangerous heights they had attained in the middle of 1964.[22] Attention was now focused on an actual shooting war and this quickly overshadowed the Sino-Soviet conflict of words. Thus, after millions of bitter words had been exchanged, neither side in the dispute seemed to have gained much satisfaction. Also, it was far from clear that anyone had a better idea of what revolution should now mean. For the Chinese, this had to await a more thorough testing and re-evaluation in the Great Proletarian Cultural Revolution.

There are obviously different kinds of revolution. Defining what revolution means for colonial territories and the newly emerging nations of the Third World concentrated on methods of coming to power. This the Chinese knew a great deal about: and they were convinced they knew more about it than the second generation of Soviet Party bureaucrats and theoreticians. Defining how to complete the business of revolution after seizing power was a different matter. On this subject, the Soviet leaders would suppose that they had the better claim to know and, until 1957–8, the Chinese seemed to have agreed. The first step in completing revolution is building socialism in a basically agrarian society. The U.S.S.R. had been through it and seemed to have succeeded; the Chinese would now do the same, only more quickly. Thus when, in 1957–8, it was felt that the Soviet model was not suitable, there were but few doubts in the mind of Mao Tse-tung about the nature of Soviet socialism. The problem was mainly one of speed and priorities. Thus the Great Leap Forward, the Mass Line, the People's Communes were conceived as more appropriate for the mobilisation of Chinese society and the rapid development of the economy. It was better suited to the size and distribution of the Chinese population to give more weight to light industry and agriculture than was prescribed in the Soviet example. They were different means of achieving the same goal.

It was really not until the Great Leap Forward had failed and the commune system had had to be greatly modified that more fundamental doubts came to the fore. These coincided with increasing concern for the way the U.S.S.R. was developing under Khrushchev. Within China, the priorities had to be changed. Agriculture became the basic index for growth. Rural light industry was encouraged to provide for its mechanisation and semi-mechanisation, but the essential feature was for agricultural units to be 'self-reliant'. Other light industry and heavy industry continued to grow but were not encouraged to grow beyond what agricultural production could support. In this way, China could avoid the mistakes of the over-centralised Soviet 'command economy', and relieve the basic units of production from bureaucratic interference. Thus the conflict with the U.S.S.R. was not only over revolutionary strategy against imperialism and capitalism, especially in the Third World, but also over the strategy of how to spark off and sustain the revolution from the countryside. But it appeared that, after the disasters of 1959–61 and the grim efforts to bring about recovery in 1961–2, the party cadres under Liu Shao-ch'i and the administrative cadres headed by Chou En-lai were too ready to rely on varieties of 'economism', that is, the use of material incentives and private plots in a mixed economy, as the safer road to socialism.[23] There was little enthusiasm for policies of mass mobilisation. The revolution was in danger of settling down to a steady but sedate pace.

The critical question was not one of pace by itself, but of the caution and timidity of ageing and stabilising élites. The Soviet model had now become a negative example. To Mao, its revolution had fallen into the hands of just such ageing, cautious and selfish élites and they had the power to thwart the growth of the revolution, even to declare that the revolution had been completed and therefore deny the need for revolution in the future. Such a development had to be prevented at all costs. It would not be true to suppose that since Soviet tendencies to élitism came from the original structure of the Bolshevik Party, the less élitist experiences of the C.C.P. could provide a safeguard against the growth of élitism in China. On the contrary, just as Soviet bureaucratic élitism owed a debt to the structure of Tsarist government, a new Chinese élitism could easily emerge along lines not dissimilar to the mandarinate and the orthodox Confucianist gentry. Therefore Mao Tse-tung was understandably alarmed at the recrudescence of élitism among party and administrative cadres at the centre and in the provinces during the years 1962–6. It was perhaps not only against the U.S.S.R. and Yugoslavia that he encouraged the fierce attacks on the 'restoration of capitalism' after 1962. In the reported parts of his speech to the Tenth Plenum in September 1962, Mao Tse-tung's warning that restoration was a real threat at all stages while socialism was being built indicated a serious concern for his own comrades as well.

There was no lack of national and local campaigns to combat élitism and the illiteracy, ignorance and lack of political consciousness which permitted élitism to develop. There were campaigns to let politics take command, to be both Red and Expert, to study Marxist–Leninist theory and the Thought of Mao Tse-tung, to promote Socialist Education in the countryside, to emulate worker-peasant heroes, to learn from the P.L.A. One campaign followed another in quick succession. But there seems no doubt that most of them lacked freshness and were rarely sustained with vigour. It would also be understandable that, when the campaigns were thought to have been directed against the new élites themselves, there would have been a certain perfunctoriness. Thus the external campaigns against Soviet revisionism were accompanied by domestic campaigns which, while weighted differently, echoed many of the same themes: revolution (within and without) cannot cease to relate to the class struggle; contradictions will remain even within socialist societies, including antagonistic ones which have to be dealt with violently; and, echoing an early precursor, 'the revolution is not yet complete, our comrades must continue to strive hard'. They made a suitable prologue to the Great Proletarian Cultural Revolution.[24]

7 To Change or Not to Change, 1966 — 71

THE years of economic recovery, 1962–5, were also years of obvious external tensions. Less obvious were the tensions developing within China. There were some much-publicised criticisms of writers, scholars, journalists and philosophers, but these seemed peripheral to the tasks of rebuilding the economy and of resisting the political pressures of the U.S.S.R. For both these tasks, unity in the leadership was most important and this the C.C.P. seemed to have. In particular, the increasingly serious struggle with the U.S.S.R. on matters of socialist ideology and authority appeared to bring out the solidarity of men like Mao Tse-tung, Liu Shao-ch'i, Chou En-lai, Teng Hsiao-p'ing (b. 1904), P'eng Chen (b. c. 1902), Lin Piao and Lo Jui-ch'ing (b. c. 1906) who, together with a host of others, seemed well agreed on Soviet errors and on going on a Chinese road. From outside, there was both respect and disbelief at the intense way the Chinese were thumbing their noses at the Russians. Also, there was both admiration and scepticism at the efforts to build a modern industrial state that was on neither Western nor Soviet lines. But no one foresaw that the combination of the insistence on independence, the need for modernity and the drive towards revolution could break the unity forged by fifteen years of struggle and fifteen years of victory and power. Since 1949, there had been a serious threat from Kao Kang and Jao Shu-shih in 1953–4 and a strong personal protest by P'eng Teh-huai against Mao Tse-tung in 1959, but neither seemed to have left any cracks in party unity. There had been no clear sign that the polemics before May 1966, including what is now recognised as the first shot in the new crisis, Yao Wen-yuan's attack on Wu Han in November 1965, had been leading to a major struggle for the power to lead the revolution on the right road.

What is now known about the Great Proletarian Cultural Revolution (G.P.C.R.) has been painfully reconstructed with the help of the unofficial and polemical writings by rival groups of Red Guards and other activists.[1] These miscellaneous and fragmentary documents not only revealed what was happening during much of the G.P.C.R. itself but also partially exposed the circumstances underlying what turned out to be a bitter struggle which broke the party bureaucracy and endangered the unity of the country. The reconstruction is still partial but the main outlines now seem clear. In this chapter, the picture will begin with the G.P.C.R. as a series of events, then go on to examine its implications for China's modernisation and its significance as part of the revolutionary process and finally return to the aftermath of disorder and what this meant for China's perception of its independence in the modern world.

There is still doubt about what is 'cultural' in the G.P.C.R. Much of the violence, whether in the form of abuse or physical destruction, was directed against things cultural, and it is tempting to describe the actions of 1966–7 as negations of culture. This is clearly a misunderstanding. The correct translation, 'The Great Revolution for Proletarian Culture', would have emphasised that the revolution was to help to create 'proletarian culture' and this could only be done, as the Chinese saw it, by first destroying the vestiges of 'bourgeois culture', the symbols of the past, nostalgia for which stood in the way of revolution itself. In practice, it was not only 'bourgeois culture' that had to be destroyed. By 1965–6 there were at least four layers of past cultures that were seen as obstructing historical progress: firstly, Chinese traditional élitist values and their manifestations; secondly, Western tastes and styles that had survived since the 1920s in the fields of art, literature and all forms of scholarship; thirdly, Soviet theories of cultural development introduced in the 1930s and 1940s and widely taught in the 1950s; finally, traditional rural conservatism causing the peasantry to cling to unacceptable longings for family and private property and enterprise. In the 1920s and 1930s, there had been many attempts to attack traditional élitism, but without success, largely because what was used to attack it was Western and alien. Since 1949, the traditional-minded élites had been physically eliminated or forcibly converted, but those who survived represented mainly a more modern form of élitism tinged with the élitism of Western professionalism and technical expertise. The blatantly 'Western' features were then removed by substituting Soviet features, but while the élitism appeared to become more 'proletarian', it was never wholly undermined. In the 1957–8 campaigns when non-party and traditional or openly 'Western' intellectuals were thought to have been thoroughly transformed, there still remained party intellectuals who maintained their mainly Soviet-type élitism. When the Soviet model became generally suspect in the early 1960s, it was perhaps not surprising that the élitism regained some of its original traditional and even 'Western' features, albeit muted and disguised in Marxist – Leninist clothing. And all this while the economic base had been changing and private property and capitalist ownership had virtually disappeared.

Thus the ideological struggle with the U.S.S.R. made clear that older forms of élitism were stubborn and did not automatically disappear when the economic base was changed. What was needed was violent revolutionary action by the progressive forces thrown up by the change in the economic base, in this case, the growing proletariat which was now strong enough to combat the élites, whether old or new. The roots of the G.P.C.R. may be found in the pervasive caution and prudence in the party élites after the disasters of 1959–61, in the relative economic stagnation even after the dangers were over, in Mao Tse-tung's failure after the Tenth Plenum in September 1962 to elicit enthusiastic response from the cadres, and in the economic, literary, philosophical, historical and artistic debates of 1962–5. But the most obvious and at the same time most vulnerable élitism was found among the intellectuals and academics and that was where Mao Tse-tung and his select vanguard chose to launch the first attack.[2] Thus Yao Wen-yuan's essay on Wu Han's representation of Hai Jui (the sixteenth-century good official whose services to the people were not appreciated by the Ming emperor) in November 1965. The attack was justified by Yao in terms of Wu Han's implied defence of P'eng Teh-huai and criticism of Mao Tse-tung. As Wu Han's earlier critical essays (with Teng T'o and Liao Mo-sha) came to light, it became clear that there was within the Peking Municipal Committee much discontent with Mao Tse-tung and some sort of confrontation with the leaders responsible was necessary. When it emerged that P'eng Chen, the Peking Chairman himself, was protecting Wu Han and his friends, it suggested that the Party at the centre had become disaffected. It then becomes understandable why Mao Tse-tung had to get Yao Wen-yuan to publish his attack in Shanghai and not in the capital itself.

The literary and historical campaign was but the beginning, the prologue to a determined effort to smoke out party leaders who were not merely opposed to Mao Tse-tung but who had become blind to the threat of conservatism and vested interests that had created the U.S.S.R. of Khrushchev and Brezhnev. In addition, the campaign opened up the possibility of exposing those who might have joined Mao Tse-tung in opposing the U.S.S.R. in theory but who really wished to emulate the stable political and economic order and the technical and military achievements of the Russians. Mao Tse-tung perceived that there was a growing gap between the young in high schools, colleges and universities who were still taught revolutionary ideals and the old and middle-aged Party cadres who had come to enjoy the years of authority and privilege and obviously did not live by the ideals they professed. He sought out the few he could still trust and encouraged those who had been disestablished, or who saw no prospect of joining the establishment, to organise opposition against the Party cadres. Whether he merely wanted to remove some of the Party leaders and clean up the Party or whether he planned from the beginning to shake the Party to its ideological foundations is still being argued.[3] What is clear is that a great force was unleashed among the young and the Party was taken by surprise. Several of the leaders then acted to contain the fury and some hastily tried to frustrate Mao Tse-tung's efforts to radicalise the Party. Liu Shao-ch'i appeared to have misjudged the extent to which Mao Tse-tung was prepared to go and, during the six months from February to August 1966, his attempts to rally the Party cadres to take the initiative and control their own cultural revolution exposed him to the radicals as the man most responsible for the decline in the Party's revolutionary image.[4] Mao Tse-tung had an overwhelming advantage in that his writings and directives had become the undisputed bases for action in the country. No one would openly act against him, everyone quoted him for what was done. But he remained still a brilliant tactician who used every opportunity provided by the growing confusion to force the Party élitists to change their ways.

In May 1966, when the G.P.C.R. was formally announced, it became clear how well prepared Mao Tse-tung had been for a major change of direction. His choice of Lin Piao as successor to P'eng Teh-huai as Minister of Defence in 1959 had ensured him of central military support. His use of Lin Piao to politicise the P.L.A., to make it the model for studying his writings (through Lin Piao's selection of Mao's quotations that became the famous Little Red Book) and to make the P.L.A. the vanguard of the campaign to 'let politics take command' paid off when the testing-time arrived.[5] This latter campaign, in particular, had spread to all activities and the Party had endorsed it. Now in 1966 the Party tasted the full implications of a slogan they had paid lip-service to but had not really taken seriously. Lo Jui-ch'ing, the P.L.A. Chief of Staff who had fallen out with Lin Piao, was the first to go. P'eng Chen, the powerful First Secretary of the Peking Committee who was accused of protecting Wu Han the historian-critic of Mao Tse-tung, was the next. Then followed the leading figures in the cultural establishment, the Ministers and Vice-ministers of Culture, Education and Higher Education, the Presidents of universities and several specialist colleges, the key men of the Party's Propaganda Department, the senior journalists and academics, all the main so-called 'cultural warlords'.[6] Mao's former secretary, Ch'en Po-ta, himself a member of this establishment as a Vice-minister of Culture, a Vice-Chairman of the Propaganda Department, the editor of the Party organ, *Hung-ch'i (Red Flag)*, a Vice-President of the Academy of Sciences and occasional lecturer at universities and the Higher Party School, led the assault. He was supported by Mao's wife, Chiang Ch'ing, whose efforts to develop a revolutionary theatre had been mocked by senior Party colleagues. Only one man saw what was demanded at the time: Kuo Mo-jo, poet, scholar and literatus par excellence and President of the Academy of Sciences, publicly confessed in April 1966 to have been fundamentally wrong and offered to burn everything that he had ever written and start afresh.

The disintegration of the Party was an astonishing event. It revealed how complacent the Party leaders and cadres throughout the country had become. They had become so confident of their authority that they could not comprehend the violence of the attacks that college and high-school students had mounted, first against their teachers, then against Party cadres and then, as they gathered force and confidence, against more senior Party leaders.[7] By August, the wall-poster war that had been started by students at Peking University with Mao Tse-tung's approval in May had brought a solidarity to the nation-wide movement which was soon to gain recognition in a grand Peking rally as the Red Guards. It was an exhilarating moment for the millions of students now joined by young workers who could legitimately challenge the drab and rigid bureaucracy that had so far ruled all aspects of their lives. It was a release, a new freedom, that echoed the great movements of modern Chinese history: the May Fourth (1919), the May Thirtieth (1925–6), and the December Ninth (1936) movements, the trek to Yenan to fight the Anti-Japanese War (1937–8), even some echo of the C.C.P.'s Long March in 1933–5. So it seemed at least to many of the students: a great adventure that brought vigour and purposefulness to the idea of revolution.

A much grimmer struggle was going on at the highest levels of the C.C.P., in the Central Committee, in the Politburo, in the Standing

Committee of the Politburo. There Mao Tse-tung and Lin Piao sought to take control by getting rid of Liu Shao-ch'i, the P.R.C. President and Teng Hsiao-p'ing, the Party's Secretary-General. Again, it was in August that they began to succeed to outvote those who had dragged their feet about the G.P.C.R. and who were alarmed at the danger that too much politics might shake the country's stability and slow its economic development. At the Eleventh Plenum of the Eighth Central Committee, Liu Shao-ch'i was demoted and Lin Piao emerged for the first time as Mao's closest comrade-in-arms. It was still only the beginning. Mao Tse-tung called for revolution in all fields of work and for the Red Guards to 'bombard the headquarters'. This would appear to be an open invitation to overthrow the Party and state structures throughout the country. But it was not intended that the Red Guards should do this on their own. They were meant to accept direction from the Cultural Revolution Group headed by Ch'en Po-ta and Chiang Ch'ing. They had as their 'leader' no less a person than Lin Piao himself and Chou En-lai was named as 'adviser'. They were to concentrate on Party headquarters and unrepentant Party leaders and cadres, on cultural values and political ideals, on reforming the superstructure. They were not to upset the centres of production, whether in the factories or in the people's communes. But the larger struggle for power could not be contained and guided without counter-measures. The party leadership at the centre was obviously divided. The leaders in the provinces, cities, towns and production units were divided too.[8] It was not a time for moderation when the stakes had become so high. Party leaders and cadres at all levels fought back, in the name of order and legitimacy, production and progress. Thus the battles continued throughout September, October and November. By that time, Liu Shao-ch'i and Teng Hsiao-p'ing had effectively been removed from power and Lin Piao had emerged supreme as the First Vice-Chairman of the Party. But the war went on unabated.

The extent of destruction and loss of production in all provinces during the G.P.C.R. will probably never be known. By December, the government was seriously alarmed and the Central Committee of the Party repeatedly warned against the excesses of the Red Guards, the factionalism that had developed in the movement and the increasing clashes between students and workers and between different factions among the workers themselves. The P.L.A. and security organs were ordered to stay neutral but they were also alerted to prevent the complete breakdown of order. Increasingly they were being involved, first 'supporting the Left' whenever the legitimised 'Rebels' were threatened with defeat, then defending themselves against attack and finally acting to re-establish authority in the provinces. The most dramatic developments were in the cities, especially in Shanghai in January 1967, when finally the old Party leadership was pulled down and a Shanghai Commune was established. Similar successes were recorded in T'ai-yuan (Shansi) and Tsingtao (Shantung). But the Shanghai Commune structure was unacceptable. The new formula of a 'three-in-one' alliance, an alliance of the revolutionary masses with the P.L.A. and some acceptable cadres, produced the first Revolutionary Committee in the north-eastern province of Heilungkiang, on the borders of the U.S.S.R. This became the model.[9] Significantly, the P.L.A. had been drawn in fully as one of the main component groups to help re-establish the new provincial governments.

This ended the first stage of the G.P.C.R. The task of arousing the literate and vocal sections of the masses, especially of the urban centres, had been all too successful and few could remain unaffected by the upheaval. The objective of removing Liu Shao-ch'i and the more orthodox Party cadres and bureaucrats had been largely achieved, the young had been given a taste of revolution, the superstructure had been overturned and older cultural values violently smashed. But there were unexpected developments: the Red Guards could not be kept together as one large amorphous group but were divided and polarised into major antagonistic factions, production had been affected in factories, communications disrupted, various organs of government at central, provincial and local levels had been taken over; 'struggle – criticism – transformation' had gone so far that the P.L.A. had to intervene and ultimately to take the lion's share of power until finally even the P.L.A. could not remain free from the political polarisations that were taking place around them. The three legs of Party, government and P.L.A. which had guaranteed orderly growth and progress for over seventeen years could no longer stand. Popular participation erased the authority structures of both Party and government and only the P.L.A. was relatively intact. There was grave danger that the P.L.A. and its own Party committees would have to take over control altogether. Thus at the second stage, the 'three-in-one' revolutionary committees had to rebuild all levels of government and rescue all production units.

This second stage may be said to have lasted another twenty months until September 1968 when all twenty-nine provinces, municipalities and autonomous areas finally had their new Revolutionary Committees. Only fragmentary information is available about the considerable difficulties some of the provinces, cities and factories experienced in trying to set up such 'alliances' of the P.L.A., the cadres and the masses. The first six that were established by April 1967 clearly had a strong worker-peasant representation. This was still a period when the P.L.A. restrained itself and simply held the ring for the battling groups while waiting for them to decide on the Committee's composition. This soon came to an end when the P.L.A. found itself the target of attack and when some of its leaders, including those who 'supported the Left', became reluctant to let the mass representatives dominate the new committees. The more the P.L.A. was taking responsibility for not only security and order but also production and administration, the less willing it was to see the fervent amateurs share its power. Thus relations between radicals of the Cultural Revolution Group who wanted more mass representation and the P.L.A. in the provinces worsened rapidly. The new fighting which occurred led to direct P.L.A. intervention. Most significantly, the accusation of 'following the capitalist road' first directed at Liu Shao-ch'i and the Party was now used against the P.L.A. itself. The idea that P.L.A. officers were themselves hardly revolutionary was dangerous, specially when the radicals of the Cultural Revolution Group began to call for the removal of some senior officers. The climax of the P.L.A. reaction against these radical voices was the Wuhan Incident of 21 July 1967 when two representatives from Peking were seized in Wuhan by the P.L.A. with the support of part of the industrial force in that city and Chou En-lai had to go there personally to rescue them from greater harm.[10]

Although the P.L.A. officers responsible were removed and the immediate results were inconclusive, the Maoist radicals and the Red Guards experienced a serious setback from which they were not to recover. The struggle continued in Peking, Shanghai and several other cities despite exhortations to the Red Guards to moderate their actions, promote production and respect state and P.L.A. property. But the P.L.A. stood firm and two of the three Revolutionary Committees formed before the end of the year were led by P.L.A. officers. By early 1968, the battle was largely over. On average three Revolutionary Committees were formed each month between January and May. Then, after a brief pause, the five remaining provinces established their committees in August and September. Most of these committees formed in 1968 were headed by P.L.A. officers (usually the political commissars), and the P.L.A. provided the leading members. The protracted struggles for power reflected the general resistance to military ascendancy in political and administrative affairs, but it also showed that mass representatives were clearly no match for senior P.L.A. officers, many of whom had had considerable Party and political experience. As the developments in 1968 evolved, it became increasingly clear that the Party had to be restored if P.L.A. power was to be curbed. Revolutionary or not, only the older cadres could stand up to the P.L.A., and only if the Party was fully restored to authority could one of the basic slogans of the revolution become meaningful again, that is, 'The Party should control the gun'.

Thus there had to be a third stage in the G.P.C.R., the stage of rebuilding the C.C.P. This had begun at the lower levels in the factories and communes almost as soon as the last Revolutionary Committee was formed in September 1968, but it was too serious a problem of power to await the slow process of struggle, bargaining and compromise that had characterised the local formations since 1967. Instead, the rebuilding began from the top, following the Twelfth Plenum of the Eighth Party Congress in October 1968 which formally stripped Liu Shao-ch'i of all his Party positions and then of his Party membership, announced the victory of the G.P.C.R. and also planned the calling of the Ninth Party Congress, the revision of the Party Constitution and the principles of party reconstruction.[11] This third stage lasted through the Ninth Party Congress in April 1969 until the last provincial Party Committee was finally decided on in 1971. This crucial stage will be considered later in this chapter because the issues of internal and external developments during this stage become more intertwined and complex and deserve separate treatment. It will also be useful if the Twelfth Plenum resolution on the victory of the G.P.C.R. is taken at its face value at this point and the significance of the events of May 1966–October 1968 is now examined before continuing on to the third stage.

The implications for revolution are not as self-evident as they appear. All actions in the G.P.C.R. were taken in the name of revolution, most of them in the name of Mao Tse-tung. 'It is right to rebel', and 'Bombard the headquarters' obviously suggest that the C.C.P. itself was not sufficiently revolutionary. Yet the unspoken fear of 'left-wing adventurism' endangering the unity of the country and the productivity of the economy was based on a concern to protect the revolution and advance it so that full socialism could be realised. It seems clear now that the example of the U.S.S.R. was the catalytic agent. It had provided a framework, but it had also provoked doubts about its revolutionary future. The greater the doubts, the greater the Soviet insistence that its road was the only correct one. And that very insistence determined the Chinese to find their own independent way. The G.P.C.R. had attacked 'revisionism' and 'the restoration of capitalism' as dangerous possibilities within the C.C.P. and described Liu Shao-ch'i as 'China's Khrushchev'. Although these attacks were not always convincing, there is no doubt that the shadow of the Soviet alternative to national power and towards technical advancement hung over the G.P.C.R. throughout this period. In particular, the bureaucratic and élitist character of the C.C.P. before 1966 was remarkably close to that of the C.P.S.U. It is in this area that the call for a genuine revolutionary spirit in 1966 appeared like an extension of the intense Sino-Soviet polemics of 1962–5.

But there was another less obvious result of the G.P.C.R. The violence and destruction of the early months and the focus on 'bourgeois values' which threatened the life-styles of a whole generation of modernisers further exposed the deep Chinese ambivalence about the concept of modernity itself. For a while, what was modern was Soviet and this formed the basis to reject the 'modern' that was Western and capitalist. Now even the 'modern' that was Soviet was suspect as 'revisionist' or 'restored capitalist'. The only criterion of what was modern, therefore, was that which was genuinely socialist and leading to the future communist society. Since no one else could point unerringly to the nature of this modernity, the Chinese would have to find it out for themselves. And the only acceptable texts they could really rely on to define that modernity were those of Marx, Engels and Lenin. As they saw it, Mao Tse-tung Thought had creatively adapted the essence of scientific materialism to Chinese conditions. The outlines drawn by the three founders of Marxism—Leninism had been filled in successively stage by stage through the growth and refinement of Mao Tse-tung Thought. Thus an evolving Chinese modernity was taking place.

The concept, however, remained fluid and elusive.[12] During the G.P.C.R., it sometimes appeared as if being revolutionary was synonymous with being modern and destroying and rejecting the old was its recurrent corollary. At other times, the essential modern change was to transform the economic base and this had to be done through an older revolution, the industrial revolution which had yet to be completed in China. For this, the secret seemed to rest with science and technology, not that which served capitalism and created new technocratic élites which could betray the cause of socialism as in Soviet Russia, but a politically committed version built upon the skills and experiences of the growing proletariat which could also eventually proletarianise the peasantry as well. It was more modern in that it conformed with the projections of Marx that a proletarian dictatorship was necessary if modernity was not to be the monopoly of new social élites or to run aground in the deep rural conservatism of the vast majority of China's peasantry. Thus the evolving Chinese modernity had to be both a bold and dramatic catching up in science and technology with the best attainable in the world today and a controlled progress that prevented the rise of new exploitative classes. In combination, it would appear to be both push and pull, a striking contradiction that must be very exhaustive to talent and resources. Yet the heart of the G.P.C.R. was the purposeful facing up to contradictions which were considered by Mao to be inevitable on the road to communism. Thus, despite the ambivalence and the uncertainty, the Chinese during the G.P.C.R. confirmed that modernity was not to be achieved during a static stage, or defined stages, of development, but was to be the product of recurring efforts to establish proletarian standards even while the proletariat was changing and expanding.[13] In this way, modernity is complementary and necessary to revolution and is itself redefined regularly by revolutionary acts themselves.

Underlying the evolving Chinese modernity and the Chinese road to communism is the deep desire to be independent and to grow independently. During the G.P.C.R., this desire took a very aggressive form in China's international relations.[14] It has since been explained that extremists in the Foreign Ministry and their Red Guard supporters had perverted Chinese foreign policy for a short while. This may well have been so. Nevertheless, the extent to which these extremists were prepared to go created an atmosphere not dissimilar to that in the U.S.A. during the McCarthy era. As the Foreign Minister Ch'en Yi found, rationality and diplomacy became almost impossible when everyone's loyalty was measured by how tough an anti-capitalist and anti-revisionist he was. Beginning with the deterioration in relations with the Netherlands in July 1966, there were fierce attacks on the Soviet embassy by Red Guard students and numerous incidents with other socialist countries, the recall of the embassy in Ghana, the riots encouraged in Macao and later Hong Kong, the anti-British actions in Peking and Shanghai, the further worsening of relations with India and perhaps most seriously, the confrontation with first the Burmese and then the Cambodian governments and finally, the long-drawn-out battle with the Indonesian government which ended when relations were suspended in October 1967. For some fifteen months, normal diplomacy became almost impossible, except possibly with North Vietnam and the P.R.G. of South Vietnam, where the escalation of American bombing raids on the north and the inflow of more U.S. and allied troops were too serious even for the Red Guards to try to change course. All ambassadors except one were recalled. From the record of China's international relations since 1949, it is obvious that most of the activities of 1966–7 were aberrations. But they did warn the Chinese leaders that it was but a short step from being aggressively independent to aggression against the independence and pride of others. What such actions could have achieved for China's own sense of independence is difficult to perceive. The negative effects of a series of retaliatory actions, especially between China and Burma and between China and Indonesia, must have confirmed that diplomatic practice and international law would be a far sounder basis for friendly relations than a misguided and virulent national pride.

Another manifestation of the desire for independence reinforced the idea of self-reliance.[15] This had surfaced soon after the Soviet withdrawal of their experts and technicians in 1960. It remained muted as the Chinese struggled to complete the projects left behind and also bought plant and equipment from Japan and Western Europe which they could not produce on their own. By the time of the G.P.C.R., self-reliance reflected the reaction against the increasing dependence on more highly developed capitalist countries for China's industrialisation. Again, it took an aggressive form within the country and spread downwards to every level of activity. Most significant of all was the way the slogan also expressed the reaction against bureaucratic and élitist central planning and control that had marked the G.P.C.R. in other fields. In particular, this ultimately had a positive effect on the policy of 'walking on two legs', of not over-stressing heavy industry but giving equal weight to the development of light industry and agriculture. By the end of the second stage of the G.P.C.R., when new local and provincial governments had been re-established and the Red Guards abolished and their members sent down to the countryside, self-reliance had become a slogan not merely of rehabilitation but also of reconstruction.

The first two stages of the G.P.C.R. had wide ramifications. To say that it was merely a struggle for power among the top leaders of the C.C.P. would be a gross misunderstanding. It is true that the immediate result of the violence was to allow Mao Tse-tung and his supporters to gain the upper hand in the Party and to eventually eliminate Liu Shao-ch'i and other opponents. The factionalism that had developed within the Party during the fifteen years of relative peace and order provided the lines of conflict once a major disagreement occurred. This is a subject that is now being studied intensely. It would be interesting to know precisely the basis of the factionalism and the actual steps at each point of disagreement which led to the final break and the outburst of violence.[16] This is still an area of academic dispute, so only an outline of the main protagonists in the struggle and the ideological issues which made the struggle inevitable has so far been attempted here. There were also obviously problems of productivity, of a slow rate of economic growth, of unemployment and disparate standards of living which might have encouraged Mao Tse-tung to act when he did and which certainly aggravated the conditions for violence. But the Chinese have written mainly in terms of ideology and power, and there is no reason to doubt that these were central to the G.P.C.R. But by ideology, they do not merely mean Marxist—Leninist theory and, by power, they do not only mean the removal of Mao Tse-tung's opponents within the Party.

From the events of 1966—8, it is clear that the ideological struggle paid great attention to questions of the style and practice of revolution, the will and commitment to push for bold and radical change as well as the institutional obstacles to revolutionary performance. The incipient élitism that lay behind these questions has already been outlined. What remains extraordinary is the way Mao Tse-tung chose to revive the revolutionary spirit and the extent to which he succeeded in identifying with the young and stirring them to such drastic action.[17] Both are quite unprecedented in Chinese history and no comparable example in world history has yet been found. The explosive mix that produced the ideological struggle is recognisably Chinese in style and Marxist—Leninist in rhetoric, but its uniqueness is hard to define except in terms of the mind and personality of Mao Tse-tung. It was his analysis of Chinese conditions, his planning and strategy and his great confidence that brought about the G.P.C.R. It is indeed remarkable that no other explanation for the events of 1966 has been as satisfactory as this simple and obvious one. What followed in 1967 and 1968, however, seems different. There was a loss of control and ultimately a diversion of purpose. The reasons are still not clear. Since the fall of Lin

Piao in 1971 and the steady withdrawal of the P.L.A. from political and economic affairs, there have been efforts to read later divisions between various factions back to 1967 and point to disagreements in the leadership as the cause of the initial loss of control. This is plausible, but it was not long before the leadership was agreed that the P.L.A. had to bring the Red Guards under its control. By that time, much of the enthusiasm in the movement had been lost, also the sense of purpose and direction which the G.P.C.R. had started out with. Perhaps Mao Tse-tung meant it to happen this way: the G.P.C.R. was only to be an outburst, a warning, a refreshing experience to waken tired bureaucratic spirits and to revolutionise the young. But it is more likely that the G.P.C.R. revealed more discord and 'antagonistic contradiction' than even Mao Tse-tung expected and undermined the Party and thrust more power on the military than he would have wanted. The G.P.C.R. confirmed that an open ideological struggle among the young must inevitably come into sharp conflict with the concern for orderly growth among their elders.

As for power, there were several layers of contention.[18] Getting rid of Lo Jui-ch'ing, P'eng Chen, Chou Yang and ultimately Liu Shao-ch'i and Teng Hsiao-p'ing was part of one layer. Removing hundreds of provincial and local Party leaders was probably related to the first, but may be described as part of another layer. Rivalry among various types of Red Guards and rivalry for leadership of local and provincial movements may, together with rivalry within the Cultural Revolution Group in Peking, be seen as a third. Factions of the P.L.A., roughly divided between those Lin Piao trusted and those he did not, formed a fourth. The battle to survive among Party cadres in the new structure of participatory democracy, the 'three-in-one' alliance of the Revolutionary Committees, against mass representatives on the one hand and P.L.A. officers on the other, was clearly a fifth and totally new layer. This last came towards the end of the second stage and was a significantly new area of contention. Although in the third stage the Party cadres were gradually to regain control over local and provincial governments, the Party's position has never been the same again.

The third stage of the G.P.C.R. from late 1968 to mid-1971 is significantly different from the first two and it may be asked if it should be considered as part of the G.P.C.R. There has never been any doubt that the violence and destruction of 1966–7 was a crucial part of the G.P.C.R.; the C.C.P. itself in October 1968 pointed to the victory of the G.P.C.R. and this suggests that the G.P.C.R. consisted of the series of events between 1966 and 1968. At the Ninth Party Congress in April 1969, the G.P.C.R. was formally brought to an end, and it may be argued that the G.P.C.R. was one major event lasting from 1966 to 1969.[19] At the same time, the Ninth Party Congress itself indicated that the restructuring of all levels of the Party would mark the final triumph of the G.P.C.R. and this would support the view that there was a third stage. The fact that Lin Piao and his closest supporters engaged in the 1969—71 struggle against the erosion of P.L.A. gains and began to fall from power about the time the last Provincial Party Committee was elected is also significant. Only in 1971 was the Party finally ready to challenge the ascendancy of the P.L.A. in various state and civilian organs and production units. The fact that 1971 was also the year when China's international position reached a new climax, with both Nixon's announcement that he was going to China and China's admission into the U.N. that October, makes it all the more convenient to group the events of late 1968 to September 1971 as the third stage of the G.P.C.R.

The third stage opened with a deep concern for questions of power. It was not only the concern for the power structure within the country but also for that within the socialist bloc following the crushing of Dubcek's Czechoslovakia in August 1968. Until then, there had appeared plenty of time for the Party to be rebuilt and the demobilised Red Guards to be tamed. Brezhnev's invasion of Czechoslovakia and enunciation of a doctrine of 'partial sovereignty' within the bloc woke the Chinese to the dangers of disunity in their country. Although they had no sympathy for Dubcek, they quickly condemned Soviet action. What was significant was the reminder that ideological struggle could lead to military action and China was vulnerable to a similar attack if its leaders were disunited. Thus questions of ideology gave way to those of power; the need was now for consolidation, unity and control.

Within the country, the ideological struggle was practically over. Many of the writings about ideological problems between 1968 and 1971 were aimed at educating the masses, 'bringing philosophy to the people' and eliciting their response to new shifts of emphasis and at consolidating gains in work-style, commitment and revolutionary spirit. Issue after issue of *Red Flag*, for example, hammered home the key points on which there had been some consensus, but there was little heat in such writings let alone any new light on theoretical matters.[20] By the end of 1968, issues of power took precedence. Consolidation in the Central Committee of the Party and in the government as well as in the provincial Revolutionary Committee was not in itself desirable. The second stage of the G.P.C.R. (1967–8) had placed the P.L.A. in a very strong position and their dominance in several key ministries and in the provinces had ensured that their representatives dominated the preparations for the Ninth Party Congress. This entitled the P.L.A. representatives to more places in the new Central Committee than had ever been open to them. The Central Committee elections confirmed that the P.L.A. had won a disproportionate amount of power in the Party, especially in the provinces where the P.L.A. had restored order in 1968, and that it would have a strong influence over the restructuring of the Party. This indeed was the case in provincial Party Committees where the chief P.L.A. leaders of the Revolutionary Committees made sure that they controlled the new Party Committees for their respective provinces. Thus the principle of consolidation would strengthen the position of the P.L.A. at the expense of the civilian Party cadres, who were now ready and encouraged to return to more responsible jobs.

The principle for Party reconstruction was still the 'three-in-one' alliance, but there had been a gradual change of emphasis from an alliance of P.L.A., Party cadres and mass representatives to one of the old, the middle-aged and the young.[21] Precisely when the emphasis shifted is still not clear. The new draft constitution considered in 1970 by the Second Plenum of the Ninth Party Central Committee permitted both kinds of alliance. But underlying the change was still the obvious imbalance in the provinces, where old Party cadres found themselves sandwiched between the inexperienced but enthusiastic worker-peasant members and senior members of the P.L.A. It was still a delicate position for the Party's civilian cadres who had yet to have their old authority restored. They could ally themselves with their P.L.A. colleagues and keep mass representation down to a minimum, or they could try to win mass support against the P.L.A., using as the central issue the idea that the Party must control the gun. It would appear that, during the struggles of 1969–71, Mao Tse-tung and his close supporters in the Party centre wanted to follow the latter course. In practice, however, this was difficult to achieve in the provinces and consequently also in the central committee already dominated by the P.L.A. Thus for the C.C.P. to be reconstructed under civilian cadre leadership it would have to depend on the lowest levels of production (on peasants in production teams and brigades and people's communes, on workers in factories, transport industries and other urban units) all electing their own Party committees, and ultimately on these committees sending representatives to provincial Party congresses to choose their members. At that point, state, P.L.A. and older Party cadres normally sent from the centre would have to compete with the new men elected from below. Through rivalry and compromise, a new kind of Party could emerge with the soldiers retreating back into their barracks, with older cadres giving way to younger ones and with fresh new faces being brought into Party leadership at every level through democratic means. In short, it was not enough to consolidate what had emerged by September 1968, it was necessary to push for a younger set of cadres and Party leaders wherever possible, ever mindful, of course, of the serious clashes and dangers on the Sino-Soviet borders and of the immediate and primary need for unity and control.

After the Ninth Party Congress in April 1969, the pressure to speed up Party rebuilding was much greater. Although the information was fragmentary, there were many indications that local Party branches at basic unit levels had begun to appear and eventually county Party committees in the provinces and ward and district committees in the cities. But it was not until a year and a half later, between 24 November and 4 December 1970, that the Hunan Party congress met and elected the first of the new provincial committees.[22] This was soon followed by three others in Kiangsi, Kwangtung and Kiangsu and by May 1971, eighteen of the twenty-nine provincial Party committees had been formed and the last of them was established in August. Most of them followed the pattern of the Revolutionary Committees and showed only slight shifts in favour of older Party cadres at the expense of mass representatives. The position of the PLA in these new committees was largely unaffected, and the line between P.L.A. and Party cadres was blurred even further. This was not surprising. P.L.A. provincial power had earlier been recognised by elections to the Central Committee and the P.L.A. Central Committeemen representing the provinces could hardly be challenged for the leadership of most provincial committees on their return to their provincial capitals. It soon became clear that the P.L.A. would remain well-entrenched in powerful positions within the Party as long as Lin Piao was the designated heir to Mao Tse-tung and his military lieutenants held key posts in the Politburo and Central Committee. And in the name of unity, this position could not easily be changed.

The obvious ascendancy of military men in the country could not long be tolerated by the C.C.P. Even more abhorrent to its principles was the possible dominance of these men in the C.C.P. itself. The difficult struggles to balance Party and P.L.A. interests can be imagined. Also understandable were the tensions that continued to be generated by radicals of the Cultural Revolution Group against the more conservative cadres. A new crisis developed in the Second Plenum of the Ninth Party Congress, which met in August – September 1970. It seemed to have centred on the new draft constitution to be presented to the Fourth People's Congress and on the question of the Presidency of the P.R.C.[23] Specifically this probably meant Lin Piao's succession to Liu Shao-ch'i as President, but it was never allowed to reach that stage. Mao Tse-tung wanted the post of President abolished, and surprisingly because it was the first known instance of an open disagreement, Ch'en Po-ta did not side with Mao Tse-tung on this issue but agreed with Lin Piao that the post should be retained and Mao Tse-gung should be elected once again to fill it. The origins of the crisis are obscure. Particularly strange is the apparent defection of Ch'en Po-ta, the longest-serving secretary to Mao Tse-tung (since 1938) and the first man to proclaim Mao Tse-tung's contributions to various aspects of Marxist – Leninist theory. If it is true that Ch'en Po-ta went over to the Lin Piao camp and opposed Mao Tse-tung, it seems hardly credible that he would have done so for reasons of ideology. A more likely explanation is that the struggle had developed into a new factionalism between Lin Piao and his P.L.A. associates and Chou En-lai and his party and executive cadres, and Mao Tse-tung had begun to support Chou En-lai. Ch'en Po-ta had been shrill in his attacks on the party and state bureaucracy during the first, and possibly also the second, stage of the G.P.C.R., and may have been responsible for the renewed extremism which continued into 1970.[24] He sided with Lin Piao either because he was disillusioned with Mao Tse-tung's tactical manœuvres to make him the scapegoat for extremism or because he miscalculated and backed Lin Piao to win against Chou En-lai. The fact that Ch'en Po-ta was in disgrace and Lin Piao was estranged and felt threatened after the Second Plenum points to the intensity of the factional struggles during the third stage. The frequent calls for unity confirm that the threat of further discord had not decreased. They became more frequent also because the U.S.S.R had become not only a threat to Party unification but also an actual threat to the Chinese border provinces if not to China's sovereignty itself.[25] By March 1969, a major border clash had occurred at Chen Pao (Damansky) Island on the Ussuri River, the border between China's north-east provinces and the Soviet maritime provinces. The reasons for the clash are still obscure – there was so little to gain on the ground and in the river. For

China, however, the message became increasingly clear. This had occurred just prior to the Ninth Party Congress and the conditions for unity were changing rapidly and external events and internal developments became more intertwined and complex than any since the Sino-Soviet break in 1960.

The threat of Soviet intervention helped to hasten the formal restructuring of the C.C.P. and highlighted a desperate need for unity against an external enemy. The fighting at Chen Pao determined the Chinese to return to the uses of diplomacy to safeguard their national interests. It reminded them of the dangerous passivity, if not virtual isolation, that the first two stages of the G.P.C.R. had brought to their international position. Once the Party Congress was over, they moved quickly to send their ambassadors back to their posts or appoint new ones.[26] Symbolically, the first was the new ambassador to Albania, China's only real ally and an irritant to the U.S.S.R. More usefully, the second was to France, the third to North Vietnam and the fourth to Cambodia: France was doubly important as a country that could yet play a valuable intermediary role in the Indo-Chinese states and one that opened a window on Western Europe. Within two months, eighteen appointments had been made. Together with Huang Hua, the ambassador to the United Arab Republic (Egypt), the only one who had not been recalled during the G.P.C.R., this made nineteen. Apart from the first four, the others may be grouped as follows: Pakistan, Nepal and Afghanistan in the neighbourhood of a hostile but pro-Soviet India; Tanzania, Zambia, Guinea, Mauritania and Congo (Brazzaville) in Black Africa, neither pro-Western nor pro-Soviet; Egypt, Algeria, Syria, Yemen and South Yemen in the Middle East where Soviet influence was strong but where the Palestinian cause was troublesome to all. Sweden was usefully neutral and open, between East and West in Europe and already crucial as the site for discussions with Canada. The success of these discussions in 1970 would open a new phase in China's diplomatic offensive. Significantly, Romania was the only Warsaw Pact country included in the first batch, marking a recognition of its desire for more independence among countries of the socialist bloc. Other connections might also be made for the first nineteen: Pakistan was also an opening to the Indian Ocean and an alternative link with East Africa and the Middle East; Guinea and Mauritania were doors to West Africa; while Tanzania, Zambia and Congo (Brazzaville) also provided contact with the various liberation movements of the Portuguese colonies of Mozambique and Angola and of Rhodesia (Zimbabwe). Altogether a select list which clearly indicated a new Chinese international policy which focused much more on China's rivalry with the U.S.S.R. than on any fears of the U.S.A. and the capitalist world.

Indeed, after the Tet offensive in early 1968 and Johnson's admission of failure in Vietnam, China had little reason to fear the U.S.A. Although China did not respond immediately to Nixon's feelers in early 1969 and attacked him continuously on his Vietnam withdrawal policy, its mood seemed far less hostile than in earlier years. Meanwhile, Sino-Soviet border relations worsened throughout 1969 not only on the Ussuri and the Amur rivers in the north east but also in Sinkiang among Turkic minorities in the north west. A series of developments in the Communist world, most notably the World Conference of seventy-five Communist Parties held in Moscow in June 1969, confirmed that renewed efforts at diplomacy were essential, including renewing talks with the U.S.A. at Warsaw in January 1970. The U.S.A. in turn had been reviewing its China policy for several years. Its failures in Indo-China and the obvious tensions between China and the U.S.S.R. persuaded more of its political leaders that the time had come for a change. In the changed atmosphere of 1970, China's progress among countries which had so far recognised the Nationalist government in Taiwan became easier. The most successful were the talks with the representatives of Canada and Italy along the lines which had enabled France to change its recognition policy in 1964. By October, the new formula had been found and Canada finally acknowledged the reality of China, and Italy did the same the next month.[27] Several others followed soon afterwards and, rather quickly, China's chances of being admitted into the United Nations became excellent.

One more step, however, was still essential: public acknowledgement by the Chinese and the Americans that they were both ready to move towards each other.[28] There were serious constraints on both sides. Twenty years of hostility made dialogue and compromise difficult. The leaders of neither side could afford to appear 'soft', and the first moves had to be careful and tentative. Throughout 1969 and 1970, Nixon had authorised small gestures of conciliation to be made, but they were too small to respond to while the war in Vietnam was going on. Cambodia was threatened first, then Sihanouk overthrown in May 1970 and the Russians were ready to denounce the Chinese for betraying the Vietnamese. Much also depended on how far factions in China were able to agree and how far Mao Tse-tung himself could be persuaded that a change was necessary. The first effort at mediation by Romania in November 1970 came at a propitious moment, only two months after the stormy Second Plenum of September and the estrangement of Lin Piao. Chou En-lai was told that the Americans really wanted to improve relations. Mao Tse-tung decided to respond and had his way at the Politburo meeting a month later. He spoke to Edgar Snow and indicated that he was prepared to meet Nixon. In March 1971, the Romanians repeated once more that the U.S.A. was ready to move. A month later, the first Chinese public gesture was made. The Chinese table-tennis team in Japan met those from Canada, Britain and the U.S.A. and an invitation to play in China was issued to them all. The Americans responded instantly, the visit became a diplomatic performance and the world was alerted to a major shift in international politics. Even then, no one could have foreseen how big a leap was to come. Nixon threw conventional practice aside and sent Kissinger to Peking. Mao Tse-tung, who had never been conventional, invited Nixon to visit Peking. Decades of prickly undergrowth were cleared away. Whatever the outcome of the meeting between Nixon and Mao, one thing was clear. No serious obstacle remained to block China's admission to the United Nations and expel the representatives of the Republic of China in Taiwan.[29] In October, the last act was played out, the ritualistic moves were followed by the Albanian – Algerian resolution to admit China, which resulted in a triumphant vote of 76 for and 35 against (with 17 abstentions). Within a week, China's representatives were welcomed into the General Assembly.

So engrossing was the drama outside China that the final stage of the G.P.C.R. was totally eclipsed. The reconstruction of the C.C.P. had suddenly taken off in late November 1970 and the new party structures in the provinces were erected in nine months. The speed in both Sino-American *rapprochement* and the completion of Party-rebuilding was no coincidence. Key decisions had been taken between September and December 1970 which related to both these developments. The precise details are still not clear, but a preliminary outline of the power struggle can be drawn from the known events. The condition of the Standing Committee of the C.C.P. Politburo during these and the following months is specially relevant. Only three men were left active. K'ang Sheng made no appearances and seemed to have been ill, and Ch'en Po-ta had just been pushed out and become an object of growing criticism. Of the three active men, Mao Tse-tung and Lin Piao seemed to have concentrated on the power relations within the Party and the

P.L.A., while Chou En-lai with the help of a vigorous new team at the Foreign Ministry worked on China's new image abroad. The crucial change was in Mao Tse-tung's disenchantment with Lin Piao at the Second Plenum. In a matter of months, the widespread rivalries below which had emerged from the first two stages of the G.P.C.R. led both leaders to act quickly. Mao Tse-tung was willing to compromise with incumbent P.L.A. leaders in the provinces and his support enabled them to be independent of the chief military leaders in Peking under Lin Piao's direction. Lin Piao used his power in the centre to enhance his position as heir-apparent and prepare the ground for the succession. The debate about a change in policy towards the U.S.A. then became important as a means of discrediting Chou En-lai. But Chou's successful policy shift emphasised Lin Piao's isolation, and Mao Tse-tung's personal tour of the provinces in August and September (after the Nixon announcement) made it increasingly clear to Lin Piao that his primacy even with the P.L.A. had been eroded away.[30] This makes credible his final act of desperation, the coup attempt, the flight to the U.S.S.R. and the crash of his plane in Mongolia on 12 September 1971.

As argued earlier, the third stage of the G.P.C.R. ended with the C.C.P. almost totally reconstructed by August 1971. No one could have foreseen that the ending should have been such an anti-climax, having been so overshadowed by the events of the next two months: the fall of Lin Piao and the leaders of his P.L.A. faction and the dramatic admission of China into the United Nations. Yet there is nothing inconsistent in the three occurring almost at the same time. The G.P.C.R. was a spectacular political and ideological divide. It marked the end of all the key Soviet elements in the C.C.P., in the state machinery and in the P.L.A. In returning to Chinese political roots to realise Marxism – Leninism in China, it had exposed the Soviet threat to Chinese sovereignty through the Brezhnev doctrine and his policy of encirclement, but it had also exposed the country to vicious factional conflicts by ambitious but frustrated men which culminated in the coup attempt by Lin Piao and his supporters. And not least, it had thrust China forward as a symbol of Third World resistance to the blandishments and manipulations of the two Super Powers, the U.S.S.R. and the U.S.A. By the *rapprochement* with the U.S.A., China stopped appearing as a disgruntled and ostracised member of one bloc in a two-bloc world but became an independent force calling attention to the dangers of such a world and advocating a wider struggle to prevent its coming about through collusion between the two Super Powers.[31]

There are obvious tactical and propagandist features in projecting this image of itself as an independent progressive force, but that the image is seriously believed in China and is credible to many Third World countries cannot be denied.

The Chinese quest for independence had come a long way. During this period, it led them to the brink of disaster where the U.S.S.R. was concerned, but it also led them to an unexpectedly credible position between the U.S.S.R. and the U.S.A. It was also particularly satisfactory to gain admittance into the United Nations and see the other 'China' ejected in a decisive and unprecedented way. But the quest had not come to an end. Taiwan survived and still called itself the Republic of China. At least two sets of Unequal Treaties still governed China's boundaries: the 'McMahon Line' on the border with India, which was an obstacle to a general settlement, and the series of treaties signed in the nineteenth century between Tsarist Russia and the Ch'ing Empire. The Ch'ing heritage was still incomplete. The third stage of the G.P.C.R. had changed little of China's concern for the integrity of that heritage. One may well ask, is this concern an expression of nationalism or even chauvinism? Is there aggressive intent underlying some sinister plan against its neighbours if China were allowed to take Taiwan or to redraw the borders with India and the U.S.S.R.? Or is China simply clinging unreasonably to the past, unwilling to face reality and accept the world for what it is? All these questions seem to de-emphasise China's commitment to the ideals of Marxism – Leninism and Mao Tse-tung Thought or the relevance of this commitment to China's international relations. There were certainly many calls for national unity in the face of the Soviet threat, but the perfunctory and ritualistic shelling of Quemoy, the minor incidents on the borders with India-Sikkim and various points of the Sino-Soviet border and even the bitter fighting at Chen Pao (Damansky) do not add up to any sinister aggressive plan. They suggest the determination not to abandon a just and righteous cause which has long marked China's quest for independence. While this might appear a stubborn reluctance to accept the world as it is, it is qualitatively different from the traditional isolationist arrogance. This stubbornness is better explained by relating the idea of independence to the Marxist – Leninist world-view which the Chinese espouse: that a socialist China must safeguard its independence at all costs, even against other socialist states, and that the cause of independence and self-reliance for all countries is not only a righteous but a progressive one which will ultimately undermine the last vestiges of capitalism.

China saw that its independence was incomplete. No less incomplete was its desire to establish new proletarian standards of modernity. The G.P.C.R., for all its initial violence against traditional, bourgeois and 'revisionist' values, confirmed that the scientific and technological skills needed for the country's industrialisation were still those which had been developed at the capitalist stage of history and were still developing outside China at a rapid rate. There was nothing proletarian about the equipment, the techniques and even the underlying ideas required to make the industrial order more productive and efficient. But their mastery by the proletariat was a different matter. This was essential if the working classes were to be freed from dependence on those whom they consider to have been exploitative, if they were to be enabled to expand the size of the proletariat and to proletarianise the peasant majority, and if they were to stay in control not only of production and distribution but also of the means of developing new standards of proletarian life. The catch, of course, is that the mastery of industrial skills might create a technocratic élite out of the proletariat itself which will then seek to perpetuate itself through political power. The third stage of the G.P.C.R. showed how complex the problem was. The Red Guards who had threatened the older élites had produced their own élitism, the élitism of those who had joined the victorious side in a series of revolutionary actions. This in turn had to be opposed by select representatives of workers, peasants and soldiers. Eventually, all of them as well as college and university students and high-school graduates were sent 'up the mountains and down to the villages'.[32] The move was partly to defuse Red Guard power in the cities and partly to channel their excess revolutionary energies, but it was also in order to support some of the ideals of the G.P.C.R.: the policies of decentralisation in economic affairs; the efforts to revive the rural People's Communes as larger production units which could become more self-sufficient in food; the capital needed to start and maintain local industry and the skills required to increase energy resources and produce agricultural machinery; the idea of diffusing scientific skills and theoretical knowledge from the urban centres to the rural areas; the re-education of the intellectuals through participation in manual labour and learning from the poor and lower-middle peasants; the balanced growth of the new popular culture through inculcating the peasantry with proletarian values; and, not least, the qualities of self-reliance which were to infuse and guide the country's desire for new standards of modernity.

Thus the G.P.C.R. redefined revolutionary ideals and revealed persistent tensions. It was a product of Mao Tse-tung's understanding of the dialectical processes of history and the skilful and at times creative use of internal and external conflicts. It sought to transform the superstructure in order to hasten the building of a strong economic base. But it was also constrained by the as yet elementary changes in China's socialist economy, and thus confirmed how incomplete the revolution was. The period from 1966 to 1971 was a major step forward in terms of historical change. They were years which produced not only significant changes in ideology and in the power structure, but also the valuable experience of how to conduct a revolution within a socialist framework. Many lessons were learnt, by the Party, the P.L.A. the mass organisations, the old, the middle-aged and the young. But perhaps the most important lesson was what a complex and protracted business it was to try and complete a revolution.

8 The Long and Complex Struggle

SINCE the fall of Lin Piao in September 1971, the pressures towards order and unity have continued and have even been intensified. Campaign after campaign has been launched to emphasise the need for the C.C.P. to control the P.L.A., to warn against treachery and to exhort workers, peasants, soldiers, intellectuals and specialist cadres to study hard the classics of Marxism —Leninism and the Thought of Mao Tse-tung. The Lin Piao affair has proved to be difficult to explain away. Fresh interpretations of a wide range of political, military, historical and cultural issues have been used to keep the affair alive, to sustain flagging interest and to disarm the sceptical. At the same time, new efforts to learn from Taching in industry and from Tachai in agriculture have been called for in order to increase production and strengthen the country's economic base as a prerequisite to order and unity. The long and complex struggle must carry on.

There have been notable successes. The brief meeting of the Tenth Party Congress in August 1973 was one: this re-established the framework for determining the goals of revolution. The long-delayed Fourth National People's Congress meeting in January 1975 was another: it defined the main criteria for socialist modernity for the next few decades. Although it did little to consolidate the leadership and guarantee the succession to Mao Tse-tung, it is remarkable that it was so effectively held under conditions of great stress and considerable uncertainty. It brought out the most characteristic features of organisation, discipline and ideology that have sustained the C.C.P. for over fifty years. At the same time, it revealed with great clarity the continuous potential for conflict or contradiction within a tightly knit system which is monopolising more power than ever before.

The Tenth Party Congress met less than two years after Lin Piao's death. Its main purpose was to exorcise Lin Piao and what he stood for from what had been affirmed at the Ninth Congress. The party constitution which had named Lin Piao as successor to Mao Tse-tung was revised, a new Central Committee shorn of all Lin Piao's supporters was elected and this in turn elected a new Politburo and Standing Committee.[1] Not surprisingly, despite the rise in total numbers from 279 to 319, P.L.A. representation fell sharply from 44 per cent of the Ninth Committee to 31 per cent. The drop is more significant than the figures suggest, because 28 new P.L.A. representatives were elected to replace the 52 who had died or been dropped (at least 24 of these for their involvement with Lin Piao) and few of these 28 held positions of power. The percentage of 'old cadres' was almost unchanged at about 30 per cent, while that of 'mass representatives' rose to about 40 per cent. In short, the Party succeeded both in reducing its military component (something that it would have found difficult to do had Lin Piao not attempted his abortive coup) and in increasing the number of new faces at the centre. The fact that about half the 124 younger alternate members represented mass organisations is an important indicator of where the Party would like to go and of the broader base the Party would like to count on for achieving its revolutionary goals.

The most surprising change and certainly a marker for the immediate future was the emergence of Wang Hung-wen (b. 1935) as the third most senior member of the Party, following Mao Tse-tung and Chou En-lai. His report on the revised party constitution and Chou's general report were the only speeches published.[2] His rise was phenomenal. Only five years earlier, he had just risen from being a junior party secretary of his textile factory to become one of the leaders of the 'rebel workers' of Shanghai at the start of the G.P.C.R. His report was the more positive and forward-looking of the two. Where Chou explained the fall of Lin Piao and emphasised the fruits of the G.P.C.R., Wang Hung-wen stressed the goals ahead. In addition to affirming that the G.P.C.R. was 'a great political revolution' and that 'revolutions like this have to be carried out many times in the future', he spoke of the need to 'train millions of successors' and alert them to the dangers within and without. Most notably, and reflecting his own experiences as a rebel, he declared: 'We must have the revolutionary spirit of daring to go against the tide . . . A true communist must act without any selfish considerations and dare to go against the tide, fearing neither removal from his post, expulsion from the Party, imprisonment, divorce nor guillotine.' Wang presumably was expected to provide the fresh start that Mao Tse-tung thought the C.C.P. needed and serve as a symbol of the 'Socialist New-born Things' produced by the G.P.C.R. His power base was still the workers of Shanghai and he lacked authority with the P.L.A. and the 'old cadres'. But that he was being carefully groomed for power was clear when he was appointed one of the vice-chairmen of the Party's Military Affairs Committee (where the other four vice-chairmen were born respectively in 1892, 1898, 1899 and 1902).[3]

Another major surprise which deserves noting had occurred earlier. This was the re-emergence of Teng Hsiao-p'ing in April 1973 after some six years in disgrace. He had been the Party's Secretary-General (since 1956) and closely linked with Liu Shao-ch'i during the violent attacks on Liu during the Cultural Revolution and had not appeared in public since late 1966. Early in 1973 he seemed to have resumed duty as one of the vice-premiers working closely with Chou En-lai and it was no longer very surprising when he was returned to the Tenth Central Committee in August. But what was astonishing was that, four months later, he was given back his place in the Politburo. This was formalised in January 1975 at the Second Plenum of the Central Committee when he was elected one of the Party's vice-chairmen and on to the Standing Committee of the Politburo. The Fourth National People's Congress then appointed him First Vice-Premier and, within months, he was acting as Premier during Chou En-lai's illness and was Chief of Staff of the P.L.A. as well. His was a remarkable recovery indeed and politically significant because he seemed not only acceptable to Mao but also to the old Party and administrative cadres and the P.L.A. He was not the only man who could provide a political bridge between the many interest groups at the centre, but there was virtually no one left who could match him in his range of administrative experience and skills. It is not surprising that almost all observers expected him to succeed Chou En-lai as Premier on Chou's death and were astonished at the way he was eased out immediately afterwards and thoroughly repudiated.

The Tenth Congress was something of an extraordinary meeting to rectify what must now appear as a gross blunder – the dependence on Lin Piao and his P.L.A. factions to round off the G.P.C.R. and prepare against the Soviet threat of intervention in late 1968 and early 1969. It also marked the first step in the Party's renewed efforts to control the gun though the initial successes were encouraging. They had set in train the series of events which was to restore the Party to full authority in the country. The Tenth Congress and the linking of the anti-Lin Piao campaign with the campaign against Confucius (and all that he represented in two thousand four hundred years of Chinese history!) helped to prepare the ground. By December 1973,[4] a major step had been taken to clip the wings of the most senior Commanders of Military

Regions: seven of the eleven were moved, one to the Peking Command itself; an eighth appointment was made to the powerful Mukden Region. In all cases, the move deprived them of control over both the provincial governments and Party committees, and trusted political commissars and administrative cadres were appointed to take over their non-military powers. By 1975, only two of the thirty-nine military commanders at regional and provincial levels still held key political posts, and one of them had not been seen in public since early 1974. There seems very little doubt that most of the soldiers outside Peking had returned to their barracks and the Party had reasserted control.

The P.L.A., of course, was not the only potential threat to the centralist power of the Party. The G.P.C.R. had shown how disaffection in various organs and institutions could be mobilised against Party personnel and could totally disrupt the work of the 'mass organisations' the Party normally controlled. Thus it was not enough to reconstruct the Communist Youth League, the All-China Federation of Labour and the Women's Federation (which was largely done in 1973 and 1974); it was necessary to devise new methods of organising the poor and lower-middle peasantry, the restless millions of urban youth now living in the countryside, the new types of tough worker-peasant-soldier tertiary students and even the new and 'liberated' cadres the Party now depended on for the 'millions of successors' the ageing Party leaders needed. Great emphasis was laid on the study of theory and political analysis, on the application of such theory to production, to history and literature, to catching out 'revisionists' and 'class enemies', to national defence and international relations. From small group study to mass meetings of hundreds of thousands, from production teams and brigades through communes counties, municipalities, provinces and autonomous regions, no one was spared in the renewed waves of intense socialisation unmatched in the period before the G.P.C.R.[5]

The Party was in full control by the end of 1973 and re-structured and institutionalised a whole range of mass activities. By the end of 1974, all preparations were ready for the calling of the Fourth National People's Congress. This had been promised in 1970—1 and had been delayed by the Lin Piao affair. In January 1975, it was finally held to pass a new State Constitution, elect a new Standing Committee and appoint a new State Council.[6] Chang Ch'un-ch'iao presented the Report on the Constitution and Chou En-lai the report on the work of the government. In the Preamble of the Constitution and in both reports are stated the main criteria of that modernity that China desired the key lies in what is considered a modern political framework, the dictatorship of the proletariat, which is continually being consolidated and strengthened by close attention to the dangers of restorationism and revisionism among those who fear the modern and glorify the past. Chang Ch'un-ch'iao then adds,

Without ample democracy, it is impossible to have a high degree of centralism, and without a high degree of centralism, it is impossible to build socialism. [The constitution] stipulates that all organs of state shall practise democratic centralism and specifies the democratic rights of citizens, and especially the rights of the fraternal minority nationalities and of women. It also stipulates that the masses shall have the right to speak out freely, air views fully, hold great debates and write big-character posters. Moreover, in accordance with Chairman Mao's proposal, the specification that citizens enjoy freedom to strike has been added.

The Preamble also emphasises 'the struggle for production and scientific experiment' and adds,

[We] should build socialism independently and with the initiative in our own hands, through self-reliance, hard struggle, diligence and thrift and by going all out, aiming high and achieving greater, faster, better and more economical results; and we should be prepared against war and natural disasters and do everything for the people.

Chou's Report was more concrete and policy-oriented. It stressed the achievements of the past ten years in economic growth and international affairs and outlined the rise in political experience and consciousness since the G.P.C.R. But it did highlight a two-stage development in the national economy:

The first stage is to build an independent and relatively comprehensive industrial and economic system in 15 years, that is before 1980; the second stage is to accomplish the comprehensive modernisation of agriculture, industry, national defence and science and technology before the end of the century, so that our national economy will be advancing in the front ranks of the world.

And it then adds,

Only when we do well in revolution is it possible to do well in production. . . . Chairman Mao pointed out, 'Rely mainly on one's efforts while making external assistance subsidiary, break down blind faith, go in for industry, agriculture and technical and cultural revolutions independently, do away with slavishness, bury dogmatism, learn from the good experience of other countries conscientiously and be sure to study their bad experience too, so as to draw lessons from it.'

Much of the desired modernity is not unfamiliar to most developing nations, or to developed nations which may find most of the above 'old hat'. The crucial difference for the Chinese is whom the modernity is for, what classes have to be destroyed before the modernity is real and to what end such modernity should be directed. In any case, China still considers itself to be 'a developing socialist country belonging to the third world'. It is modern in revolutionary spirit and political structure and therefore believes that this will ensure the transformation of the economic base that is necessary for yet another step towards the eventual achievement of a communist society.

But revolution within is never totally safe from reaction without. Lin Piao might only have sought asylum in the U.S.S.R. and might never have been a great threat to China even if he had got there. But the fact of treachery at the highest levels of leadership was a powerful reminder that the enemies of revolution will crush it no less readily than China will liquidate reactionaries if and when given the opportunity. Thus to the Chinese a conflict situation is a permanent feature not only inside China but also in international affairs until perhaps such time as 'the revolution wins the final victory over all its enemies'. Thus the triumph of China's admission to the U.N. in October 1971 was but a small step on the long road that world revolution still has to take. It was a bigger step, and a highly symbolic and visible one, for China's quest for independence, but still no more than a step.

This last is hard for the world outside to understand. By almost any standard except its own, and possibly also by the standards of the two Super Powers, China is fully independent. But it has still not, thanks to the U.S.A., regained its sovereign rights over Taiwan, a province which almost every country in the world officially acknowledges as part of China. There is also still at least one important 'Unequal Treaty', that with Russia in 1860, which has not been abolished or renegotiated to China's satisfaction. Nor can China hope to gain military equality with the U.S.A. and the U.S.S.R. for a long time to come, and without that, China does not feel it can ever be totally free from the dangers of outside interference – especially from subversion and from the readiness to take advantage of any internal dissent and rebellion. Thus China's independence appears flawed despite the efforts of a quarter of a century. The initial optimism of 1949–53 had long turned into a harsh grinding realism, with the realisation that China has little more leverage than other countries where the U.S.A. and the U.S.S.R. are concerned.

Mao Tse-tung, however, was a man accustomed to positions of military weakness and he had long applied his United Front strategy to foreign affairs. In the 1950s, when the U.S.S.R. was an ally, the strategy was concentrated on the U.S.A. In the 1960s, with so much attention focused on the southern Chinese borders and with complex wars being fought in the Indo-Chinese states, the strategy was largely ineffective. By 1969, however, it became possible to revive the strategy. There had been fighting on the Sino-Soviet border and, in Vietnam, the U.S.A. was ready to retreat. In 1971, it was beginning to look as if China needed another 'united front' against the U.S.S.R., now the greater threat to China. Once again, it might be the time to use the analogies Mao had in mind from his long-drawn-out struggle with the K.M.T. and Japanese imperialism in the 1930s and 1940s. But are the situations comparable? The only broad similarity is the desire to keep the U.S.A. and the U.S.S.R. apart and preferably in conflict as Mao had done with the K.M.T. and the Japanese. This is, however, not as easy as it used to be. The stakes are too high for either the U.S.A. or the U.S.S.R. to revert to open confrontation. But there have been some gains for China. By diluting U.S. hostility towards itself, China has found more room to manœuvre. More than sixty countries established diplomatic relations with China between 1971 and 1976. Since its admission to the U.N., China has taken part vigorously in all U.N. activities and has made itself something of an ally of all those who dare to stand up to both the U.S.A. and the U.S.S.R. and a keen supporter of those who distrust or are hostile to the U.S.S.R. for whatever reason.

Thus far, the strategy is obviously useful and helps to give a degree of consistency to all Chinese moves. The much more difficult problem is how to avoid the image that China is aspiring to rival the U.S.A. and the U.S.S.R. as the third Super Power. Despite all China's declarations to the contrary, there remains an underlying contradiction which arises from the pursuit of military equality. If this equality is a prerequisite of sovereignty and a guarantee of freedom from interference, it is also the basis for Super Power status whether China likes it or not. Furthermore, the united-front strategy involves garnering China's own set of allies, especially winning them over from the side of the U.S.S.R. Again, despite China's insistence that every country should be sovereign, equal and self-reliant, the consequences of the strategy must give China a third slate of loyal supporters in the global struggle for power and China could hardly be expected not to accept such support if offered.

There is no need to doubt that China is sincere in not wanting to be a Super Power. The word is associated with dominance and 'hegemonism', with their echoes of traditional imperialism, and China is right to reject any such association. But it is quite a different matter to think of itself as in the vanguard of world revolution and a potential leader in establishing new standards of modernity. Whether this is realistic or not at this stage, it is vital to China's image of itself and something of a safeguard against the chauvinism and expansionism that might accompany the acquisition of great power. It is significant that Mao Tse-tung had begun to take a personal hand in foreign affairs in 1970, something he had never done so openly before. This might have had something to do with the debate over whether China should have a President. Mao had disagreed with Lin Piao about this and their joint meetings with selected foreign leaders could have been a compromise arrangement whereby specific visits could be given additional political weight, for example, the delegations of Somalia, Congo (Brazzaville), Tanzania, Zambia, Sudan, South Yemen and Pakistan in June — September, not to mention those of North Vietnam, North Korea, Romania and Albania during the same period. It is more likely, however, that Mao had appreciated the complexity of the global united front and turned his mind to the challenge.

The problems with Lin Piao had distracted him for a year after September 1970 and he made few public appearances, but his decision to move the strategy to a higher gear became clear when he chose to see only Yahya Khan, Edgar Snow and Ceausescu during the eight months between November 1970 and June 1971. By that time, the stage was set for Kissinger's visit and the announcement about Nixon's visit. In 1972, he had concentrated on Nixon in February and then Tanaka in September and on China's southern flank with the visits of Bhutto, Mrs Bandaranaike and the Nepalese Foreign Minister. This was a very select list indeed for it was the year when the country was absorbed with uneasy anti-Lin Piao rectification campaigns. It was not until 1973 that Mao had felt free to devote more time towards the united front in international affairs. From January 1973 to the end of 1975, he averaged three meetings with foreign leaders every two months, an incredible number for a man of eighty who had been abroad only twice in his lifetime (and both times only to Moscow). Mao was never a man for ceremony and ritual, nor were those meetings to satisfy a new-found interest in world politics. The role Mao played here reflected his concern to stress, not only to foreign leaders, but especially to his younger colleagues, the complexity of the international situation and the long struggle ahead if China was to preserve the gains it had made and to make more gains for China's independence, modernity and revolution.

With the death of Mao Tse-tung in September 1976 the question may be asked, has not the struggle been long enough already? The struggle had begun in earnest when Mao Tse-tung first read of Marx and Lenin with Li Ta-chao in Peking in 1919. From the time he attended the First Party Congress of the C.C.P. in 1921, there had been setbacks, dangers and near-disasters for him and his party colleagues, the worst of which had lasted from 1927 to 1935. To Mao, there had been enemies not only outside but also within the Party, and he had found that there were foreign interventions not only to keep warlords fighting one another and to prevent the K.M.T. from unifying China but also to disrupt the C.C.P. by planting agents among his own Party comrades. And during the Sino-Japanese War when the C.C.P. became a legitimate partner in a patriotic war, he still had to fight to survive and to keep the vision of a modern, revolutionary Chinese future whole. Who would have expected that he would have to go through a similar cycle after the victory in 1949? That a Socialist China would have not only capitalist enemies but also 'social-imperialist' enemies of the world communist movement and that the C.C.P. would have not only residual class enemies within China but 'revisionist' 'restorationist' enemies at the very heart of the Party itself? Mao believed that struggle is an objective condition in history and no one, from the leader of the Party to the youthful Wang Hung-wen down to the urban youth in the countryside and the 'little Red Soldiers', can ever be free from its demands. The fifty to sixty years of struggle that he had personally experienced were but a beginning. After three thousand years mixed with glory, stagnation and decadence and a hundred years of shame, he may well have asked, what is there to fear from many more years of struggle? As he had discovered, the point is to know what to struggle for and how to win the ultimate victory: the twists and turns can then look after themselves.

The story of the resurgence of China cannot be concluded here. Even Mao's death marks merely the end of one stage and the start of another. What has been attempted above is an interpretation, an effort to understand. By focusing on the themes of independence, modernity and revolution, the story so far differs from those studies which have emphasised Chinese expansionism, China's sovietisation and the autochthonous nature of Mao's revolutionary goals. Only a brief summary is needed here to correct the persistent errors that have fed on unrelenting hostility and deep-seated fears about China and continue to fuel new suspicion and hatred.

It is necessary to distinguish between expansionism and the fervent desire for independence. Most of the hostile propaganda of the 1950s and early 1960s about China has been exposed by events, but there is still the will to invent more. China has been militant, but it has been so mainly because it had long suffered humiliation by not having been sufficiently so in the past. It has been threatening to those who have long threatened it, and it will continue to threaten those who still want to subvert the new Chinese spirit. It has encouraged others to be tough and challenging because it sees most of the world as manipulated and dominated by a few strong and rich powers, and most people as exploited by a minority of rich and powerful interest groups. It rejects the view that such domination and exploitation is normal and only human and insists that becoming independent is the first step towards a much-needed change. And for this reason, it seeks its own complete independence and sets an example to all others who are much less independent than it is.

There has also been too much emphasis on China's sovietisation and its position as the bearer of Stalin's heritage. This led to genuine fears in the 1950s of a giant Sino-Soviet monolith with tentacles outstretched to seize the rest of the world. What the Chinese had done was to seek Soviet help and to adopt Soviet standards of modernity. But they soon discovered their mistake. They found that the Russians, too, wanted to dominate and, even more disconcertingly, they found that Soviet modernity would distort the course of China's economic and social development. A country with such a large peasant majority must find its own way to modernise and at its own speed. Stalin's methods would have been disastrous, not to say the élitist and bureaucratic structure that was further fostered by his successors. The rejection of Soviet ways is not total, but the elusive idea of a modernity based on self-reliance does harmonise with the quest for independence.

The intensity of the Sino-Soviet quarrel has led other studies to stress the 'Chineseness' of everything that China has tried to do. Whether this 'Chineseness' is said to have begun with the Great Leap Forward in

1958 or to have become pervasive during the G.P.C.R. eight years later may still be debated, but the picture of autochthonous solutions to all China's problems has certainly gone too far. This is not to deny that China has fallen back to a large extent on its social and cultural resources when both Western values and Soviet examples have turned them off the course of imitation and adaption. The strength of tradition and the continuity in Chinese thought and behaviour are clear enough to the Chinese: hence the slogans 'Make the past serve the present', 'Treat our heritage critically'. But making Chinese contributions to the revolution is not the same as making the revolution Chinese in every way. The Chinese have never underestimated the universal features of Marxism – Leninism. They trace their revolution through the English Civil War, the American and French Revolutions, the Paris Commune and the October Revolution and no amount of reinterpretation of ancient Chinese history has shaken them from this line of descent. A *Chinese* revolution would, in fact, be meaningless. Mao Tse-tung had clearly recognised that a Chinese theory of revolution would make nonsense of at least the last 150 years of Chinese history. To China, the revolution is indisputably global and its world-wide nature has imbued the ideas of independence and modernity with great significance. However much China's own immense problems have engaged most of its energies, there is no doubt that its very understanding of the nature of historical change stems from the post-Enlightenment world that produced Marx and Engels and eventually Lenin. Without that understanding, the revolution would falter and degenerate. For Mao and the C.C.P., there could be no turning back. China is fully involved in the world and is now committed to the long and complex struggle to help to make a world that it can easily live with. The Chinese revolution is not mysterious. Its driving spirit is wholly rational. Whether or not that is enough to change the world is, of course, another story.

9 Postscript

DURING the months after the death of Chou En-lai in January 1976 and that of Mao Tse-tung in September, there was considerable uncertainty and tension about the succession to the two men. To everyone's surprise, Teng Hsiao-p'ing did not succeed Chou En-lai. Instead, Chou was followed as Premier and First Vice-Chairman of the Party by the relatively unknown Hua Kuo-feng, the Minister for Public Security. This must once again warn us how little we know about the politics of China's leadership. Since the Cultural Revolution, we have learnt to expect sudden changes and more surprises. Mao Tse-tung had long prepared China for the collective leadership that now rules the country, but it is too soon to assume that the succession question has been settled.

This introduction to China has not taken the view that to understand China since 1949, we must first understand Mao. It would, however, be foolish to deny that Mao has put his stamp on China in many ways. Much of the book has in fact described 'Maoist' China and implicitly accepted that Mao's role in moulding China has been large if not decisive. However, China without Mao will be hard to understand without taking Mao's long shadow into account.

What was this shadow where the themes of independence, modernity and revolution were concerned? Independence as the Chinese see it is a theme bound by China's history. Mao believed in it as most Chinese did, but he did not give it a unique cast. Similarly also with modernity. The Chinese had no agreed vision of it except in terms of science and technology and Mao himself did not seem to have transcended this basic image. Wherever modernity touched on versions of democracy, freedom and the civil rights of individuals, Chinese traditions intruded and the leaders became very selective about which part of the Marxist—Leninist heritage was appropriate for China. If anything, Mao Tse-tung confirmed this approach towards modernity by his rejection of both Western and Soviet criteria and his effort to find a Chinese way. And here the Chinese way came perilously close to restoring the dichotomy between a Chinese social morality and certain alien scientific ideals.

Only in the theme of revolution do we find Mao's long shadow indisputable. His was the dominant voice since the late 1930s; it was his leadership which steered the C.C.P. to victory in 1949 and it was his judgements which swayed the Party through Land Reform to the Great Leap Forward, through the quarrels with Khrushchev to the final Sino-Soviet ideological split. With the turbulent years of 1966–7, the revolution had become Mao's very own. Thereafter, there was no area of activity which was not permeated with Maoist zeal. To most Chinese, he had become the revolution personified: he alone saw the end to the Marxist–Leninist story. But in seeing him in this way, some of his keenest followers had magnified the person of Mao Tse-tung at the expense of the universalist ideas and objective conditions which inspired and determined the revolution itself. This may only be a temporary phase, arising from Mao's dominance in China for such a long period. In time, after the Chinese revolution has developed further without him, a more accurate perspective may emerge, one that Mao himself would approve: that China's independence, modernity and revolution are inseparable and that China is greater than Mao.

Chronological Table

1926	January	Second K.M.T. Congress, Canton
	July	The Northern Expedition begins under Chiang Kai-shek
	November	The Nationalist Government moves to Wuhan
1927	April	Chiang Kai-shek's coup against the C.C.P., Shanghai; Fifth C.C.P., Congress, Wuhan
	August	Nanchang Uprising, the birth of the Red Army; Mao Tse-tung's Autumn Harvest Insurrection, Hunan
1928	January	National Government formally proclaimed in Nanking
	April	Chu Teh joins Mao Tse-tung at Chingkangshan
	July — September	Sixth C.C.P. Congress, Moscow
1929	August	Mao Tse-tung well established in Kiangsi
1930	June	Wang Ming and the 'Bolsheviks' return to China
	October	The Kiangsi Provincial Soviet Government established
	December	The First K.M.T. offensive against Kiangsi (First Encirclement)
1931	January	The 'Wang Ming line' introduced at Fourth Plenum of Sixth Central Committee
	September	Japan invades Manchuria after the Mukden Incident
	December	Mao Tse-tung becomes Chairman of National Soviet Government at Juichin
1932	April	The Soviet Government declares war on Japan
1933	January	C.C.P. headquarters moves to Juichin
	October	The Fifth Encirclement campaign begins
1934	October	The Long March begins (arrives in Shensi in October 1935)
1935	January	Tsunyi Conference, Mao Tse-tung elected Chairman of the Politburo
	August	The C.C.P. proclaims its United Front Policy against Japan
1936	December	The Sian Mutiny, Chiang Kai-shek captured and released
1937	July	The Sino-Japanese War begins

	November	The National Government decides to move to Chungking
1939	April–June	K.M.T. and C.C.P. troops clash
1940	October	More clashes between K.M.T. and C.C.P. troops
1941	April	The Rectification Campaign begins in Yenan
	December	The Pacific War breaks out
1945	May	Seventh C.C.P. Congress, Yenan
	August	End of Sino-Japanese War
	November	General Marshall appointed Special Envoy to China
1946	July	The K.M.T. – C.C.P. Civil War begins
1948	August	North China People's Government established
1949	January	The P.L.A. enters Peking
	April	The P.L.A. enters Nanking
	August	Manchuria People's Government established
	September	People's Political Consultative Conference meets in Peking, adopts the Organic Law of the Central People's Government

PART II THE PEOPLE'S REPUBLIC OF CHINA SINCE 1949

1949	October	Proclamation by Mao Tse-tung of the foundation of the P.R.C.; U.S.S.R. recognises the P.R.C. (followed by Bulgaria, Romania, Poland, Hungary, Czechoslovakia, Mongolia, East Germany, North Korea, Yugoslavia; Albania in November)
	November	K.M.T. National Government established in Taiwan
	December	Burma and India recognise the P.R.C.; Mao Tse-tung visits the U.S.S.R.
1950	January	Recognition by Pakistan, Great Britain, Ceylon, Norway, Denmark, Israel, Finland, Afghanistan, Sweden, Switzerland; also the P.R.C. recognises Ho Chi Minh's government.
	February	Sino-Soviet Treaty of Friendship signed in Moscow
	March	Recognition by the Netherlands

April	Marriage Law promulgated
	Recognition by Indonesia
June	Agrarian Reform Law promulgated; beginning of Korean War
October	P.L.A. ordered to liberate Tibet; Chinese volunteers enter the Korean War
November	Wu Hsiu-ch'uan arrives at U.N. for Security Council debate
1951 July – August	Korean armistice talks at Kaesong
August	'Three-Anti' campaign begins in the Northeast Region: against corruption, waste and bureaucracy among government employees
September	Japan Peace Treaty signed in San Francisco; the Treaty is denounced by U.S.S.R. and China
October	Korean cease-fire negotiations begin again at Panmunjon
1952 February	'Five-Anti' campaign launched: against bribery, theft of State property, tax evasion, theft of State economic secrets and embezzlement
August	Chou En-lai in Moscow for further Sino-Soviet agreements
October	Liu Shao-ch'i to Moscow (stays three months); Land Reform completed
November	State Planning Commission established, headed by Kao Kang
December	First Five-Year Plan (1953–7) announced
1953 February	C.C.P. decides to implement Mutual Aid as the first step towards collectivisation
March	Death of Stalin: Chou En-lai leads delegation to funeral
July	Korean armistice agreement signed
December	C.C.P. decides to develop Agricultural Producers' Co-operatives; elections to the National People's Congress largely completed; first indication of a major power struggle in the C.C.P. (involving Kao Kang, Jao Shu-shih and others)
1954 February	Fourth Plenum of the Seventh Central Committee

April	Geneva Conference, attended by Chou En-lai
May	Fall of Dienbienphu
June	Sino-American bilateral talks begin in Geneva; Chou En-lai visits India, Burma and meets Ho Chi Minh at the Sino-Vietnamese border
July	Geneva agreement on Indo-China; Chou En-lai to E. Germany, Poland, U.S.S.R. and Mongolia
August	Chou's foreign policy report stresses the liberation of Taiwan
September	Offshore Chin-men (Quemoy) Island shelled by P.L.A. artillery; SEATO Treaty signed in Manila; First Session of the First National People's Congress in Peking; Khrushchev, Bulganin and others arrive in Peking for National Day
October	Series of New Sino-Soviet agreements signed; Prime Minister Nehru of India visits China
December	Prime Minister U Nu of Burma visits China; U.S. – Taiwan Mutual Defence Treaty signed
1955 January	Diplomatic relations established with Yugoslavia and Afghanistan (recognition in 1950)
March	Expulsion of Kao Kang and Jao Shu-shih announced
April	Bandung Conference of Asian and African States; P.R.C. treaty with Indonesia on the position of the Chinese in Indonesia
May	Prime Minister Ali Sastromidjojo of Indonesia visits China
July	Mao Tse-tung's report on agricultural co-operativisation to party secretaries in Peking
August	Diplomatic relations with Nepal
October	Sixth Plenum and 'the high tide of socialisation in rural areas' (to April 1956)
1956 February	Twentieth Party Congress of the Communist Party of the U.S.S.R.
April	Mao Tse-tung speaks on 'The Ten Great Relationships'

May	Diplomatic relations with Egypt; 'Hundred Flowers Policy' announced
July – August	Diplomatic relations with Syria and Yemen
September	Eighth National Congress of the C.C.P. (the Seventh was held 1945); First Plenum, Peking; President Sukarno of Indonesia visits China
October	P.R.C. supports U.S.S.R. in protest to Britain and France over Suez; also supports Soviet policy in Hungary
November – December	Chou En-lai visits N. Vietnam, Cambodia, India, Burma, Pakistan; Second Plenum, Peking
1957 January	Chou En-lai visits the U.S.S.R., Poland, Hungary, Afghanistan, India, Nepal, Ceylon (returns to Peking in early February)
February	Mao Tse-tung's speech 'On the Correct Handling of Contradictions Among the People'
April	Rectification Campaign begins against bureaucracy, sectarianism and subjectivism; President Voroshilov of the U.S.S.R. visits China
May	Three weeks of free expression by intellectuals
June	Anti-rightist campaigns begin
July	President Ho Chi Minh of Vietnam visits China
September	Third Plenum, Peking: First Five-Year Plan fulfilled
October	Sputnik launched; Sino-Soviet nuclear sharing agreement
November	Mao Tse-tung visits Moscow
1958 January – March	Conferences at Hangchow, Nanning (January) and Chengtu (March): Mao Tse-tung prepares for the Great Leap Forward
April	First Commune in Honan formed
May	Fourth Plenum, Peking; Second session of the Eighth Party Congress and Fifth Plenum, Peking; the Strategy of the Great Leap Forward. The new party organ *Hung-ch'i* (*Red Flag*) introduced.
July	Khrushchev in Peking

	Diplomatic relations with Cambodia
August	Enlarged Politburo meeting off Peitaiho; bombardment of Chin-men (Quemoy)
	Diplomatic relations with Iraq
September	P.R.C. recognises 'Provisional' government of Algeria
	Diplomatic relations with Morocco
November	Sixth Plenum, Wuchang, following the Chengchow and Wuchang Conferences.
	National Conference on Overseas Chinese Affairs, Canton
December	Mao Tse-tung resigns. as Chairman of the P.R.C.
	Diplomatic relations with Sudan
1959 January	Chou En-lai at Twenty-first Congress of the Communist Party of the U.S.S.R.
March	Tibetan revolt
April	Seventh Plenum, Shanghai; Second National People's Congress elects Liu Shao-ch'i as Chairman of the People's Republic
July	Lushan Politburo conference – P'eng Teh-huai's criticisms
August	Eighth Plenum, Lushan – fall of P'eng Teh-huai and his 'anti-party' clique
September	Chou En-lai and Nehru letters on Sino-Indian borders published. Khrushchev meets President Eisenhower at Camp David. Khrushchev then visits Peking for the Tenth Anniversary celebrations, but no communiqués
October	Diplomatic relations with Guinea. Dr Subandrio, Indonesian Foreign Minister, visits China: discusses problems of Chinese nationals in Indonesia
December	On the anniversary of Stalin's birth, China says his achievements far outweighed his defects
1960 January	Prime Minister Ne Win of Burma visits China: signs a treaty of friendship and also an agreement settling Sino-Burmese border problems

February	K'ang Sheng at meeting of Warsaw Pact countries
March	Border agreement signed with Nepal
April	Following Khrushchev's visits to south and south-east Asia, Chou En-lai visits Burma, India, Nepal (and Cambodia and Vietnam in May)
June	P'eng Chen at Bucharest Conference; Eisenhower visits Taiwan
July	Diplomatic relations with Ghana
August	Soviet technicians withdrawn from China
September	Diplomatic relations with Cuba
October	Diplomatic relations with Mali
November	Moscow 'summit' meeting on the forty-third anniversary of the October Revolution, Liu Shao-ch'i in Moscow
December	Prince Sihanouk of Cambodia in Peking to sign a treaty of friendship
	Diplomatic relations with Somalia
1961 January	Ninth Plenum, Peking: decides that agriculture was the foundation and industry the leading factor in economic development
February	First large grain purchases from Canada and Australia
March	Central Work Conference, Canton, adopts 'Draft Regulations on the Rural People's Communes'
August	President Nkrumah of Ghana in Peking, treaty of friendship signed
October	Chou En-lai in Moscow for Twenty-second Congress of the Communist Party of the U.S.S.R.
December	Diplomatic relations with Tanganyika
1962 January – February	C.C. Work Conference reappraises all economic policies
March	Supreme State Conference presided over by Liu Shao-ch'i; meetings of the National People's Congress and the People's Political Consultative Conference
April – October	Series of protest notes between India and China

June	China recognises Laos (diplomatic relations in September)
August – September	Central Work Conference, Peitaiho and Peking: Mao Tse-tung stops the retreat from the Great Leap policies
September	Tenth Plenum, Peking, return to 'class struggle'; agrees on the Socialist education campaign
October	Serious fighting on the Sino-Indian border (10 October – 22 November); diplomatic relations with Uganda
October – December	Relations with U.S.S.R. worsen, over Khrushchev's backdown in Cuba and sympathy for India
1963 January	Sino-Soviet quarrel totally open (Wu Hsiu-ch'uan at East Berlin), fierce attacks throughout the year
April – May	Liu Shao-ch'i visits Indonesia, Burma, Cambodia, Vietnam
May	Anti-Chinese riots in Indonesia; Central Work Conference, Hangchow, adopts the 'First-Ten-Points' on Rural Work
September	Liu Shao-ch'i visits Korea
December	Chou En-lai to Africa (13 December – 5 February 1964), visits United Arab Republic, Algeria, Morocco; diplomatic relations with Kenya and Burundi; recognition by Tunisia
1964 January – February	Chou En-lai visits Albania, Tunisia, Ghana, Mali, Guinea, Sudan, Ethiopia and Somalia; after return to Peking, visits Burma, Pakistan and Ceylon
	Diplomatic relations with France and Congo (B); later, with Central African Republic, Zambia and Dahomey; also recognised by Malawi
June	Central Work Conference adopts rules for Poor and Lower-Middle Peasants Association
July	Chou En-lai to Burma
September	Prince Sihanouk (of Cambodia), President of Congo-Brazzaville, President of Mali in Pek-

	ing for Fifteenth Anniversary celebrations
October	Fall of Khrushchev; China's first nuclear test
November	Chou En-lai visits Moscow
December	Supreme State Conference; Third National People's Congress (21 December –4 January 1965)
1965 January	Central Work Conference adopts the 'Twenty-Three Points' on the Rural Socialist Education Campaign; Burundi breaks off relations; Foreign Minister Dr Subandrio in Peking, following Indonesia's withdrawal from United Nations
February	Soviet Premier Kosygin in Peking; American bombing of North Vietnam; President Nyerere of Tanzania in Peking, signs a treaty of friendship
March	President Ayub Khan of Pakistan in Peking; Chou En-lai visits Romania, Albania and Algeria; Ch'en Yi visits Afghanistan, Pakistan and Nepal
April	Chou En-lai visits United Arab Republic, Pakistan and Burma; later, he visits Indonesia
May	Second nuclear test; P'eng Chen to Indonesia; Lo Jui-ch'ing's speech on the twentieth anniversary of V.E. Day
June	Chou En-lai visits Pakistan and Tanzania, and returns via Ethiopia, United Arab Republic and Syria; Ch'en Yi in Algiers, and Chou En-lai in Cairo (to meet Presidents Ayub Khan, Nasser and Sukarno) on postponing the Afro-Asian Conference
July	Diplomatic relations with Mauritania; visits to Peking by Prime Minister of Uganda, President of Somalia and Prime Minister Ne Win of Burma
August	Ch'en Yi visits Indonesia
September	Ch'en Yi visits Pakistan, Syria, Algeria, Mali, Guinea and Afghanistan; China supports Pakistan in war with India; Prince Sihanouk

	visits Peking; GESTAPU coup in Indonesia crushed by the Army; Lin Piao's article on People's War published
October	Sino-Indonesian relations deteriorate; China decides not to attend Afro-Asian Conference
November	Attack on historian Wu Han, the first shot of the Cultural Revolution
December	Politburo Standing Committee meeting, Shanghai, where Lin Piao attacks Lo Jui-ch'ing
1966 January	Dahomey and Central African Republic break off relations; Sino-Indonesian relations worsen throughout the year
February	Coup in Ghana while President Nkrumah in Peking
March	Mao Tse-tung and Lin Piao move firmly against intellectuals; Liu Shao-ch'i visits Pakistan
April	Liu Shao-ch'i visits Afghanistan, Pakistan and Burma
May	Chou En-lai officially announces beginning of the Cultural Revolution; 'May 16 Circular' and removal of P'eng Chen and Lo Jui-ch'ing; third nuclear test
June – July	Chou En-lai visits Romania, Albania and Pakistan; Cultural Revolution moves into high gear
August	Eleventh Plenum adopts 'Decisions Concerning the Great Proletarian Cultural Revolution'; Lin Piao promoted at expense of Liu Shao-ch'i; Red Guards received by Mao Tse-tung
September	Schools and universities closed
October	Fourth nuclear test
November	Red Guard Rallies in Peking; Ghana breaks off relations; Lin Piao the sole Vice-Chairman of the C.C.P.
December	Fifth nuclear test
1967 January	Fierce struggles for power in the provinces begin; 'rebels' seize power in Shanghai and

establish the Shanghai Commune; First Re-volutionary Committee established in Heilungkiang – the'three-in-one alliance' of P.L.A., Party cadres and mass repre-sentatives

February – April	Revolutionary Committees in Shanghai, Shantung, Shansi, Peking and Kweichow
May – June	Troubles in Hong Kong and Kowloon and attacks on British diplomats
June	Sixth nuclear test: first hydrogen bomb exploded
July	Wuhan Incident, arrest of Peking Political Commissar and *Red Flag* senior deputy editor
August	Attacks on Mongolian, British, Soviet, Kenyan embassies and Italian trade mission; Re-volutionary Committee in Chinghai
September	Recall of embassy staff from Indonesia and Tunisia
October	Relations with Indonesia suspended
November – December	Revolutionary Committees in Inner Mongolia and Tienstin; recognition by South Yemen; seventh nuclear test
1968 January – May	Revolutionary Committees in all but five pro-vinces
April	Protocols with Zambia and Tanzania to build the Tanzam Railway
June	President Nyerere of Tanzania in Peking; Kwangsi fighting stops Soviet arms shipment by rail to Vietnam
August – September	China condemns Soviet invasion of Czechoslo-vakia; increased control of Red Guard acti-vities by P.L.A. and Propaganda Teams; Revolutionary Committees in the final five provinces, marking the 'victory' of the Cul-tural Revolution; intensification of the 'youth to the countryside' movement and the campaign to re-educate intellectuals
October	Twelfth Plenum sacks Liu Shao-ch'i and expels him from C.C.P., confirms the success of the Cultural Revolution and need to rebuild the

C.C.P.

December	Eighth nuclear test, 3-megaton hydrogen bomb
1969 January	New Year editorials call for order and unity; negotiations begin for diplomatic relations with Canada and Italy.
March	Clashes on Sino-Soviet border at Chenpao/Damansky Island on the Ussuri river
April	Ninth National Party Congress, report by Lin Piao and adoption of a new Party Constitution; strong P.L.A. representation on the new C.C.; First Plenum elects the new Politburo
May	Sino-Soviet border clashes in Sinkiang; China sends out ambassadors to Albania and France (only Huang Hua in Cairo had not been recalled)
June	China not present at World Conference of Communist Parties in Moscow, Brezhnev openly attacks China; more ambassadors to Vietnam, Cambodia, Pakistan, Tanzania, Guinea, Zambia, Romania, Sweden, Congo (B) and Syria; continued tensions on Sino-Soviet borders
July	Ambassadors sent out to Nepal, Mauritania, Afghanistan, South Yemen, Algeria and Yemen
September	Chou En-lai to Hanoi on death of Ho Chi Minh; Chou En-lai meets Soviet Premier Kosygin at Peking airport; announcement that China now self-sufficient in oil; ninth nuclear test (first underground) and a new hydrogen bomb
October	Twentieth Anniversary celebrations, rally at Tienanmen Square
1970 January	Sino-U.S. Warsaw Talks resumed after break of two years
April	Chou En-lai to Korea; first earth 'satellite launched
May	Prince Sihanouk overthrown, forms government in exile in Peking

July	New agreements signed to help build Tanzam Railway
August	Second Plenum of Ninth C.C., break with Ch'en Po-ta and beginnings of struggle with Lin Piao
October	Diplomatic relations with Canada; tenth nuclear test
November	Diplomatic relations with Italy; President Yahya Khan vists China
December	Politburo meeting on *détente* policy with U.S.A. First new Party Committee established in Hunan province, then in Kiangsi, Kwangtung and Kiangsu. During the year, diplomatic relations established with Equatorial Guinea and Ethiopia
1971 January	Diplomatic relations with Chile
March	Second satellite launched; Chou En-lai visits Vietnam
April	'Ping-pong' diplomacy, invitation to the U.S. team
June	President Ceausescu in Peking
July	President Nixon's visit to China announced after Dr Kissinger's first visit.
August	President Ne Win visits China; last provincial Party Committees established (Szechuan, Tibet, Ningsia and Heilungkiang)
September	Lin Piao abortive coup, killed in air crash
October	Admission to U.N.; Emperor Haile Selassie visits China
November	Eleventh nuclear test; President Bhutto visits China
December	Anti-Lin Piao campaign begins; Chinese criticism of India's role in the creation of Bangladesh During the year, diplomatic relations also established with Nigeria, Kuwait, Cameroons, San Marino, Austria, Sierra Leone, Iran, Turkey, Belgium, Lebanon, Peru, Rwanda, Iceland, Senegal
1972 January	Twelfth nuclear test; President Bhutto visits

	China
February	President Nixon visits China
June	Mrs Bandaranaike in Peking
July	Mao Tse-tung meets French Foreign Minister Schuman
September	Prime Minister Tanaka in Peking, diplomatic relations with Japan
October	Diplomatic relations with West Germany
December	Diplomatic relations with Australia, New Zealand
	During the year, diplomatic relations also established with Cyprus, Malta, Argentina, Mexico, Mauritius, Greece, Guyana, Togo, Malagasy, Luxemburg, Jamaica, Chad, Zaire
1973 January	President Mobutu (Zaire) visits China
February	First Communist Youth League Committee re-established in Shanghai (the rest in quick succession, completed in July)
April	President of Mexico visits China; First Trade Union Committees in Peking and Shanghai (the rest in quick succession, completed in December)
July	First Women's Federation Committee (the rest in quick succession, completed in December)
August	Tenth National Party Congress, reports by Chou En-lai and Wang Hung-wen
September	President Pompidou of France visits China; beginnings of the Anti-Lin Piao and Anti-Confucius campaign
October	Prime Ministers Trudeau (Canada) and Whitlam (Australia) visit China
December	King of Nepal visits China; Senior Regional Commanders reshuffled
	During the year, Spain and Upper Volta establish diplomatic relations.
1974 January	Paracel Island firmly restored to Chinese control, also restates claims over the Nansha (Spratly) island group
February	President Kaunda of Zambia and President

	Boumedienne of Algeria visit China
March	President Nyerere of Tanzania visits China
April	Teng Hsiao-p'ing leads delegation to Special Session of the U.N. General Assembly
May	Prime Minister Tun Razak visits China, diplomatic relations with Malaysia; Presidents Senghor (Senegal) and Makarios (Cyprus) and Prime Minister Bhutto (Pakistan) visit China
June	Thirteenth nuclear test
November	After Kissinger's seventh visit, announcement that President Ford will be visiting China in 1975
	During the year, diplomatic relations also established with Guinea-Bissau, Gabon, Trinidad and Tobago, Venezuela, Niger, Brazil, Gambia
1975 January	Fourth National People's Congress adopts a new State Constitution, appoints the State Council and the Standing Committee; Second Plenum of the Tenth C.C.; Teng Hsiao-p'ing appointed Chief of General Staff and Chang Ch'un-ch'iao Director of P.L.A. General Political Department
February	President Samora Machel of Mozambique visits China
April	President Kim Il-sung (North Korea) visits China
May	Teng Hsiao-p'ing visits France; official relations established with the European Economic Community
June	President Marcos visits China, diplomatic relations with the Philippines; Prime Minister Kukrit visits China, diplomatic relations with Thailand
July	Third earth satellite launched
August	Mao Tse-tung meets Prince Sihanouk with Khieu Samphan of Cambodia; recognition of Bangladesh (diplomatic relations in October)

September	National Conference on 'Learn from Tachai' in agriculture
October	Completion of the Tanzania–Zambia Railway; underground nuclear test
November	President Ne Win visits China; fourth earth satellite launched
December	President Ford of the U.S.A. visits China; fifth earth satellite launched
	During the year, diplomatic relations also established with Botswana, São Tomé and Príncipe, Fiji, Western Samoa
1976 January	Death of Chou En-lai; nuclear test.
February	Hua Kuo-feng as Acting Premier; former President Nixon visits China
April	Violent demonstrations in Tienanmen Square; Teng Hsiao-p'ing removed from all posts; Hua Kuo-feng appointed Premier and First Vice-Chairman of the C.C.P.; Prime Minister Muldoon of New Zealand visits China
May	Prime Minister Lee Kuan Yew of Singapore visits China.
June	Prime Minister Fraser of Australia visits China
July	Death of Chu Teh; Tanzam Railway completed and handed over; severe earthquake in T'ang-shan
August	Sixth earth satellite launched
September	Death of Mao Tse-tung

Notes and Guide to Further Reading

The amount of material published on contemporary China in and outside the country is now very large. For the readers of this history, I limit my notes to those publications which are more easily accessible to the English-speaking world. I call attention as much as possible to the more important recent writings in the hope that the reader may find time to pursue the subject much further than the better-known introductory surveys. A considerable part of the key Chinese documents may be found in English translation, most notably in *Survey of China Mainland Press, Selections from China Mainland Magazines, Current Background*, published by the U.S. Consulate General, Hong Kong, and special series of translations from newspapers, magazines and books published by the U.S. Joint Publications Research Service. A more selective set of translations are published in China in *People's China* (1950–7) and then in *Peking Review* (since 1958). In addition, there are daily news releases issued by China and monitored radio broadcasts issued in the U.S.A. and Britain. More scholarly translations of documents may be found in *The China Quarterly* and the China Translation Series published by International Arts and Sciences Press, New York. For information about other series and collections before 1965, *Contemporary China: A Research Guide* by Peter Burton and Eugene Wu (Stanford, 1967) is invaluable.

I. INTRODUCTION

1. A recent stimulating introduction is C. P. FitzGerald, *The Chinese View of their Place in the World* (London, 1964; with postscript 1966; addendum, 1969). A number of scholarly studies which break new ground may be found in J. K. Fairbank (ed.), *The Chinese World Order* (Harvard U.P., 1968).

2. Some notable recent studies which bring out China's 'international' perspectives before the tenth century are Yü Ying-shih, *Trade and Expansion in Han China* (California U.P., 1967) and E. H. Schafer, *The Golden Peaches of Samarkand* (California U.P., 1963). An excellent introduction to early Chinese history is E. O. Reischauter and J. K. Fairbank, *East Asia: The Great Tradition* (Boston, 1960).

3. Some broad philosophical issues concerning Sung Confucianism are discussed in a number of essays by W. T. de Bary, James T. C. Liu, F. W. Mote, H. Wilhelm, H. Franke and C. M. Shirokauer, collected in A. F. Wright (ed.), *Studies in Chinese Thought* (Chicago U.P., 1953); D. S. Nivison and A. F. Wright (eds), *Confucianism in Action* (Stanford U.P., 1959); A. F. Wright (ed.), *The Confucian Persuasion* (Stanford U.P., 1960); A. F. Wright and Denis Twitchett (eds), *Confucian Personalities* (Stanford U.P., 1962).

4. This is discussed by Wang Gungwu in 'Early Ming Relations with South-east Asia: A Background Essay', in Fairbank (ed.), *Chinese World Order*, pp. 34–62; and in 'China and South-east Asia, 1402–1424' in J. Ch'en and N. Tarling (eds), *Studies in the Social History of China and South-east Asia: Essays in Memory of Victor Purcell* (Cambridge U.P., 1970) pp. 375–401. An excellent study of the change of policy is Lo Jung-pang, 'The Decline of the Early Ming Navy', *Oriens Extremus*, v (1958–9) 149–68.

For the Mongol Yuan transition period, see I. de Rachewiltz, 'Personnel and

Personalities in North China in the Early Mongol Period', *Journal of the Economic and Social History of the Orient*, IX (1966) 88—144, and John W. Dardess, *Conquerors and Confucius, Aspects of Political Change in Late Yuan China* (Columbia U.P., 1973).

5. Chang Tien-tse, *Sino-Portuguese Trade from 1514 to 1644* (Leiden, 1934; repr. 1969); Arnold H. Rowbotham, *Missionary and Mandarin: the Jesuits at the Court of China* (California U.P., 1942); Wolfgang Franke, *China and the West*, trans. R. A. Wilson (Oxford, 1967).

6. A number of recent publications have reopened the serious study of the early Ch'ing dynasty, most notably Fu Lo-shu, *A Documentary Chronicle of Sino-Western Relations, 1644–1820* (Arizona U.P., 1966); L. D. Kessler, 'Chinese Scholars and the Early Manchu State', *Harvard Journal of Asiatic Studies*, XXXI (1971) 179–200; Jonathan D. Spence, *Emperor of China: Self-Portrait of K'ang-hsi* (New York, 1974); Mark Mancall, *Russia and China, their Diplomatic Relations to 1728* (Harvard U.P., 1971), and Robert B. Oxnam, *Ruling from Horseback, Manchu Politics in the Oboi Regency, 1661–69* (Chicago U.P., 1975).

7. This large and fascinating subject is still being explored by Joseph Needham and his colleagues in the multi-volume *Science and Civilisation in China* (Cambridge U.P., 1954–   ). Vol. V, part 2 appeared in 1974. A recent bold attempt to draw some conclusions for economic history is Mark Elvin, *The Pattern of the Chinese Past* (London, 1973).

8. A useful survey of some of the efforts can be seen in James P. Harrison, *The Communists and Chinese Peasant Rebellions: A Study in the Rewriting of Chinese History* (New York, 1969); also several essays in Albert Feuerwerker (ed.), *History in Communist China* (New York, 1968).

9. Wang Gungwu, ' "Burning Books and Burying Scholars Alive": Some Recent Interpretations Concerning Ch'in Shih-huang', *Papers on Far Eastern History*, IX (March 1974) 137–86; Li Yu-ning (ed.), *The Politics of Historiography: The First Emperor of China* (New York, 1975).

10. Wang Gungwu, 'Juxtaposing Past and Present in China Today', *The China Quarterly*, LXI (March 1975) 1–24.

11. The number of studies of Mao Tse-tung has increased remarkably in recent years. The best introductions remain those of Stuart Schram, *Mao Tse-tung* (Harmondsworth, 1966), and Jerome Ch'en, *Mao and the Chinese Revolution* (Oxford U.P., 1965). Two stimulating studies, Richard H. Solomon, *Mao's Revolution and the Chinese Political Culture* (California U.P., 1971), and Frederic Wakeman Jr, *History and Will, Philosophical Perspectives of Mao Tse-tung's Thought* (California U.P., 1973), are important.

12. There have been a small number of studies of leaders other than Mao Tse-tung, notably Hsu Kai-yu on Chou En-lai, *Chou En-lai: China's Grey Eminence* (New York, 1968) and the recent study of Liu Shao-ch'i by Lowell Dittmer, *Liu Shao-ch'i and the Chinese Cultural Revolution* (California U.P., 1974). Shorter but well-researched biographies may be found in the invaluable *Biographic Dictionary of Chinese Communism 1921–1965*, ed. Donald W. Klein and Anne B. Clark (Harvard U.P., 1971) in two vols.

2. NEW PRESSURES FOR CHANGE: HISTORICAL BACKGROUND UP TO 1949

1. For good surveys of this period see J. K. Fairbank, E. O. Reischauer and A. M. Craig, *East Asia: The Modern Transformation* (Boston, 1965) and Immanuel C. Y. Hsü, *The Rise of Modern China* (Oxford U.P., 1970).

2. By 1900, legations were opened in only three countries which were not empires: Italy, Peru and Korea. Of these, only Korea had a specially appointed minister; the minister in London looked after Italy (and Belgium) and the one in Washington looked after Peru (and Spain). For details, see J. V. A. MacMurray (ed.), *Treaties and Agreements with and concerning China*, vol. I (Oxford U.P., New York, 1921); H. B. Morse, *The International Relations of the Chinese Empire*, vol. III (London, 1918).

3. The active political life of these four men spanned nearly eighty years. They and their colleagues have been the subject of several fine studies. Two important studies published in 1957–8 may still be read with profit: Mary C. Wright, *The Last Stand of Chinese Conservatism, the Tung-chih Restoration, 1862–1874* (Stanford U.P., 1957) and Joseph R. Levenson, *Confucian China and its Modern Fate: The Problem of Intellectual Continuity* (California U.P., 1958). More recently, an excellent study is Chang Hao, *Liang Ch'i-Ch'ao and Intellectual Transition in China 1890–1907* (Harvard U.P., 1971).

4. Harold Z. Schiffrin, *Sun Yat-sen and the Origins of the Chinese Revolution* (California U.P., 1968); Michael Gasster, *Chinese Intellectuals and the Revolution of 1911* (Washington U.P., 1969).

5. There is still no authoritative study of China's foreign relations and border problems in the decade after 1912. Several special studies touch on different aspects of this period, but these are based mainly on Western and Japanese archives. Chinese foreign-affairs documents have begun to appear, but very few are available in English translation. Good general surveys of the period may be found in H. M. Vinacke, *A History of the Far East in Modern Times* (New York, 1959) and H. F. MacNair and D. F. Lach, *Modern Far-Eastern International Relations* (New York, 1955). For an American view, an excellent study is Russell H. Fifield, *Woodrow Wilson and the Far East* (New York, 1952).

6. Sun Yat-sen, *San Min Chu I: The Three Principles of the People*, trans. F. W. Price, ed. L. T. Chen (Shanghai, 1929). His later views on race and nationalism may be contrasted with the anti-Manchu phase before 1911; see Schiffrin, *Sun Yat-sen*, pp. 283–99.

7. Since the early 1950s, the government of the People's Republic of China has taken firm steps to eradicate 'Great Han chauvinism' from textbooks and maps, especially in books published for foreign readers, notably Hu Sheng, *Imperialism and Chinese Politics, 1840–1925* (Peking, 1955), Ho Kan-chih, *A History of the Modern Chinese Revolution* (Peking, 1959), and Wang Chun-heng, *A Simple Geography of China* (Peking, 1958).

8. Allen S. Whiting, *Soviet Policies in China, 1917–1924* (Columbia U.P., 1954) and Leong Sow-theng, *China and Soviet Russia: Their Diplomatic Relations, 1917–1924* (Australian National U.P., 1976).

9. C. Martin Wilbur, 'Military Separatism and the Process of Reunification under the Nationalist Regime, 1922–1937' in Ho Ping-ti and Tang Tsou (eds), *China in Crisis*, vol. 1: *China's Heritage and the Communist Political System* (Chicago U.P., 1968) pp. 203–63; Lucian W. Pye, *Warlord Politics, Politics and Coalition in the Modernisation of Republican China* (New York, 1971).

10. Two recent studies bring this out clearly: Tien Hung-mao, *Government and Politics in Kuomintang China, 1927–1937* (Stanford U.P., 1972); Lloyd E. Eastman, *The Abortive Revolution, China Under Nationalist Rule 1927–1937* (Harvard U.P., 1974).

11. The most outstanding reports on this subject are still the contemporary ones by Edgar Snow, *Red Star over China*, rev. ed. (New York, 1944), and George E. Taylor, *The Struggle for North China* (Institute of Pacific Relations, New York, 1940).

12. After considerable neglect, this subject has recently been well served by the publication of two books on it in one year: Gerald E. Bunker, *The Peace Conspiracy, Wang Ching-wei and the China War, 1937–1941* (Harvard U.P., 1972) and John H. Boyle, *China and Japan at War, 1937–1945, the Politics of Collaboration* (Stanford U.P., 1972).

13. Herbert Feis, *The China Tangle, the American Effort in China from Pearl Harbour to the Marshall Mission* (Princeton U.P., 1953); U.S. State Department, *United States' Relations with China* (Washington, 1949; reissued in two vols by Stanford U.P., 1967).

14. Chow Tse-tsung, *The May Fourth Movement, Intellectual Revolution in Modern China* (Harvard U.P., 1960) in two vols.

15. Mary C. Wright (ed.), *China in Revolution, the First Phase 1900–1913* (Yale U.P., 1968); Albert Feuerwerker *et al.* (eds), *Approaches to Modern Chinese history* (California U.P., 1967).

16. Sun Yat-sen, *Memoirs of a Chinese Revolutionary, a Programme of National Reconstruction*

for China (London, 1927); *The International Development of China* (London, 1928; Taipei, 1953); and *Fundamentals of National Reconstruction* (Taipei, 1953).

17. Lucien Bianco, *Origins of the Chinese Revolution 1915–1949* (Stanford, 1971), captures the atmosphere of near-chaos to be followed by tight controls after 1928. Examples of regional change include studies by James Sheridan on Feng Yü-hsiang (Stanford, 1966), Donald G. Gillin on Yen Hsi-shan (Princeton, 1967), Robert A. Kapp on Szechuan (Yale U.P., 1973), Diana Lary on Kwangsi (Cambridge U.P., 1974) and John Hall on Yunnan (Monographs on Far Eastern History, A.N.U., Canberra, 1976).

18. Various discussions are to be found of the contributions of foreign 'modernisers' in the issues of *Chinese Social and Political Science Review* (1916–37). More specific examples may be found in Shirley S. Garrett, *Social Reformers in Urban China, The Chinese Young Men's Christian Association 1895–1926* (Harvard U.P., 1970); Daniel W. Y. Kwok, *Scientism in Chinese Thought 1900–1950* (Yale U.P., 1965); Charlotte Furth, *Ting Wen-chiang, Science and China's New Culture* (Harvard U.P., 1970), and Jerome B. Grieder, *Hu Shih and the Chinese Renaissance, Liberalism in the Chinese Revolution 1917–1937* (Harvard U.P., 1970).

19. A major study of the period is Benjamin Schwartz, *In Search of Wealth and Power, Yen Fu and the West* (Harvard U.P., 1964). See also Jerome Ch'en's historical background chapter in J. Gray (ed.), *Modern China's Search for a Political Form* (London, 1969) pp. 1–40.

20. A sample of the variety can be found in E. R. Hughes, *The Invasion of China by the Western World* (New York, 1938); Hu Shih, *The Chinese Renaissance* (Chicago U.P., 1934) and O. Briere, *Fifty Years of Chinese Philosophy 1898–1950*, trans. L. G. Thompson (London, 1956).

21. See note 17 of this chapter for regional examples of 'warlord patriotism'; also Li Chien-nung, *The Political History of China 1840–1928*, trans. Teng Ssu-yü and J. Ingalls (Princeton, 1956). The more radical varieties are better known, as for example in biographies of Chiang Kai-shek by Hollington Tong (Shanghai, 1937), two vols, and Hsiung Shih-i (London, 1948), and of Wang Chin-wei by T'ang Leang-li (Peiping, 1931).

22. There are several Peking and Taipei versions of what happened during the years of K.M.T.-C.C.P. alliance. Two accounts available in English are Ho Kan-chih, *Modern Chinese Revolution*, and Hu Chiao-mu, *Thirty Years of the Chinese Communist Party* (Peking, 1959). These may be compared with Benjamin Schwartz, *Chinese Communism and the Rise of Mao* (Harvard U.P., 1951); Conrad Brandt, *Stalin's Failure in China 1924–27* (Harvard U.P., 1958); C. Martin Wilbur and Julie Lien-ying How (eds), *Documents on Communism, Nationalism and Soviet Advisers in China 1918–1927* (Columbia U.P., 1956).

23. There is as yet no authoritative study of the new managerial élites and urban workers of this period except in Chinese and Japanese. On the C.C.P. and the peasants, there have been some notable recent studies: Hsiao Tso-liang, *Power Relations within the Chinese Communist Movement 1930–1934* (Washington U.P., 1961, 1967) two vols, and *The Land Revolution in China 1939–1934* (Washington U.P., 1969); Ilpvong J. Kim, *The Politics of Chinese Communism, Kiangsi Under the Soviets* (California U.P., 1973).

24. The question of *ko-ming* is closely linked to the idea of the Mandate of Heaven. This idea is most clearly stated by Mencius: a good introduction is Arthur Waley, *Three Ways of Thought in Ancient China* (London, 1939) pp. 123–62. An excellent new translation of Mencius by D. C. Lau was published in Penguin Classics (Harmondsworth, 1970).

25. Norman D. Palmer and Leng Shao Chuan, *Sun Yat-sen and Communism* (New York, 1961); Maurice Meisner, *Li Ta-chao and the Origin of the Chinese Marxism* (Harvard U.P., 1967).

26. See references in note 22 of this chapter. A vivid account of the rise and fall of the 'alliance' is in Harold R. Isaacs, *The Tragedy of the Chinese Revolution*, 2nd rev. ed. (Stanford U.P., 1962).

27. Chen Po-ta, *Notes on Ten Years of Civil War 1927–1936* (Peking, 1954); also the studies of Mao Tse-tung by Schram and Ch'en. Another version of interest is Han Suyin,

The Morning Deluge, Mao Tse-tung and the Chinese Revolution, 1893–1953 (London, 1972). Yet another version is provided by Chang Kuo-t'ao, *The Rise of the Chinese Communist Party* (Kansas U.P., 1971, 1972) two vols, especially vol. II.

28. Chiang Kai-shek, *China's Destiny*, trans. Wang Chung-hui (New York, 1947); a critique of this work by Ch'en Po-ta is partially translated in Stuart Gelder (ed.), *The Chinese Communists* (London, 1946) pp. 256–90.

29. The consequences of the campaigns in the name of Sun Yat-sen's revolution were serious; see John Israel, *Student Nationalism in China, 1927–1937* (Stanford U.P., 1966), and the background chapters of Lyman P. Van Slyke, *Enemies and Friends: The United Front in Chinese Communist History* (Stanford U.P., 1967).

30. Mao Tse-tung's May 1937 statement 'The Tasks of the C.C.P. in the Period of Resistance to Japan', and his October 1938 essay, 'The Role of the C.C.P. in the National War', *Selected Works* (London, 1954) vol. I, pp. 258–81; vol. II, pp. 244–61. In addition to Van Slyke, *Enemies and Friends*, see Tetsuya Kataoka, *Resistance and Revolution in China: The Communists and the Second United Front* (California U.P., 1974).

31. See note 12 of this chapter.

32. On this point, see the two views represented by Chalmers A. Johnson, *Peasant Nationalism and Communist Power: The Emergence of Revolutionary China, 1937–1945* (Stanford U.P., 1962) and Mark Selden, *The Yenan Way in Revolutionary China* (Harvard U.P., 1971). Selden emphasises how much the C.C.P. treated the war as a protracted revolutionary struggle.

33. Mao Tse-tung, 'Strategic Problems in the Anti-Japanese War', *Selected Works* (London, 1954) vol. II, pp. 119–56; 'The Chinese Revolution and the C.C.P.', vol. III, pp. 72–101; 'On New Democracy', vol. III, pp. 106–56.

34. Hsü Yung-ying, *A Survey of Shensi – Kansu – Ninghsia Border Region* (Inst. of Pacific Relations, 1945); also see Selden, *The Yenan Way*.

35. Lionel Max Chassin, *The Communist Conquest of China: A History of the Civil War, 1945–49* (London, 1966) and J. Guillermaz, *The History of the Chinese Communist Party*, trans. Anne Destenay (London, 1972).

The best collection of documents is still U.S. Department of State's *United States' Relations with China*.

3. BUILDING A NEW MODEL, 1949–53

1. Tang Tsou, *America's Failure in China 1941–50* (Chicago U.P., 1963) chs 2–4.

2. Carsun Chang, *The Third Force in China* (New York, 1952); Jack Belden, *China Shakes the World* (New York, 1949). Still one of the best books for this period is C. P. FitzGerald, *Revolution in China* (London, 1952) reissued as *The Birth of Communist China* (Harmondsworth, 1964).

3. Chou Shun-hsin, *The Chinese Inflation 1937–49* (New York, 1963); for a vivid account of the last years of K.M.T. rule, see A. Doak Barnett, *China on the Eve of Communist Takeover* (New York, 1961).

4. Chassin, *Communist Conquest*; and the analysis by O. Edmund Clubb, 'Chiang Kai-shek's Waterloo: The Battle of the Hwai-Hai', *Pacific Historical Review*, xxv (1956) 389–99.

5. Two works of a documentary nature captured some of the atmosphere of the post-war years and should be read together with Belden, *China Shakes the World* and Barnett, *China on the Eve*: John F. Melby, *The Mandate of Heaven: Record of a Civil War, China 1945–49* (Toronto U.P., 1968), and Derk Bodde, *Peking Diary 1948–1949, A Year of Revolution* (New York, 1950).

There is still nothing more revealing and authoritative than *United States' Relations with China*.

6. Mao Tse-tung, *Selected Works*, vol. IV (Peking, 1961) pp. 411—24.

7. The full text of this report may be found in *People's China* (16 October 1950) pp. 4—9, 30—2; and is reproduced in *The First Year of Victory* (Peking, 1951).

8. This emerges clearly in Mao Tse-tung's 'On People's Democratic Dictatorship' in *Selected Works*, vol. IV, pp. 417—18; if there is any doubt, see Ch'en Po-ta, 'Stalin and the Chinese Revolution', published in Chinese in December 1949 and 'On the Thought of Mao Tse-tung', published in June 1951. English editions of both these appeared in 1953: *Stalin and the Chinese Revolution, in Celebration of Stalin's Seventieth Birthday* (Peking, 1953), and *Mao Tse-tung and the Chinese Revolution, Written in Commemoration of the 30th Anniversary of the Communist Party of China* (Peking, 1953).

9. Mao Tse-tung, *Selected Works*, vol. IV, p. 422.

10. *The Common Program and other Documents of the First Plenary Session of the Chinese People's Political Consultative Conference* (Peking, 1950).

11. The question has again been asked following the publication of Joseph W. Esherick (ed.), *Lost Chance in China, The World War II Despatches of John S. Service* (New York, 1974); John Paton Davies, *Dragon by the Tail; American, British, Japanese, and Russian Encounters with China and One Another* (New York, 1972); John S. Service, *The Amerasia Papers: Some Problems in the History of U.S. — China Relations* (Center for Chinese Studies, Berkeley, 1971). The most sophisticated recent analysis is John Gittings, *The World and China, 1922—72* (London, 1974), chs 5, 6 and 7.

12. 'The Thought of Mao Tse-tung' had appeared at the end of the war. The background to this may be examined in the rectification campaigns of 1942—4; see *Mao's China, Party Reform Documents 1942—44*, trans. and introduction by Boyd Compton (Washington U. P., 1952). After 1949, Chen Po-ta states it clearly in *Mao and the Chinese Revolution*.

13. For the text of the treaty and agreements see O. B. van der Sprenkel (ed.), *New China: Three Views* (New York, 1951) pp. 227—35.

14. Don C. Price, *Russia and the Roots of the Chinese Revolution, 1896—1911* (Harvard U.P., 1975).
   The first knowledge of the U.S.S.R. came through Ch'ü Ch'iu-pai's (1899—1935) accounts of his journeys in 1920—3, *O-hsiang Chi-ch'eng* (Journey to the Land of Hunger) and *Ch'ih-tu hsin-shih* (Impressions of the Red Capital). Lu Hsun (1881—1936) gave authoritative support to the quality of Russian and Soviet writings in the late 1920s. But it was not until the Second World War that the Russians were given a generally good press for a brief period, especially after the visit of Kuo Mo-jo (b. 1892) in 1945 (*Su-lien chi-hsing*) and Shen Yen-ping (Mao Tun, b. 1896) in 1946—7 (*Su-lien chien-wen lu*).

15. The activities of the Sino-Soviet Friendship Association may be read about in the issues of *People's China* (1950—7), but there are many more accounts of Soviet friendship in Chinese-language sources, especially newspapers and magazines like the *Sino-Soviet Friendship*. A brief survey may be found in P'eng Ming, *Chung-Su yu-yi shih* (A History of Sino-Soviet Friendship, Peking, 1957).

16. In contrast to the despatches of John S. Service and the later books by John Paton Davies and John Service, there are the policy speeches and editorials issued in *Daily News Release* (Hong Kong, May 1948—50) and *China Digest* (Hong Kong, 1947—9), some of which have been collected in V. P. Dutt (ed.), *East Asia: China, Korea, Japan, 1947—1950* (Oxford U.P., 1958).

17. Some choice examples of anti-U.S. campaigns before and after the start of the Korean War may be found in Richard L. Walker, *China under Communism, The First Five Years* (Yale U.P., 1955) chs 10—12.

18. Two most useful introductions to the state structure are Franz Schurmann, *Ideology and Organisation in Communist China* (California U.P., 1966), ch. 3, and D. J. Waller, *The Government and Politics of Communist China* (London, 1970) ch. 3.

19. Li Choh-ming, *Economic Development of Communist China: An Appraisal of the First Five*

Years of Industrialisation (California U.P., 1959). There is an interesting near-contemporary account in ch. 13 of W. W. Rostow *et al.*, *The Prospects for Communist China* (Massachusetts Institute of Technology Press, 1954).

20.   N.C.N.A., Peking, 30 September 1953; *New China's Economic Achievements 1949–52* (Peking, 1952), policy statements by Po I-po and Ch'en Yun.

21.   The articles by Hsueh Mu-ch'iao, Po I-po and Li Fu-ch'un in *People's China* (17 September 1952) pp. 18, 23–8; (16 October 1952) pp. 10–15; (1 November 1952) pp. 8–11.

22.   Chou En-lai's Political Report to the Third Session of the First National Committee of the Chinese People's Political Consultative Conference, 23 October 1951–text in *People's China* (16 November 1951) Supplement, pp. 1–10.

23.   Of the several general surveys of Soviet-type industrialisation during the early years of the P. R. C., the best is still Chao Kuo-chun, *Economic Planning and Organisation in Mainland China, a Documentary Study, 1949–1957* (Harvard U.P., 1959 and 1960) two vols. For the north east, see also Chao's *North-east China (Manchuria) Today* (M.I.T. Press, 1953).

24.   *The Agrarian Reform Law of the People's Republic of China*, 4th ed. (Peking, 1953). This includes Liu Shao-ch'i's 'Report on the Agrarian Reform Law (16 July 1950)'.

25.   Chao Kuo-chun, *Agrarian Policy of the Chinese Communist Party, 1921–1959* (London, 1960); also the interesting study by Daniel H. Bays, 'Agrarian Reform in Kwangtung, 1950–1953', in *Early Communist China: Two Studies* (Michigan Chinese Studies, 1969), pp. 28–77.

26.   *The Marriage Law of the People's Republic of China* (Peking, 1950); see C. K. Yang, *The Chinese Family in the Communist Revolution* (M.I.T. Press, 1959).

27.   John Gardner, 'The Wu-fan Campaign in Shanghai: A Study in the Consolidation of Urban Control', in A. Doak Barnett (ed.), *Chinese Communist Politics in Action* (Washington U.P., 1969) pp. 477–539; Sherwin Montell, 'The San-fan Wu-fan Movement in Communist China', *Papers on China* (Harvard Regional Studies Seminar, 1954) pp. 136–96. There are several contemporary accounts by visitors; these two are still interesting to read today: Raja Huthessing, *The Great Peace* (New York, 1953), and Frank Moraes, *Report on Mao's China* (New York, 1953).

28.   The principles of thought reform were those enunciated in Mao Tse-tung's Lecture to the Party School on 1 February 1942; see 'Reform in Learning, the Party, and Literature', in *Mao's China*, trans. Boyd Compton, pp. 9–32. Another version of this important document may be found in Conrad Brandt, Benjamin Schwartz and John K. Fairbank, *A Documentary History of Chinese Communism* (Harvard U.P., 1952) pp. 375–92. There have been several sensational studies of 'brain-washing' in China. The one that is still worth reading is Robert Jay Lifton, *Thought Reform and the Psychology of Totalism, a Study of 'Brainwashing' in China* (New York, 1961; Pelican ed. Harmondsworth, 1967).

29.   Two good surveys of various aspects of education in China are found in Hu Chang-tu *et al.*, *China: Its People, its Society, its Culture* (New Haven: H.R.A.F. Press, 1960) ch. 20, and R. F. Price, *Education in Communist China* (London, 1970). A near-contemporary account by K. E. Priestley, 'Education in the People's Republic of China: Beginnings', in *The Yearbook of Education, 1952* (London, 1953) is still useful; reprinted in Stewart E. Fraser (ed.), *Education and Communism in China* (Hong Kong, 1969) pp. 49–80.

30.   This is evidenced by the large number of non-C.C.P. intellectuals who published their writings from 1951 to 1953: in scholarly journals as well as in newspapers and openly propagandist magazines. Also, an increasing number of scholarly books and traditional texts were published; for example, see Merle Goldman, *Literary Dissent in Communist China* (Harvard U.P., 1967) chs 5 and 6.

31.   There are many calculations. The most thorough seem to be those in Alexander Eckstein, *Communist China's Economic Growth and Foreign Trade* (New York, 1966) pp. 94–5.

Cf. Chu-yuan Cheng, *Economic Relations between Peking and Moscow, 1949–63* (New York, 1964) p. 14, where the figure is as low as 51·5 per cent.

32. Mao Tse-tung and Ch'en Po-ta on Stalin and Lenin are the best examples of the concern with the early years of the October Revolution; also numerous articles and essays in *Hsuch-hsi* (1949–53) and *Hsin-hua yueh-pao* (1949–53).

33. It was not obvious during the first four years of the P.R.C. that the Chinese leaders disagreed about Soviet ideological polemics and development debates, but the tensions that arose during the next four make it clear that there had been earlier deep disagreements. Much more open were hesitations and doubts about Soviet views about literature and history, see D. W. Fokkema, *Literary Doctrine in China and Soviet Influence, 1956–1960* (The Hague, 1965).

34. Wu Hsiu-ch'uan's speech in *U.N. Security Council Official Records*, 5th Year, 527 Meeting (28 November 1950) no. 69, pp. 2–25; also in *People's China* (16 December 1950) Supplement. Long extracts are quoted in Roderick MacFarquhar (ed.), *Sino-American Relations, 1949–71* (Newton Abbot, 1972) pp. 86–98.

35. Liu Shao-ch'i *Collected Works*, vol. 1 (Hong Kong, 1969) pp. 259–67.

36. This is brilliantly discussed in Gittings, *The World and China*, pp. 155–62.

4. TOWARDS INDEPENDENCE, 1953–8

1. *People's China* (16 March 1953).

2. Byron S. J. Weng, *Peking's U.N. Policy, Continuity and Change* (New York, 1972).

3. Contrast the agreements before 1954 to those of 1954–8, especially after the agreement with France on 5 June 1953; see Douglas M. Johnston and Hungdah Chiu, *Agreements of the People's Republic of China, 1949–1967: A Calendar* (Harvard U.P., 1968) pp. 19–89.

4. Robert F. Randle, *Geneva 1954: The Settlement of the Indo-Chinese War* (Princeton U.P., 1969) reviews the impact of China's presence in its first international conference. Also see Melvin Gurtov, *The First Vietnam Crisis: Chinese Communist Strategy and United States Involvement, 1953–54* (Columbia U.P., 1967) for a different perspective.

5. For a background to the Taiwan Crisis of 1954, see Harold C. Hinton, *Communist China in World Politics* (Boston, 1966) pp. 258–63.

6. Chou En-lai, Report on Foreign Affairs to the Thirty-third Session of the Central Government Council 11 August 1954, *People's China* (1 September 1954) Supplement. See also his Report on the Work of the Government, First Session of the First National People's Congress on 23 September 1954.

7. U.S. Department of State, *American Foreign Policy, 1950–55*, vol. 1 (Washington D.C., 1957) pp. 945–7. Extracts of the treaty may be found in McFarquhar (ed.), *Sino-American Relations*, pp. 108–11.

8. *Documents of the First Session of the First National People's Congress of the People's Republic of China* (Peking, 1955).

9. Text of Sino-Soviet Communiqués and declarations of 12 October 1954 may be found in *Survey of China Mainland Press*, no. 906 (12 October 1954); see also Khrushchev's speech in *Survey*, no. 902 (6 October 1954). There are useful references in Howard L. Boorman *et al.*, *Moscow–Peking Axis, Strengths and Strains* (New York, 1957).

10. The statements by the P.R.C. are themselves unambiguous where Tibet was concerned, but China's position vis-à-vis the autonomy of Tibet has been controversial since the eighteenth century; see Li Tieh-tseng, *The Historical Status of Tibet* (New York, 1956), and Alastair Lamb's two valuable studies, *Britain and Chinese Central Asia: The Road to Lhasa, 1767 to 1905* (London, 1960), and *The McMahon Line: A Study in the Relations between India, China and Tibet, 1904 to 1914* (London, 1966) two vols.

11. *China and the Asian – African Conference (Documents)* (Peking, 1955); George McT. Kahin, *The Asian – African Conference: Bandung, Indonesia, April 1955* (Cornell U.P., 1956).

12. Two books provide a useful contrast: Robert S. Elegant, *The Dragon's Seed: Peking and the Overseas Chinese* (New York, 1959), and Lea E. Williams, *The Future of the Overseas Chinese in South-east Asia* (New York, 1966). An authoritative account of the main shifts in P.R.C. policy is Stephen FitzGerald, *China and the Overseas Chinese: a Study of Peking's Changing Policy, 1949 – 1970* (Cambridge U.P., 1972).

13. Mao Tse-tung's visit to Moscow for the fortieth anniversary of the October Revolution marked a significant shift in his views about the socialist camp; see his speeches, *Current Background*, no. 480 (13 November 1957), and no. 534 (12 November 1958). A comprehensive survey of Chinese policy concerning nuclear power in the 1950s may be found in Alice Langley Hsieh, *Communist China's Strategy in the Nuclear Era* (Englewood Cliffs, N. J., 1962).

14. The best analysis of this critical stage in Sino-Soviet relations is still Donald S. Zagoria, *The Sino-Soviet Conflict, 1956 – 1961* (Princeton U.P., 1962).

15. Two of the best short accounts of this stage of Sino-Soviet relations are Ishwer C. Ojha, *Chinese Foreign Policy in an Age of Transition: The Diplomacy of Cultural Despair* (Boston, 1969) ch. 5; and Gittings, *The World and China*, chs 10 – 12.

16. Speech to Party leaders at Chengtu Conference, 10 March 1958, from *Mao Tse-tung ssu-hsiang wan-sui* (Peking, 1969), trans. in Stuart Schram (ed.), *Mao Tse-tung Unrehearsed, Talks and Letters: 1956 – 71* (Harmondsworth, 1974) pp. 96 – 103.

17. State Statistical Bureau, P.R.C., *Ten Great Years: Statistics of the Economic and Cultural Achievements of the People's Republic of China* (Peking, 1960); *Ten Glorious Years* (Peking, 1960). There are many critical Western studies examining these achievements. The two that are still helpful are Joint Economic Committee of the U.S. Congress, *An Economic Profile of Mainland China* (Washington D.C., 1967) two vols, and Chen Nai-ruenn, *Chinese Economic Statistics* (Edinburgh U.P., 1967).

18. Until 1958, P.L.A. spokesmen were fairly open on this subject, usually at Army Day celebrations, notably speeches by Chu Teh, Liu Ya-lou, Hsiao Hua, P'eng Te-huai and Su Yü. For a brief account of some aspects of the P.L.A. and modernisation, see John Gittings, *The Role of the Chinese Army* (Oxford U.P., 1967) ch. 7.

19. The best study of this subject is Eckstein, *China's Economic Growth*. For some examples of concern to 'catch up', see Liu Shao-ch'i and Chou En-lai, speeches to the First National People's Congress in 1954, *People's China* (1 and 16 October 1954). This concern is also implicit in the *First Five-Year Plan for Development of the National Economy of the P.R.C. in 1953 – 57* (Peking, 1956); see Li Fu-ch'un's Report on the First Five-Year Plan to the National People's Congress in July 1955, *People's China* (16 August 1955) Supplement.

20. *Ten Great Years*; and Kuan Ta-tung, *The Socialist Transformation of Capitalist Industry and Commerce in China* (Peking, 1960).

21. Theodore H. E. Chen, *Thought Reform of the Chinese Intellectuals* (Hong Kong U.P., 1960).

22. Of the vast amount published during the Hundred Flowers campaign, the most important statements have been collected in *Hsin-hua Pan-yueh k'an (New China Semi-monthly)* (June – August 1957). A selection of these, as well as some others, may be found in Roderick McFarquhar (ed.), *The Hundred Flowers Campaign and the Chinese Intellectuals* (London, 1960). A recent authoritative analysis of the complex background of this campaign is Roderick McFarquhar, *The Origins of the Cultural Revolution*, vol. I: *Contradictions among the People 1956 – 57* (Oxford U.P., 1974) parts I and II.

23. McFarquhar, *Contradictions among the People*, part III; Janos Radvanyi, 'The Hungarian Revolution and the Hundred Flowers Campaign', *The China Quarterly*, XLIII (July – September 1970) 121 – 9.

24. A valuable new study of this question is Parris H. Chang, *Power and Policy in China* (Pennsylvania State U.P., 1975) ch. I.

170   CHINA AND THE WORLD SINCE 1949

25. *Mao Tse-tung ssu-hsiang wan-sui* (Peking, 1967 and 1969), made available by the Institute of International Relations, Taipei, Taiwan in mid-1973; introduced by Stuart Schram in a review article, 'Mao Tse-tung: A Self-portrait', *The China Quarterly*, LVII (January–March 1974) 156–65; then in the same periodical specific topics, notably those discussed by John Gittings, 'New Light on Mao: His View of the World', LX (December 1974) 750–66; and by Richard Levy, 'New Light on Mao: His Views on the Soviet Union's *Political Economy*', LXI (March 1975) 95–117. See also Schram's Introduction and Notes to *Mao Tse-tung Unrehearsed*, pp. 7–47, 49–57.

26. Thomas P. Bernstein, 'Leadership and Mass Mobilisation in the Soviet and Chinese Collectivisation Campaigns of 1929–30 and 1955–56: A Comparison', *The China Quarterly*, XXXI (July–September 1967) 1–47.

27. Since the Cultural Revolution, this period has been almost wholly reassessed. The most interesting discussions have been McFarquhar, *Contradictions among the People*; Chang, *Power and Policy*; and Gittings, *The World and China* (see notes 15, 22 and 24 above). See also the issue of *The China Quarterly* devoted to the Twentieth Anniversary of the P.R.C., XXXIX (July–September 1969) 1–75.

28. In Jerome Ch'en (ed.), *Mao* (Englewood Cliffs, N.J., 1969) pp. 65–85; the *People's Daily* article (5 April 1956) is the well-known *On the Historical Experience of the Dictatorship of the Proletariat* (Peking, 1956); reproduced in R. R. Bowie and J. K. Fairbank (eds), *Communist China, 1955–59: Policy Documents with Analysis* (Harvard U.P., 1962) pp. 144–51.

29. In *People's China* (1 July 1957), Supplement; also separately (Peking, 1957); reproduced in *Communist China, 1955–59* , pp. 275–94.

30. For the Draft Regulations of the Weihsing People's Commune (dated 7 August 1958), see E. Stuart Kirby (ed.), *Contemporary China*, III, 1958–9 (Hong Kong U.P., 1960) pp. 235–52. See also the Resolution on Some Questions Concerning the People's Communes, 10 December 1958, in Union Research Institute, *Documents of Chinese Communist Party Central Committee, September 1956–April 1969*, vol. 1 (Hong Kong, 1971) pp. 123–48.

5. FACING THE STORMS, 1958–66: PART 1

1. Zagoria, *Sino-Soviet Conflict*, chs 8 and 9; for some key documents, see G. F. Hudson *et al.*, *The Sino-Soviet Dispute* (London, 1961); also see notes in following chapter.

2. The significance of these numbers has been examined by Donald W. Klein, 'Peking's Diplomats in Africa', *Current Scene* (1 July 1964); see a special issue on Sino-African relations in *Race* (London) 5/4 (April 1964), and especially articles by George T. Yu and W. A. C. Adie. A broad and useful survey is Bruce D. Larkin, *China and Africa, 1949–70: the Foreign Policy of the P.R.C.* (California U.P., 1971) pp. 38–88.

3. For Cuba, see *Peking Review* (19 July, 2 August, 23 August 1960). This exciting breakthrough coincided with the first Treaty of Friendship with an African country when President Sekou Touré of Guinea visited China; see the extra-large issue of *Peking Review* (14 September 1960).

For Laos, see *Peking Review* (15 June, 27 July 1962) on the end of the Second Geneva Conference, prelude to formal diplomatic recognition in September.

For France, there was much writing on General de Gaulle's decision throughout 1964: see Stephen Erasmus, 'General de Gaulle's Recognition of Peking', *The China Quarterly*, XVIII (April–June 1964) 195–200 and Hinton, *Communist China in World Politics*, pp. 148–52.

4. There was a considerable literature on this published between 1959 and 1964. The key documents concerning the 1959 revolt may be found in *Concerning the Question of Tibet* (Peking, 1959); Ministry of External Affairs (India), *White Paper: Notes, Memoranda and*

Letters Exchanged and Agreements Signed between the Governments of India and China, 1954–1959, vols I and II (New Delhi, 1959).

5. On this subject, the Indian government and various Indian scholars have published a large number of books; the two key collections are the Ministry of External Affairs, *Report of the Officials of the Governments of India and the People's Republic of China* (New Delhi, 1961), and Indian Society of International Law, *The Sino-Indian Boundary: Texts of Treaties, Agreements and Certain Exchange of Notes Relating to the Sino-Indian Boundary* (New Delhi, 1962). The two main Chinese collections are *Documents on the Sino-Indian Boundary Question* (Peking, 1960) and *The Sino-Indian Boundary Question* (Peking, 1962).

6. For examples of works hostile to China, see Rodney Gilbert (ed.), *Genocide in Tibet* (New York, 1959); Chanakya Sen (ed.), *Tibet Disappears: A Documentary History of Tibet's International Status, the Great Rebellion and its Aftermath* (Bombay, 1960); and George N. Patterson, 'China and Tibet: Background to the Revolt', *The China Quarterly*, I (January–March 1960) 87–102.

7. Two recent books illustrate some of the tragic and complex elements in Han–Tibetan relations, both by Tibetans: Tubten Jigme Norbu and Colin Turnbull, *Tibet: Its History, Religion and People* (London, 1968; Pelican ed. Harmondsworth, 1972) and Dewa Norbu, *Red Star over Tibet* (London, 1974). The Chinese government had been rather silent about Tibet after the Cultural Revolution, but during the past three years there have been regular reports about life and developments in the Autonomous Province in *People's Daily, Kuang-ming Daily, China Reconstructs, China Pictorial* and other media. A few select foreign visitors have also been invited to visit Tibet.

8. Ministry of External Affairs (India), *White Paper*, vols 8 and 9 (see note 4 of this chapter). The literature in English on the war has been largely by Indians and friends of India, and most of them brand China as the 'aggressor'. A remarkably objective account by an Indian is Ojha, *Chinese Foreign Policy*, ch. 6. Of the vast amount written on the subject, only two scholarly books have suggested that India might have been equally, if not more, responsible for this war; Alastair Lamb, *The China–India Border: The Origins of the Disputed Boundaries* (Oxford U.P., 1964) and Neville Maxwell, *India's China War* (London, 1970).

9. *Peking Review*, XVI–XXIII (20 April–8 June 1962). The negotiations with Pakistan were announced on 3 May in the midst of increasingly serious accusations about Indian intrusions into Chinese territory, and comments appeared on 5 June.

10. Maxwell, *India's China War* did not appear until 1970.

11. Three sets of documents illustrate the stepping up of Chinese activities in the Afro-Asian world, beginning with *China Supports the Arab People's Struggle for National Independence* (Peking, 1958). The second is *The Chinese Resolutely Support the Just Struggle of the African People* (Peking, 1961). This leads to the point when Chou En-lai was directly lobbying for the second Afro-Asian conference, *Afro-Asian Solidarity against Imperialism* (Peking, 1964). Also see Charles Neuhauser, *Third World Politics: China and the Afro-Asian People's Solidarity Organisation, 1957–1967* (East Asian Research Center, Harvard, 1968).

12. *Concering the Situation in Laos* (Peking, 1959).

13. Of the many American writings in the 1950s concerned about China's ambitions, one that was sober and influential at the time and is still worth reading is A. Doak Barnett, *Communist China and Asia: A Challenge to American Policy* (New York, 1960).

14. For the Chinese record, *Peking Review* (31 March 1961) has a short history of military operations since December 1960 for which China held the U.S.A. responsible; then the visits of Laotian leaders to Peking in April (*Peking Review*, 28 April 1961), and then regular reports of the proceedings of the enlarged Geneva Conference from May 1961 to July 1962, when the declaration on Laotian neutrality was finally passed. Two useful studies from a different point of view are J. J. Cyzak and C. F. Salans, 'The International Conference on Laos and the Geneva Agreement of 1962', *Journal of Southeast Asian History*, 7/2 (September 1966) 27–47, and Arthur J. Dommen, *Conflict in Laos:*

The Politics of Neutralisation (New York, 1964). A recent study is Lee Chae-jin, *Communist China's Policy towards Laos: A Case Study, 1954–1967* (Kansas U.P., 1970).

15. See FitzGerald, *China and the Overseas Chinese*; Elegant, *The Dragon's Seed*; and Williams, *The Future of the Overseas Chinese* for three contrasting views on this subject. A new survey of importance is Mary F. Somers Heidhues, *South-east Asia's Chinese Minorities* (Melbourne, 1974).

16. *Ch'iao-wu pao* (Peking) for 1958–60; some important documents have been translated; e.g. in *Current Background*, no. 579 (25 May 1959), no. 623 (29 June 1960) and no. 627 (18 July 1960), especially those by Fang Fang and Wang Yueh. FitzGerald, *China and the Overseas Chinese* shows that the P.R.C. government had changed its Overseas Chinese policy in 1955. But shedding the Overseas Chinese was something like 'decolonisation' and this could not be done overnight. Some of the residual responsibilities were very embarrassing to national policy.

17. Donald E. Willmott, *The National Status of the Chinese in Indonesia 1900–1958* (Cornell U.P., 1961); J. A. C. Mackie (ed.), *The Chinese in Indonesia: Five Essays* (Melbourne, 1976).

18. *Peking Review*, especially issues in December 1959, May and July 1960, April and June 1961. Some of the key documents have been collected in G. M. Ambekar and V. D. Divekar (eds), *Documents on China's Relations with South and South-east Asia (1949–1962)* (Bombay, 1964) pp. 60–71, 229–74.

19. This must be placed in the context of Sino-Indonesian relations; Mohd Ghazali bim Shafie, *Confrontation: A Manifestation of the Indonesian Problem* (Kuala Lumpur, 1964); *Indonesian Intentions towards Malaysia* (Kuala Lumpur, 1964); J. M. van der Kroef, 'The Sino-Indonesian Partnership', *Orbis*, VIII, 2 (1964) 332–56. Another feature to be emphasised is China's keen support for D. N. Aidit and the Indonesian Communist Party; see Peking's publication of Aidit's speeches: *The Indonesian Revolution and the Immediate Tasks of the Communist Party of Indonesia* (Peking, 1964), *Dare, Dare and Dare Again!* (Peking, 1963), *Set Afire the Banteng Spirit! Ever Forward, No Retreat!* (Peking, 1964).

20. Two most important analyses of the result are David Mozingo, 'China's Policy toward Indonesia', and Ruth T. McVey, 'Indonesian Communism and China', in Tang Tsou (ed.), *China in Crisis*, vol. II: *China's Policies in Asia and America's Alternatives* (Chicago U.P., 1968) pp. 333–52 and 357–94. Also, see Sheldon W. Simon, *The Broken Triangle: Peking, Djakarta and the PKI* (Johns Hopkins P., 1968). A useful and thoughtful survey is C. P. FitzGerald, *China and South-east Asia since 1945* (Melbourne, 1973) ch. 2.

21. Peace and diplomacy in Burma, Nepal and Pakistan are contrasted with conflict and tension in Vietnam, Laos and India and accusations of subversion in Thailand, Malaysia and Indonesia – a very complex picture; see the excellent analysis by Ojha, *Chinese Foreign Policy*, ch. 7. Two other useful works to consult are Harold C. Hinton, *China's Turbulent Quest, an Analysis of China's Foreign Relations since 1949*, rev. ed. (Indiana U.P., 1972) chs 9 and 10; and Peter Van Ness, *Revolution and Chinese Foreign Policy: Peking's Support for Wars of National Liberation* (California U.P., 1971).

22. Richard Lowenthal, 'China', in Z. Brzezinski (ed.), *Africa and the Communist World* (Stanford U.P., 1963) pp. 142–203; Colin Legum, 'Africa and China: Symbolism and Substance', in A. M. Halpern (ed.), *Policies toward China: Views from Six Continents* (New York, 1965) pp. 389–436; W. A. C. Adie, 'Chou En-lai on Safari', *The China Quarterly*, XVIII (April–June 1964) 174–94. Also see note 2 of this chapter.

23. *Afro-Asian Solidarity against Imperialism* (Peking, 1964), for example his speech in Ethiopia about 'the main spirit of the Bandung Conference and the Addis Ababa Conference', pp. 247–52.

24. Chen Yi, *Vice Premier Chen Yi Answers Questions put by Correspondents* (Peking, 1966).

25. Wang, 'Juxtaposing Past and Present', *China Quarterly*, LXI (March 1975) 7–12.

26. Larkin, *China and Africa* (California U.P., 1971) chs 6–8.

6. FACING THE STORMS, 1958–66: PART II

1. Chinese sources since the Sino-Soviet split tend to overstate Soviet emphasis on heavy industry and the armaments industry. Western studies have been strongly influenced by Chinese writings to concentrate on differences in ideology, but there is growing awareness that economic achievements are relevant; cf. Kurt London (ed.), *Unity and Contradiction: Major Aspects of Sino-Soviet Relations* (New York, 1962) parts I, III and VIII, and Donald W. Treadgold (ed.), *Soviet and Chinese Communism: Similarities and Differences* (Washington U.P., 1967) part V.

2. Schurmann, *Ideology and Organisation*, pp. 380–403, 472–500; Chang, *Power and Policy*, ch. 3; also see Edgar Snow, *The Other Side of the River: Red China Today* (New York, 1961).

3. *Peking Review* (23 and 30 September, most of October, November and December 1958).

4. Chang, *Power and Policy*, ch. 4, has an admirably clear summary of the events of 1959. There has been a vast amount of Red Guard material on the role of P'eng Te-huai, Liu Shao-ch'i and others; a good example of this may be found translated in *Chinese Law and Government*, 1/4 (1968); another in *Current Background*, no. 851 (26 April 1968). See also Schram, *Mao Unrehearsed*, pp. 131–57.

5. *Documents of C.C.P. Central Committee*, vol. I, pp. 167–72.

6. *Peking Review*, issues of late 1959, 1960 and 1961 stress the efforts to develop the economy but reveal little of the economic difficulties China experienced. In contrast, see the documents captured by Taiwan commandos from Lienchiang, Fukien in 1964; C. S. Chen (ed.), *Rural Peoples' Communes in Lienchiang* (Stanford, 1969).

7. *Sixth Plenary Session of the Eighth Central Committee of the Communist Party of China* (Peking, 1958).

8. Documents in Union Research Institute, *The Case of P'eng Teh-huai, 1959–1968* (Hong Kong, 1968); see also Byung-joon Ahn, 'Adjustments in the Great Leap Forward and their Ideological Legacy, 1959–62', in Chalmers Johnson (ed.), *Ideology and Politics in Contemporary China* (Washington U.P., 1973) pp. 257–300.

9. 'Speech at Tenth Plenum of the Eighth Central Committee', in Schram, *Mao Unrehearsed*, pp. 188–96; also see *Peking Review* (28 September 1962). An interesting analysis may be found in Michel C. Oksenberg, 'Policy-making under Mao, 1949–68: An Overview', in John M. H. Lindbeck (ed.), *China: Management of a Revolutionary Society* (Washington U.P., 1971) pp. 79–115.

10. The literature on the 'Red' and 'Expert' debate is vast. One study which has direct bearing on the question of modernity is Rensselaer W. Lee III, 'The Politics of Technology in Communist China', in Johnson (ed.), *Ideology and Politics*, pp. 301–25.

11. A most readable book which provides a background to the stresses which affected Sino-Soviet relations at the 'state-to-state' and 'people-to-people' levels in the late 1950s is Klaus Mehnert, *Peking and Moscow*, trans. Leila Vennewitz (London, 1963) pp. 313–48; but it was not until later that the world learnt of Khrushchev's 'treachery' in July–August 1960 and the extent to which this hurt the Chinese economy.

12. After Mao's Tenth Plenum Speech, most of the vehemence against revisionism and the restoration of capitalism was openly directed against the U.S.S.R.; beginning with *Leninism and Modern Revisionism* (Peking, 1963) and reaching a climax in 1964 with letters between the Central Committees of the two Communist Parties, and the well-known 'On Khrushchev's Phoney Communism and Its Historical Lessons for the World', see the collected statements, letters and editorials in *The Polemic on the General Line of the International Communist Movement* (Peking, 1965). But there were domestic echoes of this revisionism: see Richard H. Solomon, *Mao's Revolution and the Chinese Political Culture* (California U.P., 1971) ch. 19.

13. A very fine study of this complex problem may be found in Jack Gray, 'The Two

Roads: Alternative Strategies of Social Change and Economic Growth in China', in Stuart R. Schram (ed.), *Authority, Participation and Cultural Change in China* (Cambridge U.P., 1973) pp. 109–57.

14. A full study of this campaign is Richard Baum, *Prelude to Revolution: Mao, the Party, and the Peasant Question, 1962–66* (Columbia U.P., 1975).

15. The renewed intellectual ferment in 1961–2 and the preliminary struggles against scholars, writers and journalists soon afterwards produced a considerable volume of publications; these have been partially examined in Merle Goldman, 'Party Policies toward the Intellectuals: The Unique Blooming and Contending of 1961–62', in John Wilson Lewis (ed.), *Party Leadership and Revolutionary Power in China* (Cambridge U.P., 1970) pp. 268–303; and 'The Chinese Communist Party's "Cultural Revolution" of 1962–64', in Johnson (ed.), *Ideology and Politics*, pp. 219–54. Also see Wang, 'Juxtaposing Past and Present', 7–12. An elaborate study which links the ferment with key political issues is William F. Dorrill, 'Power, Policy, and Ideology in the Making of the Chinese Cultural Revolution', in Thomas W. Robinson (ed.), *The Cultural Revolution in China* (California U.P., 1971) pp. 21–112.

16. The Chinese published virtually no statistics for this period and reconstructing quantitative data has been attempted by several economists. Some conservative figures have been collected together in Wu Yuan-li (ed.), *China: A Handbook* (Newton Abbot, 1973) part I, p. 123, tables, and part III, pp. 850–94. A systematic survey which throws considerable light on the economy during the early 1960s is Audrey Donnithorne, *China's Economic System* (London, 1967).

17. See note 12 of this chapter.

18. Zagoria, *Sino-Soviet Conflict*, chs 12–15; see also *Peking Review* (9 February, 12 and 26 April, 28 June, 13 and 20 December 1960).

19. *Peking Review* (27 October 1961).

20. The key documents are collected and analysed by William E. Griffith in three volumes: *Albania and the Sino-Soviet Rift, The Sino-Soviet Rift, Sino-Soviet Relations, 1964–1965* (M.I.T. Press, 1963, 1964 and 1967). They should be read together with John Gittings, *Survey of the Sino-Soviet Dispute: A Commentary and Extracts from the Recent Polemics 1963–1967* (Oxford U.P., 1968).

21. *The Origin and Development of the Differences Between the Leadership of the C.P.S.U. and Ourselves; On the Question of Stalin; Is Yugoslavia a Socialist Country?; Apologists of Neo-Colonialism; Two Different Lines on the Question of War and Peace; Peaceful Coexistence – Two Diametrically Opposed Policies* (all Peking, 1963); *The Leaders of the C.P.S.U. are the Greatest Splitters of Our Times; The Proletarian Revolution and Khrushchev's Revisionism; On Khrushchev's Phoney Communism and Its Historical Lessons for the World* (all Peking, 1964).

22. A subject that has attracted much attention is the political nuances of the two statements in the context of the Vietnam War, Lo Jui-ch'ing's 'Commemorate the Victory over German Fascism! Carry the Struggle against U.S. Imperialism Through to the End!' in *Peking Review* (14 May 1965), and Lin Piao, 'Long Live the Victory of People's War' in *Peking Review* (3 September 1965); see also later Chinese attacks on Lo Jui-ch'ing, e.g. *Peking Review* (24 November 1967), 'Basic Differences between the Proletarian and Bourgeois Military Lines', for another set of nuances.

23. For various themes along the 'capitalist road', including economic themes, see Lowell Dittmer, *Liu Shao-ch'i and the Chinese Cultural Revolution: The Politics of Mass Criticism* (California U.P., 1974) ch. 7.

24. Stuart Schram has produced the best essay so far on the Cultural Revolution, including the most useful prologue, 'Introduction: The Cultural Revolution in Historical Perspective', in Schram (ed.), *Authority, Participation . . .* pp. 1–108.

7. TO CHANGE OR NOT TO CHANGE, 1966-71

1. The amount published in English on the G.P.C.R. is now so large that it is difficult to select a few truly authoritative studies. They range from documentary translations and collections and foreign residents' reports to various levels of analysis and interpretation: for example *The Great Socialist Cultural Revolution in China* (Peking, 1966); Union Research Institute, *C.C.P. Documents of the G.P.C.R., 1966–1967* (Hong Kong, 1968); reports by Neale Hunter, *Shanghai Journal: An Eye-witness Account of the Cultural Revolution* (New York, 1969), and D. W. Fokkema, *Report from Peking: Observations of a Western Diplomat on the Cultural Revolution* (London, 1971); works mentioned in the notes to ch. 6 by Schram in *Authority, Participation and Cultural Change*; Robinson (ed.), *Cultural Revolution*, Dittmer, *Liu Shao-ch'i*, and Solomon, *Mao's Revolution;* broader interpretations by Robert J. Lifton, *Revolutionary Immortality: Mao Tse-tung and the Chinese Cultural Revolution* (New York, 1968), E. L. Wheelwright and Bruce McFarlane, *The Chinese Road to Socialism: Economics of the Cultural Revolution* (New York, 1970).

2. Parris H. Chang, *Radicals and Radical Ideology in China's Cultural Revolution* (New York, 1973); James R. Pusey, *Wu Han: Attacking the Present through the Past* (East Asian Research Center, Harvard, 1969); Schram, *Mao Unrehearsed*, pp. 234–79.

3. 'Decision of the C.C.P. Central Committee Concerning the G.P.C.R.', *Peking Review* (12 August 1966). Compare, for example, Dittmer, *Liu Shao-ch'i*; Chang, *Radicals and Radical Ideology* and Simon Leys, *Les Habits Neufs du Président Mao* (Paris, 1971).

4. Dittmer, *Liu Shao-ch'i*, ch. 4; A. E. Kent, *Indictment without Trial; The Case of Liu Shao-ch'i* (Canberra, 1969).

5. Gittings, *The Chinese Army*, chs 11 and 12; and his 'Army–Party Relations in the Light of the Cultural Revolution' in Lewis (ed.), *Party Leadership*, pp. 373–403. Also see Ellis Joffe, 'The Chinese Army under Lin Piao: Prelude to Political Intervention', in Lindbeck (ed.), *China: Management*, pp. 343–74.

6. The most detailed information on fallen intellectuals generally has been collected by Ting Wang in Hong Kong in his several volumes on the Cultural Revolution; some idea of the size of these élite groups may be seen in Sydney Leonard Greenblatt, 'Organisational Elites and Social Change at Peking University', in Robert A. Scalapino (ed.), *Elites in the People's Republic of China* (Washington U.P., 1972) pp. 451–97. For Kuo Mo-jo's self-confession, 'Learn from the Masses of Workers, Peasants and Soldiers and Serve Them', *Kuang-ming Daily* (28 April 1966), in *Survey of Chinese Mainland Press*, no. 3691 (5 May 1966).

7. A fascinating account of one centre of rebellion is William Hinton, *Hundred Day War; The Cultural Revolution at Tsinghua University* (New York, 1972); compare with Ken Ling, *Red Guard: From Schoolboy to 'Little General' in Mao's China* (London, 1972), and Gordon A. Bennett and Ronald M. Montaperto, *Red Guard: The Political Biography of Dai Hsiao-ai* (New York, 1972). A fine and interesting analysis of class politics is Gordon White, *The Politics of Class and Class Origin: The Case of the Cultural Revolution* (Contemporary China Papers, A.N.U., Canberra, 1976).

8. Parris H. Chang, 'Provincial Party Leaders' Strategies for Survival during the Cultural Revolution', in Scalapino (ed.), *Elites in the P.R.C.*, pp. 501–39; Richard Baum, 'The Cultural Revolution in the Countryside: Anatomy of a Limited Rebellion', in Robinson (ed.), *Cultural Revolution*, pp. 367–476, are two detailed studies. Also see Hunter, *Shanghai Journal* and Ezra F. Vogel, *Canton under Communism: Programs and Politics in a Provincial Capital, 1949–1968* (Harvard U.P., 1969) ch. 8.

9. Jürgen Domes, *The Internal Politics of China 1949–1972*, trans. Rüdiger Machetzki (London, 1973) chs 12–14; also his 'The Role of the Military in the Formation of Revolutionary Committees, 1967–68', *The China Quarterly*, XLIV (October–December 1970) 112–45.

10. Thomas W. Robinson, 'The Wuhan Incident: Local Strife and Provincial

Rebellion during the Cultural Revolution', *The China Quarterly*, xlvii (July – September 1971) 413–38; for a broader view of the P.L.A. during the G.P.C.R., see William W. Whitson and Chen-hsia Huang, *The Chinese High Command: A History of Communist Military Politics, 1927–71* (New York, 1973) chs 7–8.

11. *Union Research Institute, Documents of Chinese Communist Party Central Committee* (Hong Kong, 1971) pp. 227–50.

12. The ideological background of this debate has wide ramifications; an early attempt to encapsulate its main features is Arthur A. Cohen, *The Communism of Mao Tse-tung* (Chicago U.P., 1964), who acknowledges the influence of the writings of Benjamin I. Schwartz and Karl A. Wittfogel. See also London (ed.), *Unity and Contradiction*, articles by Cyril E. Black, T. H. Rigby, Robert C. North, H. F. Schurmann and Boris Meissner, pp. 3–99, 122–41. Two excellent essays are Benjamin I. Schwartz, 'Modernisation and the Maoist Vision: Some Reflections on Chinese Communist Goals (1965)' reproduced in *Communism and China: Ideology in Flux* (Harvard U.P., 1968) pp. 162–85 ; and part iii of James Chieh Hsiung, *Ideology and Practice: The Evolution of Chinese Communism* (New York, 1970) pp. 169–290.

13. As seen in economic achievements, see Dwight Perkins, 'Economic Growth in China and the Cultural Revolution (1960–April 1967)', *The China Quarterly*, xxx (April–June 1967) 33–48; Carl Riskin, 'The Chinese Economy in 1967', *The Cultural Revolution: 1967 in Review* (Michigan Chinese Studies, 1968) pp. 45–71; Richard K. Diao, 'The Impact of the Cultural Revolution on China's Economic Elite', *The China Quarterly*, xlii (April–June 1970) 65–87.

14. Melvin Gurtov, 'The Foreign Ministry and Foreign Affairs in the Chinese Cultural Revolution', and Thomas W. Robinson, 'Chou En-lai and the Cultural Revolution in China', in Robinson (ed.), *Cultural Revolution*, pp. 313–66; 165–312.

15. Jack Gray, 'The Two Roads', Marianne Bastid, 'Levels of Economic Decision-making'; Jon Sigurdson, 'Rural Industry and the Internal Transfer of Technology', in Schram (ed.), *Authority, Participation*, pp. 109–57, 159–97, 199–232; see also Audrey Donnithorne, *The Budget and the Plan in China* (Contemporary China Papers, A.N.U., Canberra, 1972).

16. Schram, 'Introduction' to Schram (ed.), *Authority, Participation*, pp. 1–108; McFarquhar, *Contradictions among the People*, chs 11, 15, 18; Chang, *Power and Policy*, chs 4–6.

17. Lifton, *Revolutionary Immortality* and Solomon, *Mao's Revolution*, ch. 19, offer 'psychocultural' explanations for this which tend to diminish Mao's deep concern to be a genuine Marxist revolutionary.

18. The most helpful single source of information is Klein and Clark (eds), *Biographic Dictionary*, esp. Appendices, vol. ii, pp. 1041–1169. This has been brought up to date in Malcolm Lamb, *Directory of Central Officials in the People's Republic of China, 1968–1975* (Contemporary China Papers, A.N.U., Canberra, 1976). For provincial levels, see Frederick C. Teiwes, *Provincial Party Personnel in Mainland China, 1956–1966* (Columbia University East Asian Institute, 1967). For P.L.A. factions, see Whitson, *Chinese High Command*, pp. 364–435, 498–517. For Red Guards and others, Hunter, *Shanghai Journal* and Hinton, *Hundred Day War* provide good examples; see also White, *The Politics of Class*, pp. 19–63.

19. *Peking Review* (2 May 1969), Gerald Tannebaum, 'The Working Class Must Occupy the Superstructure' and 'Highlights of the Historical Struggle between the Two Lines in the Communist Party of China', *Eastern Horizon*, viii/2 (1969) 7–22; viii/4 (1969) 6–27; viii/5 (1969) 5–23.

20. Key *Red Flag* articles are found in translation in *Peking Review*; otherwise most of them are translated in *Selections from China Mainland Magazines*, nos 610–53 (22 January 1968–5 May 1969).

21. The Draft Constitution of the P.R.C. considered in September 1970 was later

released in Taipei in November 1970; see *China News Analysis* (Hong Kong, 4 December 1970). By the time of the Tenth Party Congress in August 1973, the new Party Constitution had retained only 'the principle of combining the old, the middle-aged and the young', *Peking Review* (7 September 1973). This seems to have led to a change of wording in the P.R.C. Constitution. When this was passed in January 1975 the last sentence in article 11 read, 'Its leading body must be a three-in-one combination of the old, the middle-aged and the young', *Peking Review* (24 January 1975).

22. For the progress of party committees, see section, 'Quarterly Chronicle and Documentation', *The China Quarterly*, xlv – xlviii (January – March to October – December 1971).

23. See subsequent accounts of the Lin Piao affair following Chou En-lai's Report to the Tenth Party Congress in August 1973, *Peking Review* (7 September 1973); also *Chinese Law and Government*, v/3 – 4 (autumn and winter 1972 – 3), Documents of the Central Committee of the C.C.P. (Chung-fa no. 4 and no. 24), 'Struggle to Smash the Counter-revolutionary Coup d'état by the Lin Piao Anti-party Clique', two parts, pp. 43 – 57, 58 – 67.

24. Parris H. Chang, 'The Role of Ch'en Po-ta in the Cultural Revolution', *Asia Quarterly*, 1 (1973) 17 – 58.

25. The Chinese view may be found in two statements issued on 24 May 1969 and 7 October 1969, both published in Peking 1969, and *Down With the New Tsars! Soviet Revisionists' Anti-China Atrocities on the Hei Lung and Wusuli Rivers* (Peking, 1969). Two useful background books are O. Edmund Chubb, *China and Russia: The 'Great Game'* (Columbia U.P., 1971) and Harold C. Hinton, *The Bear at the Gate: Chinese Policy-making under Soviet Pressure* (Washington, 1971).

26. Wang Gungwu, *The Re-emergence of China* (Wellington, New Zealand, 1973).

27. *Peking Review* (16 October, 13 November 1970).

28. Richard H. Moorsteen and Morton Abramowitz, *Remaking China Policy: U.S. – China Relations and Governmental Decision-making* (Harvard U.P., 1971); MacFarquhar (ed.), *Sino-American Relations*, part I, pp. 3 – 56; and part II, pp. 246 – 57; also Bruce Douglass and Ross Terrill (eds), *China and Ourselves: Explorations and Revisions by a New Generation* (Boston, 1970).

29. *Speeches welcoming the Delegation of the P.R.C. by the U.N. Assembly President and Representatives of Various Countries, at the Plenary Meeting of the Twenty-sixth Session of the U.N. General Assembly, 15 November 1971* (Peking, 1971).

30. *Chinese Law and Government*, v/3 – 4 (autumn – winter 1972 – 73), Document of the Central Committee of C.C.P. (Chung-fa no. 12) 'Summary of Chairman Mao's Talks to Responsible Local Comrades during his Tour of Inspection (mid-August to 12 September 1971)', pp. 31 – 42.

31. See Chiao Kuan-hua's speech at the United Nations, *Irresistible Historical Trend* (Peking, 1971); *Unite to Win Still Greater Victories – New Year's Day editorial by Renmin Ribao, Hongqi and Jiehfangjun Pao* (Peking, 1972); *Speech by Chiao Kuan-hua at the Plenary Meeting of the Twenty-seventh Session of the U.N. General Assembly* (Peking, 1972) and issues of *Peking Review* since 1972.

32. Martin Singer, *Educated Youth and the Cultural Revolution in China* (Michigan Chinese Studies, 1971) chs 3 and 4. For a background study, see John Gardner, 'Educated Youth and Urban Rural Inequalities, 1958 – 1966', in John Wilson Lewis (ed.), *The City in Communist China* (Stanford U.P., 1971) pp. 235 – 86. A more recent study is D. Gordon White, 'The Politics of *Hsia-hsiang* Youth', *The China Quarterly*, lix (July – September 1974) 491 – 517.

8. THE LONG AND COMPLEX STRUGGLE

1. Lamb, *Directory of Central Officials*, part A and Appendices.
2. *Peking Review* (7 September 1973) 29–33; Parris H. Chang, 'Political Profiles: Wang Hung-wen and Li-Teh-Sheng', *The China Quarterly*, LVII (January – March 1974) 124–8.
3. Liu Po-ch'eng (b. 1892), Yeh Chien-ying (b. 1898), Nieh Jung-chen (b. 1899) and Hsü Hsiang-ch'ien (b. 1902).
4. See *Current Scene*, XII/2 (February 1974) 19–23.
5. *People's Daily* and *New China News Agency* reports, 1973 and 1974; also summaries in 'Quarterly Chronicle and Documentation', *The China Quarterly*, from issue LIII.
6. *Peking Review* (24 January 1975).

Select Bibliography

(Including books not mentioned in Notes.)

G. M. AMBEKAR AND V. D. DIVEKAR (eds), *Documents on China's Relations with South and South-east Asia, 1949–62* (Bombay, 1964).

A. DOAK BARNETT, *Cadres, Bureaucracy and Political Power in Communist China* (Columbia U.P., 1967).

A. DOAK BARNETT, *Uncertain Passage: China's Transition to the Post-Mao Era* (Washington, 1974).

A. DOAK BARNETT, *Communist China and Asia* (New York, 1960).

RICHARD BAUM, *Prelude to Revolution: Mao, the Party and the Peasant Question* (Columbia U.P., 1973).

JACK BELDEN, *China Shakes the World* (New York, 1949; Harmondsworth, 1973).

LUCIEN BIANCO, *Origins of the Chinese Revolution 1915–1949* (Stanford U.P., 1971).

R. R. BOWIE AND J. K. FAIRBANK (eds), *Communist China, 1955–59: Policy Documents* (Harvard U.P., 1962).

C. BRANDT, B. SCHWARTZ AND J. K. FAIRBANK, *A Documentary History of Chinese Communism* (Harvard U.P., 1952).

A. BUCHAN (ed.) *China and the Peace of Asia* (New York, 1965).

PARRIS H. CHANG, *Power and Policy in China* (Pennsylvania State U.P., 1975).

JEROME CH'EN (ed.), *Mao Papers* (Oxford U.P., 1970).

JEROME CH'EN (ed.), *Mao* (Englewood Cliffs, N.J., 1969).

JEROME CH'EN, *Mao and the Chinese Revolution* (Oxford U.P., 1965).

CH'EN PO-TA, *Notes on Ten Years of Civil War 1927–1936* (Peking, 1954).

CH'EN PO-TA, *Mao Tse-tung and the Chinese Revolution* (Peking, 1953).

CH'EN PO-TA, *Stalin and the Chinese Revolution* (Peking, 1953).

CHESTER J. CHENG (ed.), *The Politics of the Chinese Red Army* (Stanford, 1966).

CHIANG KAI-SHEK, *Soviet Russia in China* (New York, 1957).

CHIANG KAI-SHEK, *China's Destiny*, trans. Wang Chung-hui (New York, 1947).

China, State Statistical Bureau, *Ten Great Years* (Peking, 1960).

China, *Afro-Asian Solidarity against Imperialism* (Peking, 1964).

China, *Leninism and Modern Revisionism* (Peking, 1963).

China, *The Great Socialist Cultural Revolution in China* (Peking, 1966).

B. COMPTON, *Mao's China — Party Reform Documents 1942–44* (Washington U.P., 1952).

L. DITTMER, *Liu Shao-ch'i and the Chinese Cultural Revolution* (California U.P., 1974).

J. DOMES, *The Internal Politics of China, 1949–72*, trans. R. Machetzki (London, 1973).

A. DONNITHORNE, *China's Economic System* (London, 1967).

A. ECKSTEIN, *Communist China's Economic Growth and Foreign Trade* (New York, 1966).

C. P. FITZGERALD, *Revolution in China* (London, 1952; rev. ed. entitled *The Birth of Communist China*, Harmondsworth, 1964).

S. FITZGERALD, *China and the Overseas Chinese — A Study of Peking's Changing Policy, 1949–1970* (Cambridge U.P., 1972).

J. GITTINGS, *Survey of the Sino-Soviet Dispute* (Oxford U.P., 1968).

J. GITTINGS, *The Role of the Chinese Army* (Oxford U.P., 1966).

J. GITTINGS, *The World and China, 1922–72* (London, 1974).

W. E. GRIFFITH, *The Sino-Soviet Rift* (M.I.T. Press, 1964).

W. E. GRIFFITH, *Sino-Soviet Relations, 1964–65* (M.I.T. Press, 1967).

J. GUILLERMARZ, *A History of the Chinese Communist Party*, trans. A. Destenay (London, 1972).

M. GURTOV, *China and South-east Asia — The Politics of Survival* (Lexington, Mass., 1971).

HAN SUYIN, *The Morning Deluge* (London, 1972).

HAN SUYIN, *Wind in the Tower* (London, 1976).

J. P. HARRISON, *The Long March to Power — A History of the C.C.P., 1921–71* (New York, 1972).

HAROLD C. HINTON, *China's Turbulent Quest* (New York, 1970).

HAROLD C. HINTON, *Communist China in World Politics* (Boston, 1966).

WILLIAM HINTON, *Fan Shen: A Documentary of Revolution in a Chinese Village* (New York, 1966).

WILLIAM HINTON, *Hundred Day War: The Cultural Revolution at Tsinghua University* (New York, 1972).

HO KAN-CHIH, *A History of the Modern Chinese Revolution* (Peking, 1959).

ALICE LANGLEY HSIEH, *Communist China's Strategy in the Nuclear Era*

(Englewood Cliffs, N.J., 1962).

JAMES C. HSIUNG, *Ideology and Practice: The Evolution of Chinese Communism* (New York, 1970).

HSU KAI-YU, *Chou En-lai: China's Grey Eminence* (New York, 1968).

ARTHUR HUCK, *The Security of China* (Columbia U.P., 1970).

NEALE HUNTER, *Shanghai Journal* (New York, 1969).

Institute for Far East (U.S.S.R. Academy), *Leninism and Modern China's Problems* (Moscow, 1972).

International Meeting of Communist and Workers' Parties (Moscow, 1969).

S. KARNOW, *Mao and China: from Revolution to Revolution* (New York, 1972).

DONALD W. KLEIN AND ANNE B. CLARK (eds), *Biographic Dictionary of Chinese Communism 1921—1965* (Harvard U.P., 1971) 2 vols.

ALASTAIR LAMB, *The China—India Border* (Oxford U.P., 1964).

BRUCE D. LARKIN, *China and Africa, 1949—70* (California U.P., 1971).

LI CHOH-MING, *Economic Development of Communist China* (California U.P., 1959).

LIU SHAO-CH'I, *Collected Works*, 3 vols (Hong Kong, 1969).

LIU TA-CHUNG AND YEH KUNG-CHIA, *The Economy of the Chinese Mainland* (Princeton U.P., 1965).

R. McFARQUHAR (ed.), *Sino-American Relations, 1949—71* (Newton Abbot, 1972).

R. McFARQUHAR (ed.), *The Hundred Flowers Campaign and the Chinese Intellectuals* (London, 1960).

R. McFARQUHAR, *The Origins of the Cultural Revolution*, vol. 1 (Oxford U.P., 1974).

MAO TSE-TUNG, *Selected Works*, 4 vols (London, 1954 —6; Peking, 1961).

N. MAXWELL, *India's China War* (London, 1970).

K. MEHNERT, *Peking and Moscow*, trans. L. Vennewitz (London, 1963).

New China's Economic Achievements 1949—52 (Peking, 1952).

A. OGUNSANWO, *China's Policy in Africa, 1958—71* (Cambridge U.P., 1974).

ISHWER C. OJHA, *Chinese Foreign Policy in an Age of Transition: The Diplomacy of Cultural Despair* (Boston, 1969).

LUCIAN PYE, *The Spirit of Chinese Politics* (M.I.T. Press, 1968).

THOMAS W. ROBINSON (ed.), *The Cultural Revolution in China* (California U.P., 1971).

STUART SCHRAM, *The Political Thought of Mao Tse-tung* (New York, 1963; rev. ed., Harmondsworth, 1969).

STUART SCHRAM, *Mao Tse-tung* (Harmondsworth, 1966).

STUART SCHRAM (ed.), *Mao Tse-tung Unrehearsed* (Harmondsworth, 1974).

FRANZ SCHURMANN, *Ideology and Organisation in Communist China* (California U.P., 1966).

BENJAMIN SCHWARTZ, *Chinese Communism and the Rise of Mao* (Harvard U.P., 1951).

BENJAMIN SCHWARTZ, *Communism and China: Ideology in Flux* (Harvard U.P., 1968).

J. D. SIMMONDS, *China's World: The Foreign Policy of a Developing State* (A.N.U., Canberra, 1970).

SHELDON SIMON, *The Broken Triangle: Peking, Djakarta and the P.K.I.* (Johns Hopkins U.P., 1968).

EDGAR SNOW, *Red Star over China* (London, 1937; rev. ed., Harmondsworth, 1972).

EDGAR SNOW, *The Other Side of the River* (New York, 1961).

RICHARD H. SOLOMON, *Mao's Revolution and the Chinese Political Culture* (California U.P., 1971).

J. STALIN, *Economic Problems of Socialism in the U.S.S.R.* (Moscow, 1952).

J. B. STARR, *Ideology and Culture* (New York, 1973).

SUN YAT-SEN, *San Min Chu I: Three Principles of the People*, trans. F. W. Price, ed. L. T. Chen (Shanghai, 1929).

D. W. TREADGOLD (ed.), *Soviet and Chinese Communism: Similarities and Differences* (Washington U.P., 1967).

Union Research Institute, *C.C.P. Documents of the G.P.C.R., 1966–67* (Hong Kong, 1968).

Union Research Institute, *Documents of Chinese Communist Party Central Committee, September 1956– April 1969* (Hong Kong, 1971) 2 vols.

U.S. Congress, *An Economic Profile of Mainland China* (Washington, 1967).

U.S. Congress, *P.R.C.: An Economic Assessment* (Washington, 1972).

U.S. State Department, *United States' Relations with China* (Washington, 1949; reissued in two vols by Stanford U.P., 1967).

PETER VAN NESS, *Revolution and Chinese Foreign Policy* (California U.P., 1971).

RICHARD L. WALKER, *China under Communism, The First Five Years* (Yale U.P., 1955).

E. L. WHEELWRIGHT AND B. MACFARLANE, *The Chinese Road to Socialism* (New York, 1970).

GORDON WHITE, *The Politics of Class and Class Origin: The Case of the*

Cultural Revolution (A.N.U., Canberra, 1976).
W. W. WHITSON AND C. H. HUANG, *The Chinese High Command* (New York, 1973).
IAN WILSON (ed.), *China and the World Community* (Sydney, 1973).
WU YUAN-LI (ed.), *China: A Handbook* (Newton Abbot, 1973).
DONALD S. ZAGORIA, *The Sino-Soviet Conflict, 1956–1961* (Princeton U.P., 1962).

JOURNALS AND PERIODICALS

Asian Survey (Berkeley, California).
China News Analysis (Hong Kong).
The China Quarterly (London).
China Report (New Delhi).
Chinese Economic Studies (New York).
Chinese Law and Government (New York).
Chinese Studies in History (New York).
Current Background (Hong Kong).
Current Scene (Hong Kong).
Far Eastern Economic Review (Hong Kong).
International Affairs (Moscow).
Issues and Studies (Taiwan).
Pacific Affairs (Vancouver).
Peking Review (Peking).
People's China (Peking).
Selections from China Mainland Magazines (Hong Kong).
Survey of China Mainland Press (Hong Kong).

Index